The Bear Hunter

*The Life and Times of Robert Eager Bobo
in the Canebrakes of the Old South*

BY

JAMES T. McCAFFERTY

Second EDITION (First Paperback Edition)

CANEBRAKE PUBLISHING COMPANY
McCOMB, MISSISSIPPI

Printed in the United States of America

ISBN 978-0-9966559-6-5

Library of Congress Control Number: 2023911860

Publisher's Cataloging-in-Publication
(Provided by Quality Books, Inc.)

McCafferty, Jim, author.
    The bear hunter : the life and times of Robert Eager
Bobo in the canebrakes of the Old South / by James T.
McCafferty. -- First paperback edition.
        pages cm
        Includes bibliographical references and index.
        LCCN 2023911860
        ISBN 978-0-9966559-1-0
        ISBN 978-0-9966559-0-3
        ISBN 978-0-9966559-6-5
        1. Bobo, Robert Eager, 1847-1902. 2. Big game
hunters--United States--Biography. 3. Bear hunting--
Mississippi--History. 4. Delta (Miss. : Region)--
History--19th century. 5. Biographies. I. Title.

SK17.B62M33 2015   799.292
                 QBI15-600185

Dust jacket design by James T. McCafferty
Interior design and layout by Six Penny Graphics

In Loving Memory of Malinda

Wisdom of Solomon 3:1-9

Robert Eager Bobo (1847–1902)

Contents

Illustrations

Cover: from a work by William Ludwell Sheppard (1833–1912) that appeared in the October 1881 issue of Scribner's Monthly as a woodcut illustration (engraving by C. Culler) for "Bear-Hunting in the South," by Col. James Gordon of Pontotoc, Mississippi.

Preface

Over a century ago readers of sporting journals in America and Europe relished the tales of Mississippi Delta bear hunter Robert Eager Bobo. Yet, in the intervening decades, this most famous bear hunter of the late 1800s has been all but forgotten. To my great blessing, though, over the years I have been fortunate enough to meet and to know some persons to whom his memory remains a cherished reality.

The story of *The Bear Hunter* began for me in the fall of 1964 when I entered the fifth grade at St. George Episcopal Day School in Clarksdale, Mississippi. There were seven boys in our little class of 20. Among them was a lively dark-haired youngster with the curious name of Fincher Gist "Jack" Bobo. It was from Jack that I first heard about a man with that same interesting last name—his great, great grandfather, Robert (Bob) Eager Bobo—who had hunted bear in Coahoma County with a gun the family still owned.

The next year our family moved about 65 miles down U. S. Highway 61 to Leland, Mississippi, in Washington County. I do not recall hearing anything about Bob Bobo the Bear Hunter in Leland, but I did hear a lot about old time bear hunters. It was 1965. The Delta, even then, was a relatively young country. As late as 1940 the region still had been half-covered with timber and swamps. There were persons yet alive in the Leland of the mid-1960s who had pioneered the area, who remembered the glory days of Delta hunting, and who had seen the bears, wolves, and panthers that inhabited those dark woods at the turn of the last century. The old people there remembered when Theodore Roosevelt had come South and hunted with Washington County men like Holt Collier and LeRoy Percy and the Metcalfe brothers. Many others had heard about those times from their parents and grandparents.

Still, I did not think of the Bobos again until August 1976 when I entered law school at the University of Mississippi. In my freshman class there were three of the seven boys who had started the fifth grade together back at St. George in 1964. One of them was Jack Bobo. Our paths had crossed again.

Eleven years later my wife and I were living in Oxford, Mississippi, and I was working as a freelance magazine writer, selling articles primarily to hunting and fishing magazines. In addition to producing the usual "hook and bullet" type stuff that it is the staple of the outdoor press, I maintained my lifelong interest in history.

History was at least a nurtured, if not a natural, interest for me. I had grown up hearing stories from my father about our family and kin and old times in Mississippi. All four of my grandparents were from families that had been in Mississippi at least from the early 1800s. The McCafferty branch of my forebears, in fact, had come to Mississippi about the same time and from the same South Carolina county (Union) as the Bobos. Both of my father's grandfathers had been Civil War veterans. One of them, Yewing McCafferty, had served in Gen. Nathan Bedford Forrest's cavalry corps, as had Bob Bobo.

When we lived in Marks, Mississippi, in the Delta, in the 1950s, my father showed me a small island in the Coldwater River that had formed around the wreckage of a Civil War gunboat. When we lived in Iuka, in the northeast Mississippi hills, a friend's family had displays of Civil War bayonets and pistols and uniform buttons and buckles, all picked up from a gravel bar near their home by the Tennessee River in Tishomingo County. We had in my grandmother McCafferty's home in Kosciusko, Mississippi, a double-barreled muzzle-loading 12 gauge shotgun and a powder horn that had belonged to her husband, my grandfather, and to his father before him. My grandfather had used them on his deer and bear hunting trips to Sunflower County in the Mississippi Delta in the 1880s and 1890s. In my family, and, indeed, in the Mississippi of my childhood, the past was very much present.

In February 1987 *Field & Stream*—a magazine that bought my writing from time to time—reprinted a story by Col. James Gordon, the Confederate veteran, writer, and bear hunter who had lived in Pontotoc County, just a few miles east of my home in Oxford. I began researching Gordon's life and discovered the many articles he had written about hunting in nineteenth century Coahoma County, Mississippi. All the talk of bear and panther I had heard growing up came back to me, and I determined to learn more about the old days in the Delta.

Much of my initial research involved Col. Gordon, who had written articles for a wide variety of magazines during the post civil war period—the 1870s, 80s, and 90s. In collecting his writings I discovered the big three outdoor magazines of that era: *Turf, Field and Farm*; *The American Field*; and *Forest and Stream*. To my delight, I found that I could obtain bound volumes of the *Turf, Field and Farm* and microfilmed versions of *The American Field* and *Forest and Stream* through the University of Mississippi library through the wonder of inter-library loan. My thinking was that I would write a book on nineteenth century bear hunters of the Mississippi Delta.

Many an hour I probably should have devoted to more economically profitable pursuits I spent pouring over old volumes of the *Turf* or winding my way through microfilms of *The American Field* or *Forest and Stream* searching for Mississippi Delta bear hunting stories. I collected quite a few. Now I am glad I did. Many of those microfilms and ancient volumes are no longer lent through inter-library loan and only a very few libraries, most of them far distant from me, have them in their stacks and file cabinets. Had I not collected those stories then, many of them would be practically unavailable to me now.

It is a frustrating fact for the researcher of hunting history that most of the nineteenth century outdoor writers signed their articles with pseudonyms. Unless you just happen upon something like an obituary that identified the deceased as the person who used such-and-such a pen name you might never know who the writer whose works you discovered and love actually was.

In the late 1980s, while rooting around in the history of Delta bear hunting, I came across a reference to Bob Bobo in an article by a hunter/writer from Rushville, Indiana, who signed only his initials ("C. C.") to his account of his 1892 camping and hunting trip to Mississippi. While hunting along the Delta's Sunflower River, C. C. had met "R. E. Bobo" whom he called "an enthusiastic hunter" who owned a large pack "of the very best bear dogs."

I immediately thought of my classmate from St. George and law school, Jack Bobo. I assumed that C. C.'s R. E. Bobo must have been Jack's ancestor, but I wasn't sure. I wrote a letter to Jack to see if C. C.'s Bobo was indeed his ancestor. Jack replied that, yes, he was—a great, great grandfather, in fact. Jack suggested I talk to his father—the fourth R. E. Bobo—who at that time was the storehouse of family information on the first R. E. Bobo, the bear hunter.

I called Jack's father soon afterwards. Mr. Bobo sent me several photo copies of old news clippings on the Bear Hunter from the family scrapbook. He also agreed to meet with me to discuss his great-grandfather.

Within a few days I was with Mr. Bobo in his insurance agency office in the Bobo building—now the Clarksdale city hall—appropriately situated on the bank of the Sunflower River, the stream that figured so prominently in his ancestor's hunts. Mr. Bobo showed me and graciously permitted me to copy the three extant photos of the Bear Hunter that were hanging on the wall in his office.

I have learned in my years of research that if the facts about a person are not set down in writing they generally will be lost to history by the third generation. While the Bobos had retained more information than most about their ancestor, time and two premature deaths in the family tree had taken their toll. Although the materials Mr. Bobo had and the stories the Bobo family retained in their oral tradition and scrapbook were interesting, there did not seem to be enough there for a lengthy magazine article, much less a book.

Not long afterward the pressures of supporting a growing family prompted my return to law practice and a move to Jackson, Mississippi. I did write two children's books about Holt Collier, the bear hunter and former slave who had guided Theodore Roosevelt on his 1902 Mississippi Delta bear hunt. The first, *Holt and the Teddy Bear*, was published in 1991. The second, *Holt and the Cowboys*, came out in 1993. Both were published by Pelican Publishing Company, Gretna, Louisiana, and are available through local bookstores, online companies, and from me. I did not write the larger book on Delta bear hunting I had envisioned. Rather, I filed my research away with the idea that one day I would return to it. Nonetheless, I continued to make notes and collect information and mull over the subject.

Then, about four years ago, I determined to revive that project. At first I thought I would write a single book on a half a dozen or so of the hunters I had discovered in my research, some of whom had been known to me only by their pen names. Thanks to the internet I was able to use clues from many of the articles I had collected to uncover the identities of some of those mysterious writers and hunters. Thus I was able to discover, for example, that the writer whom for three decades I had known only as "A. Mule" was in fact Mississippi born Memphis lawyer George R. Phelan, and that the author, "Coahoma," whose articles I had collected, was actually Mississippi levee engineer Thomas Gregory Dabney.

What I especially enjoyed was being able to tell some persons of this present time things about their ancestors they did not know. For instance, in researching Asa Edwards, one of the bear hunters mentioned in this book, I came across one of his descendants on *Ancestry.com*. I was able to provide her with several articles by James Gordon about hunting trips he took with "old Asa, the Bear Hunter." She had no idea that such materials existed or that her ancestor had been a celebrated Delta hunter mentioned in major national magazines.

My research expanded and expanded until I realized I had the material, not just for one book, but for at least three or four. One of the persons about whom I found more information than I had ever imagined existed was Robert Eager Bobo. Bob Bobo may well have been the most written about bear hunter of the latter nineteenth century. In the five years from 1892 through 1896 at least nine major magazine articles appeared in the sporting press entirely about Bobo and his bear hunting. Eight of them were written by Bobo's friend, Chicago writer Emerson Hough. Besides the big magazine pieces, dozens of smaller articles about or mentioning Bobo appeared in the local and national press from the 1870s through the turn of the twentieth century.

The stories about Bobo described a dauntless man who, after coming home as a boy from the Civil War with little more to his name than the clothes on his back, carved a profitable plantation and logging business out of a wilderness. Through hard work and enterprise, he built a life and prosperity for himself and his progeny that has persisted now for five generations.

Bob Bobo's story is not without its troubling aspects. The strong-willed Bobo had an obsession with bear hunting that undeniably led to much unnecessary killing and waste of the animals. In considering that, however, we must remember that for the Delta pioneers bears were destructive nuisances; eradicating them was seen as a public service.

Bob Bobo was not killing bears, though, out of a sense of civic duty. He was driven to pursue them as surely as Captain Ahab was obsessed with harpooning Moby Dick. He was not the only one. Many sportsmen of that day had found chasing the bruin with horse and hound to be an absolute compulsion. "Once you try it," said one hunter, "it sticks, and the fondness for it will not shake or wear off." Bobo was an addict, purely and simply. He could not have stopped bear hunting even had he wanted to. Only death would put an end to his habit.

Bobo, however, despite his compulsive ways, was an extremely gracious and hospitable man—"the soul of generosity," according to Emerson Hough.

This project has been my attempt to put all the information on Bobo the Bear Hunter I could find into a readable package. In that effort I have tried to bring into the narrative, not just the events from Bobo's life, but stories that would expound upon and explain—or at least shed some light on—the nineteenth century Mississippi Delta backwoods country that was the world of Robert Eager Bobo. The result, I hope, is something that not only will entertain the reader but will contribute to a better understanding of the way of life of the Delta pioneers of the 1800s. I also hope this book will give some relatively little known but substantial characters of the Delta's past a more prominent place in our collective memory.

In an effort to save the reader from the tedium of citations I have tried to keep endnotes to a minimum—a difficult task since I wanted to give credit to all the many of the past who contributed so much to this book. Rather than inserting a note each time I quoted from some work, I put notes only at the conclusions of passages that relied upon one source. That is, if I had a series of paragraphs containing quotes from only one source, I would place a footnote at the conclusion of that series of paragraphs to separate it from the next quote from a different source.

"History would be an excellent thing," Leo Tolstoy is supposed to have said, "if only it were true." I believe what I have written is true. I can promise you this: what I have written accurately reflects and synthesizes my sources to the best of my abilities. At least such accuracy has been my goal throughout this process, as I trust my many scores of endnotes and my dozen or so pages of bibliography bear witness. I hope my effort has done Robert Eager Bobo, the Bear Hunter, and you, my friend the reader, justice.

But let us not delay! The hunters are gathered; the horses are champing at their bits; the dogs are spoiling for a fight; Bobo is sounding his horn. It is time to ride!

1   A Divine Appointment

"**A**n invitation has been extended by Governor Longino, of Mississippi, to President Theodore Roosevelt," the press announced in June 1902, "to take part in a grand bear hunt in the Yazoo canebrake. ...The Hon. R. E. Bobo, of Bobo, Miss., will be master of ceremonies if the President accepts."[1]

The President accepted. The hunt was set for November of that year. The big day came. The presidential train rolled into the little Mississippi Delta plantation depot called Smedes Station. A host of dignitaries, including a United States senator, a presidential cabinet secretary, a future governor of Louisiana, and a railroad president,[2] were on hand, but Robert Eager Bobo was not present. He had made other plans and did not accept his invitation to the hunt.

Some called him "champion bear hunter of the world." Robert Eager Bobo, though, was not the kind of man who required titles, especially those bestowed by others. He knew exactly who he was and what he was. Plenty others knew, too. Illinois Central Railroad agent Thomas A. Divine knew. Chicago journalist Emerson Hough would soon know, as well.

The three men sat together in Tom Divine's Memphis office. It was the opening week of November 1894, almost exactly eight years before Bobo would fail to appear for the presidential bear hunt. Hough had met Divine for the first time only a few days earlier. Never before had he met Bobo. Like any regular reader of the sporting press, however, Hough already knew *of* Bob Bobo, the Mississippi planter reputed to have killed 304 bear in a single year. For more than twenty years articles trumpeting Bobo's bear hunting exploits had appeared in publications around the country. It was Divine's intention, Hough learned, that he go bear hunting in the Mississippi Delta with Bobo.

Bobo made clear that he was no commercial outfitter at just anyone's beck and call. Bob Bobo and Tom Divine, though, were the closest of friends. Tom called Bobo "Rob." Except for Divine, only Bobo's kin did that, and each man honored the request of the other without hesitation. That was the only reason Hough was going hunting with Bob Bobo: Divine had proposed it.

Indeed, a hunt with Bobo was the rarest of things for a stranger uninvited by the man himself. Someone, in fact, once offered money to Bobo to host a hunting party. The Bear Hunter was incensed. "I'm no guide!" boomed Bobo, "and I don't hire out."[3]

Hough, on the other hand, did hire out. As a lawyer turned writer, selling his time and talents had long been Hough's stock in trade. Born in 1857, Hough grew up in Newton, Iowa. Following his graduation from the state university with a degree in philosophy, Hough apprenticed in a Newton law office and soon was admitted to the bar. Finding the small town Midwestern life far too tame for his liking, Hough relocated to White Oaks, Lincoln County, New Mexico Territory, in 1881. Billy the Kid had been killed in that same locale only a few weeks before. There Hough opened a law office, camped, hunted, wrote for the local newspaper, freelanced articles to magazines, and acquired a life-long love for things western.

In 1886 Hough moved to the Chicago area where he made his living as a fulltime writer working for a variety of publications. The following year Hough took the position of "Chicago and Western" editor for one of the leading sporting publications of the day, *Forest and Stream*. The country, being yet young enough in those days for the lower Mississippi River valley to be thought of as the west, Memphis and the southern Mississippi River country fell within Hough's "Western" responsibilities at *Forest and Stream*.

The considerable following Hough would develop from his writing for *Forest and Stream* would help assure his commercial success in later years. Before his death in 1923 he would become one of the more prominent authors of the early twentieth century, writing for magazines as diverse as *Field & Stream* and the *Saturday Evening Post* and penning numerous novels and popular histories. Hough would be among the first to write for the nascent motion picture industry and at least two of his books would become the bases for silent films. One of those, *North of Thirty-Six*, would be remade twice as the sound movies entitled *The Conquering Hordes* (1931) and *The Texans* (1938). Hough would also become a leading light in the embryonic conservation movement, using his influential post at *Forest and Stream* to spearhead the fight to save the American buffalo from extinction.[4]

Emerson Hough had long wished to meet Bob Bobo and welcomed his Memphis encounter with the celebrated hunter. Hough, 37, found in Bobo that November day a man ten years his senior: in build, strong and "bear-like"; in complexion, ruddy, with a "sweeping, sandy mustache"; a "hardy-looking" man, reminiscent of the "the old frontier type." The Bear Hunter's healthy glow, Hough thought, would have been the ideal advertisement for attracting immigrants to the Mississippi Delta. Bobo's radiant countenance, Hough said, as much as shouted, "No malaria here!"

Bobo, Hough concluded, surely had a temperament to match his vigorous appearance. "Impetuous," is how Hough described him, "crashing through things, not going around them." Summarizing and manifesting all those physical and mental traits was the Bear Hunter's "cold blue shooting eye," an aspect of the man Hough surely felt as much as he saw. Hough, who had lived among desperados, bad men, and generally tough hombres while in New Mexico, knew and respected a real man when he saw one. He immediately liked Bob Bobo. Whether Bobo truly was the world's champion bear hunter, who could know? Champion, after all, Hough mused, was often an "empty title." He was confident, however, that when he had "blundered" onto Bob Bobo, he had crossed paths with the man who at least appeared most worthy of that designation. [5]

Certainly during the post-war years of the nineteenth century Bobo's home in Mississippi's Delta country had become, as one writer put it, a "headquarters for the hunters of large game from all parts of the United States. Men traveled from New England and from the Pacific Slope, from New Orleans, from Chicago and even from abroad, to enjoy his hospitality and to hunt under his guidance and over his preserves."[6] Bob Bobo, in fact, may well have been the only man who ever hosted the notorious and fugitive outlaw, Jesse James, for a bear hunt.

What kind of enigmatic character would take an infamous gang leader bear hunting yet decline an opportunity to do the same for the nation's chief executive? Any just and worthwhile answer to that question requires a study of Bobo and his environment.

2 The Delta

Of all the fascinating regions of the American South, that part of the State of Mississippi called the Delta, where Bob Bobo lived, is among the most distinctive in culture and landscape. Shaped roughly like a flattened football with its ends near Memphis, Tennessee, to the north, and Vicksburg, Mississippi, to the south, the Delta is bordered by the Mississippi River to the west, and a range of abruptly rising wooded hills to the east.* Also historically known as the "Mississippi Bottom,"[1] the Great Swamp,"[2] or just "the Swamp,"[3] the country is not a proper delta in the sense of the alluvium that accumulates at the mouth of a river. Neither is it a swamp insofar as that term implies a perpetually marshy piece of land. Rather, it is some 6,500 square miles of great river bottom, almost tabletop flat, irregularly inscribed with myriad lakes and meandering water courses often called bayous or bogues, terms derived from the French and Choctaw words for creek or stream. A land of plantations, bottomland hardwood forests, cypress swamps, delicious food, rugged men, and beautiful women, it justifiably has been called "the most Southern Place on Earth."[4]

Today the Delta may be known best as a focal point of the 1960s civil rights movement or as the home of famous blues singers, such as B. B. King and Muddy Waters. In the nineteenth century, however, the Delta, at least among America's sportsmen, was celebrated as a bear hunter's mecca. Contributing to the legendary status of the Delta as bruin country were the tall tales of yarn spinners such as Yazoo County's William C. Hall and Mississippi governor Alexander G. McNutt. Writing for the widely read *Spirit of the Times* in the 1840s under the pseudonyms of A Missourian[5] and Turkey Runner,[6] respectively, they related the supposed—and, usually, comic—adventures of real life Delta characters and bear hunters like Yazoo County's

---

* This description, of course, refers only to the portion of Mississippi called "the Delta." The term "Delta" is also used by residents of Arkansas and Louisiana (and sometimes in this book) to refer to the portions of those states located in the bottomlands associated with the Mississippi River.

panther fighter and preacher, Mike Hooter,[7] and Issaquena County's Calvin Belcher,[8] who once tried to ride an alligator across the Yazoo River.[9]

Later, after the War Between the States, bear hunting stories set in the Delta and frequently involving narrow escapes from death appeared regularly in the outdoor press. Often written about or by romantic figures like former Confederate officers Gen. Wade Hampton[10] and Col. James "Pious Jeems" Gordon,[11] such tales captured the imaginations of sportsmen in the United States and abroad. Little wonder that hunters of means and often those without flocked to Mississippi during the latter half of the nineteenth century and the beginning of the twentieth to hunt the Delta's black bear.

Surely the Delta bear hunting fraternity included as wide a variety of persons as ever pursued any particular activity in any particular locale. From plantation slave to English nobleman, from backwoods squatter to an American president, and from every station in between, they hunted bear in the Mississippi Delta. For many of them, Bob Bobo's Coahoma County was the preferred destination.

Lying along the Mississippi River in the Delta's northwest quadrant, Coahoma County was yet a young country when Bobo and Hough first met in Tom Divine's office in 1894. The Choctaws, in fact, had ceded the land to the United States in 1832,[12] little more than half a century earlier. The very name, Coahoma, which means "red panther" in the Choctaw tongue, suggests the wilderness that county was in its early years.

To conceive the magnificence of the Delta forests in those times strains the modern imagination. Memphis lawyer George R. Phelan, a Confederate veteran, writer, duelist, and adventurer who had led Fenian cavalry against the British in Ireland,[13] confessed that he could not enter the Delta's "fertile morass… without a certain weird, mysterious sensation." Descending "from the open fields and stunted vegetation of the uplands into the gloomy aisles and among the great trees" of the swamp, he wrote, would "impress the most careless with a sense of the wonderful in nature."

Virtually all who encountered the great woodlands of the Mississippi bottoms before extensive clearing began were astounded by their magnitude. The "giant forms" of the huge trees seemed to lift "themselves to the clouds," rising to heights almost "terrifying to the 6-foot gazer below," wrote Phelan in 1882.[14] "In stature, in towering majesty, they are unsurpassed by any trees of our eastern forests," observed Theodore Roosevelt, after hunting in the Delta woods of Mississippi and Louisiana. "[L]ordlier kings of the green-leaved world are not to be found until we reach the sequoias and redwoods of the Sierras."[15]

Other writers were more specific: "Many lofty oaks measured... five feet in diameter" and were "60 to 70 feet to the first limb,"[16] reported a Jackson, Mississippi, newspaper in 1890. James Gordon of Pontotoc County, Mississippi, wrote of Delta sycamores and cottonwoods ten feet in diameter.[17] One yellow poplar tree cut around 1890 in Holmes County, Mississippi, measured twelve feet through the middle.[18]

Expansive stands of bamboo-like cane (*Arundinaria gigantea*) formed a singular feature of that virginal wilderness. Often called blue cane,[19] the plant, which did not tolerate inundation well, grew on the better drained, higher rises.[20] A member of the grass family, cane thrived only where it received plenty of light. As a result, it proliferated in dense stands in clearings in the forests where trees had been removed or felled by fire or tornadoes or otherwise. Composed of individual stalks commonly more than 20 feet high, sometimes as big around as a man's wrist,[21] and spaced hardly more than an inch or two apart, these cane thickets, called "brakes," often grew in patches covering several square miles of the Delta. An integral component of the bottomland ecology, the canebrake served as habitat for creatures as diverse as the Bachman's warbler and the black bear and the swamp rabbit and the panther.

The exact origin of the term brake in relation to cane is not entirely clear. Some dictionaries link the name to an antiquated Germanic word for bush (*brake*); others say it is derived from *bracken*, the archaic English noun for a dense growth of ferns. From there, say such theories, the word came to mean a thicket of any kind of vegetation. No less of an authority than D. B. Weir, horticulturist, author, and chronicler of the White River Delta country in Arkansas, disagreed. What is more, he rejected the standard spelling—brake—in favor of "break."

"Webster is undoubtedly wrong," Weir said of the dictionary entries that used the brake spelling. "Break, as used here, was not derived from any word... and has in no sense the meaning of brake." The term "break," as opposed to "brake," Weir explained, meant "a sudden change in the growth of anything, especially timber." Thus, said Weir, "I say I struck a break of cypress," meaning "I passed out of some other kind of timber into a growth of cypress...." Similarly, he added, there may be "a break of ash, a break of cane." Weir was not alone in his spelling. Until the late nineteenth century, when brake became the standard, both spellings were used. Even today, one occasionally sees the term break used in reference to cane.

Weir, one suspects, gave the word something of a folk etymology that sought more to make sense of the way a word sounded than to account for its true origins. In any event, both Webster's definition and Weir's describe a brake as a stand of some generally uniform type of vegetation. While cane is the plant most commonly associated with the term brake, to this day in the Delta there are locales known as "Cypress Brake," "Persimmon Brake," "Pecan Brake," and others, all named for the predominant species of tree in their respective areas.

Weir ultimately concluded that the spelling made "no difference." After all, in the Delta swamps, he said, one "was many miles from people who had, or had any need of books of reference, dictionaries and many other of the discomforts of life." We will not know the true way to spell the word, he suggested, until "we get a dictionary to the Arkansas language...."[22]

Regardless of one's choice of spelling, how the unspoiled Delta country appeared to its first white settlers depended upon the soul of the observer. One very practical old timer remembered the early Delta as "nothing but a wilderness of sloughs and canebrakes, filled with all kinds of wild animals."[23]

More poetic witnesses seemed to have found something of their own reflections in the Delta forests. The Byronically intense George Phelan, for example, sensed gloom among those towering trees. Without doubt, the deeper woods, composed of mature timber and having few clearings, could appear forbidding. The leaves on the tree branches, Phelan said, were so high above the forest floor they appeared black to the observer below. Except for the snippet of "cane or... bunch of mistletoe" that showed the rare hint of green, "the prevailing colors [were] deep somber browns and funereal grays." Only the white bark of an occasional sycamore "gleam[ed] out of the darkness like a tombstone." Over all that "wild and lonely" scenery lay what George Phelan believed to be the most impressive feature of the Delta climax forest: a deep, brooding, death-like silence.

From spring through early fall, the forest's overarching canopy admitted little sunlight, creating "shade... too dense for grass" and the other plants needed by wildlife for cover and browse. Consequently, game animals preferred the clearings cut by fires or windstorms and the edges of those places to the mature forests. Song birds flitted about such openings in the woods and frogs croaked around the waterholes, but in the deepest "recesses of the swamp the still[ness] experienced by day [was] almost unbroken." [24]

Canebrake, Tensas Parish, Louisiana, 1905. *U. S. Department of Agriculture photo.*

A more lighthearted pioneer thought those same Delta woods enchanting with a loveliness that defied description: "I have seen carpets of beautiful moss," he said, "which would completely cover the ground and old rotten logs. It would be in sheets large enough to carpet a large hall, all studded with all kinds of colored flowers. It looked for the world like a Brussels carpet; and so closely knit together that it would turn water."[25] At night that same forest floor luminesced with the foxfire adorning the innumerable decaying tree trunks strewn throughout the woods in all directions.[26]

For plainspoken Tunica County pioneer Shelby McPeak the early nineteenth century Delta "was like the place you read about in the good

Book—a real Paradise." Annual high water kept the flood intolerant cane off all but the highest land yet rarely affected the game. The yearly fall burning of grass by the Delta's original Indian inhabitants, according to McPeak, had rendered the forests relatively free from underbrush, "leaving the noblest, biggest, fairest open woods that ever a moccasin made a track in." [27]

The Delta's many lakes, sloughs, and bayous teemed with life. Geese, swans, ducks, and pelicans paddled upon them by the thousands during the fall and winter months. Because the lands surrounding those early Delta waters had not yet been greatly disturbed by the plow, they suffered little from silty run-off. Consequently, during the dry, low-water months (approximately July through November) they often had a clarity rarely seen in those same lakes and streams today.[28] Nineteenth century Delta sportsmen described them in terms ranging from "semi-transparent"[29] to "as pure and clear as though they gurgled through the gorges of the Catskill Mountains."[30]

In the shallows of those waters vast stands of American lotus (*Nelumbo lutea*), or yonkapin, with their great white and yellow long-stemmed flowers, towering three, four, or even six feet above the surface, blossomed continually from spring until fall. On stems above their giant floating pads they bore pods of nuts the pioneers considered a delicacy when roasted.

Under the lily pads lurked largemouth and spotted basses (called trout[31] by early Delta folk), chain pickerel, and warmouth, always poised to seize the insect or minnow that might get too careless. Alligators cruised those waters, as well, as did that crocodilian's namesake, the huge alligator gar, often weighing 200 pounds or more.[32] The big fish basked in the sun on lake surfaces, occasionally leaping half-way out of the water and falling with resounding reports.

Although neither the alligator nor the gar named for it normally posed any serious threat to humans, they could sometimes be dangerous. While hunting in Louisiana in 1907, Theodore Roosevelt met a planter who "had lost part of his hand by the bite of an alligator; and had seen a [swimming] companion seized by the foot by a huge garfish, from which he was rescued with the utmost difficulty by his fellow swimmers."[33]

The Delta woods, too, were a biological wonder. Like the Biblical Promised Land, they "were full of honey" and other wild offerings. In the spring, the clearings and sunny woodland edges bore "wild strawberries... far sweeter and better" than the domestic varieties raised on settlers' farms. In the first weeks of summer "blackberries and dewberries loaded the vines in every little opening." Later, and into the fall, on the higher grounds, "dense thickets of paw-paws, plums, cherries, grapes, and all sorts of other" plants produced their wild fruits. "As for nuts," in the fall "they were in places so thick that... a man might walk... for hundreds of yards" on pecans and [black] walnuts and his feet "not touch the ground."

Not surprisingly, such a rich country supported game in lavish numbers. "The deer," remembered pioneer Shelby McPeak, referring to the Delta's native white-tailed deer (*Odocoileus virginianus*), went "about in regular droves, sometimes fifteen or more in a bunch, and it was almost impossible to miss killing one anywhere if a man sat still on a log for an hour. The b'ar and turkeys, to say nothing of the wild hogs and cattle, were just running about in every direction...."[34]

The "wildcats, panthers, bears, and other wild animals" that "roamed the woods"[35] of the Delta were bold enough on rare occasions to attack humans. Once during those early days a group of men and women were returning to their plantation homes after trading at the river port of Friars Point. As they walked through the woods a wildcat[36] jumped on the back of a woman in the party. It took the help of a man wielding his newly purchased ax to drive the cat away.[37] Little wonder many early Delta residents who found themselves out after dark carried lit tallow candles to discourage unwanted attention from aggressive predators.[38]

Snakes were also an ever present danger. The canebrakes and sloughs provided ideal habitat for cottonmouths, copperheads, and a variety of rattlesnakes.[39] One Dr. Upshauer of Carrollton, Mississippi, writing in 1880, reported that in his eight years of practice in the swamp he had "attended many cases of snake bite, both of rattlesnakes and moccasins." Dr. Upshauer treated the bites with "a salt of carbonate of ammonia" and "attach[ed] but little importance" to the time-honored "whiskey treatment,"[40] no doubt to the great disappointment of many of his backwoods patients.

Greater threats to early settlers than predatory mammals and venomous reptiles, though, at least during the warm weather months, were the malaria bearing mosquitoes and the biting buffalo gnats. The vast swarms of those insects that plagued that bottomland country can scarcely be appreciated by anyone who has not spent a warm day in the Delta woods. Whenever possible Delta pioneers ate and slept under mosquito bars, tent-like hangings of fine netting designed to keep insects away. The women sewed under mosquito bars and the men wore netting over their faces when they went hunting.

The settlers also regularly built "smokes," smoldering fires that produced clouds of sooty fumes insect pests could not tolerate. They made special stands on their porches to hold those smokes to discourage mosquitoes and gnats from swarming near their houses.[41] With open windows in the hot, pre-air conditioning South being a necessity from late spring through early fall, the smell, taste, and feel of smoke must have been a constant in the lives of Delta pioneers during insect season.

Even more painful than the mosquitoes were the relentlessly biting buffalo gnats. So-called because of the hump on its back, the buffalo gnat is a type of tiny black fly about one sixteenth of an inch long.[42] Pharaoh's Biblical plague of gnats[43] could not have caused the Egyptians more misery than the Delta's black flies inflicted upon the settlers of the Mississippi bottom. The pests began swarming in the early spring, typically peaking in May. The constant harassment of clouds of biting gnats about one's head was aggravation enough. Some humans, though, suffered from allergic reactions to the flies' bites and developed fevers within hours or even minutes of gnat attacks.[44] Domestic livestock fared even worse. In years of especially bad gnat infestations, hundreds of mules, horses, and cows died from the bites of the great masses of flies that descended upon them.[45]

The heat and the drier weather of summer usually abated the nuisance substantially, if not completely. Even so, A. B. Wingfield, a Chattanooga, Tennessee, engineer who built railroad bridges and surveyed in Bolivar County, Mississippi, recalled in 1888 that even as late as June, July, and August he had at times been forced to wrap his face with a wet towel to keep the flies out of his nose and mouth. Only the first frosts of fall brought sure relief from the buffalo gnats' torments.

In the interim, smoke was the most effective relief from the flies for man and beast alike. "Anyone could go out in the woods and build up a smoke and in twenty minutes there would be deer there, seeking relief from the bites of" the insects, W. A. Alcorn told his son more than 100 years ago. The flies even drove wildlife almost to the pioneers' doorsteps. Alcorn once counted 13 deer standing with the domestic cattle in the smoke from a backwoods Delta porch.[46]

Since the flies require clean, flowing water for reproduction, the modern levee system, which has eliminated the frequent overflows of the old days, has rendered the buffalo gnat almost a forgotten foe in most parts of the Delta.[47] Still, in some years, even in this present century, the flies swarm in numbers great enough to cause considerable aggravation.[48]

As deadly as the buffalo gnats were to farm stock and as painful and frequent their bites, they were but a seasonal misery causing no lasting harm to humans. The clouds of mosquitoes, on the other hand, often carried a disease that could be deadly: malaria.

Also known as the ague, malaria was and is in some countries, still, a serious illness that may well have killed more human beings than any other disease in history. As late as the World War I era, some 50 percent of the residents surveyed in the central Delta counties of Sunflower and Bolivar had suffered from the malady.

Essentially an infection caused by microscopic organisms, malaria is transmitted by mosquitoes of the *Anopheles* genus. No doctor was needed to determine when someone in the family had the ague, wrote one old frontiersman. The shivers from the chills were so violent they "shook the house."

While that pioneer may have stretched the truth a bit, he hardly could have exaggerated the devastating effect of malaria on Delta residents. Besides the standard chills and fevers that accompanied the illness, complications from the disease included yellowing of the skin and eyes and bleeding from the kidneys.

While the disease was readily treatable with quinine, many Deltans, either untreated or insufficiently treated, suffered from recurring bouts of the ague all their lives. Some who contracted the disease died from it. Small children were especially vulnerable to the sickness, as the seven tiny graves in one family plot in Sunflower County bear sad witness.[49] Although campaigns against the *Anopheles* mosquito drastically reduced the threat of malaria in the 1930s and 40s, even today an occasional case of the disease is reported in Mississippi.

The Delta truly was a land of blessings and curses; a paradise, but a fallen one. Perhaps the great chronicler of the canebrakes, Col. James

Gordon,[50] offered the soberest view of the nineteenth century Delta: "The great swamp…abounds in game, is charming in scenery, luxurious in products," and has "a most enchanting Winter climate"; but "the trail of the serpent is over all, for the deadly miasma guards this beautiful Eden with the sword of death."[51]

3   Pioneer Ways

Whether perceived as the original Paradise or as a malarial purgatory, the Delta was undeniably fertile, so loamy that a man would sink down to his shoe tops in the soil of the canebrakes.[1] "Rich as cream" is how one old-timer described it.[2] Beginning before the War Between the States settlers arrived and began clearing the land to make way for King Cotton, the crop that would reign in Mississippi for almost a century and a half. Little by little "the cane was cut and small trees cut down and other trees deadened (i.e., girdled by stripping a swath of bark from around the tree with an ax, which killed the tree)"[3] in preparation for the plantation and the plow.

Bob Bobo's father, Fincher Gist Bobo, was among the first of those pioneers, arriving in the upper Delta in the 1840s. Born in 1815 of Huguenot* stock,[4] Fincher hailed from Union County, South Carolina, where his father, Barram[5] Bobo, had been a prosperous merchant.[6] Besides his business interests, Barram had owned a 900 acre plantation and had built a fine, two story brick home, which he named "Cross Keys." Fincher was one of a dozen children Barram and his wife, Frances Woodson Bobo, had brought into the world.[7]

Sometime after Barram's death in 1829 a relative acquired Cross Keys. Probably around late 1836 or early 1837,[8] Frances and an unknown number of her children, including Fincher, set out to start life anew in Mississippi.[9]

The Bobos traveled in the winter to prevent spoilage of their food supply, which consisted of a hogshead[10] of dressed turkeys and pots of frozen beans from which they cut slices for eating with their turkey. Fincher also brought along a pack of foxhounds, the descendants of which would serve him and his progeny for at least three generations.[11]

In 1837 Fincher married Sarah Louisa Eager (b. 1815), daughter of Robert Eager, of Lowndes County, Mississippi. Sarah and Fincher first

---

* The Bobo name had been spelled "Beaubeaux," "BauBeau," or "Baubau" in France.

settled with other Bobos from South Carolina in Panola County, Mississippi, about 50 miles south of Memphis, Tennessee.[12] There was cheap fertile acreage to be had a little further west, though, in the Mississippi bottom.
In 1842 Fincher went prospecting for that good land in Coahoma County,
leaving his family behind temporarily in Panola.[13] Fincher was back and
forth between the wilds of Coahoma and the slightly more settled Panola
County as he readied a farmstead for his family.

Coahoma County's total population as tallied by the 1840 census
had been a meager 1290 souls,[14] most of whom lived in and around a
few villages—Delta, Friar's Point, and Port Royal[15]—on the bank of the
Mississippi River. The remainder, including Fincher Bobo, dwelt on isolated
plantations and farms or in simple cabins sparsely scattered about the
primeval forest of the county's interior.

Most settlers developed their lands slowly. First, a family cleared off a
quarter acre or so, built a one-room log cabin, and got along as best it could,
growing no crops except perhaps a subsistence patch of corn and vegetables.
Until plantable land could be hacked out of the Delta jungle, life was hard.
As former Mississippi House of Representatives speaker Walter Sillers put it,
"the mere physical work of keeping alive and clearing the woods challenged
all the energies" of the men and women who settled that country.[16]

While engaged in the slow process of clearing their land, many Coahoma pioneers survived by hunting and fishing. One antebellum resident
of Friars Point recalled that his family often dug for softshell turtle eggs on
nearby Mississippi River sandbars. "We treasured these eggs," he said in a
1937 interview. "They were round, beautiful, white[, and] about the size of
a very large marble. When scrambled, we relished them."[17]

The settlers sold or swapped their surplus game and fish for flour,
sugar, coffee and other staples on the trading boats that plied the rivers or
they traded with the stores in Friars Point or in Helena, Arkansas,[18] on the
opposite bank of the Mississippi. There being no refrigeration or access to
ice in the summer months, the early Coahoma residents often buried stocks
of some perishables, like butter or cream, to keep them cool so as to prevent
spoilage as long as possible.[19]

James Gordon described the life of one Delta pioneer, George
Washington "Wash" Dye, like this: "Along the streams and bayous his traps
were set for beaver, and his lines were stretched across the river for fish.

Bear, deer, wild turkeys and wild honey abounded on his table. His peltries bought his bread and ammunition...."[20]

Similarly, Bolivar County (directly below Coahoma County), Mississippi, pioneer "Uncle" John Randolph Martin "hunted and fished for a living 'mostly,'" while "cultivat[ing] a small field of corn." In contrast with Bob Bobo, who hunted only "for fun," Martin was a "pot-hunter or pot-fisherman," who "always hunted, just as he fished, for meat and not for sport or glory." Uncle John also maintained "a large drove of hogs that lived the year around on the heavy mast," as well as a "considerable herd of cattle that fattened on switch cane[21] and bull weeds."[22] The settlers all had their individual brands or ear notches for their livestock, which ranged freely, "and it [was] considered a greater crime to kill and steal a steer or hog that belong[ed] to one of the neighbors than to kill a man," or so asserted A. B. Wingfield, who wrote a number of articles about Uncle John Martin and the other folk he met while working in the Delta backwoods.[23]

Fincher Bobo built a cabin near the Sunflower River on a cleared spread of 160 acres just south of the present location of the city of Clarksdale in time for the birth in 1847 of his only son, Robert Eager Bobo.[24] Farm implements were few and simple in those days. Often the "corn was planted with an ax. The ax was stuck in the ground, the corn dropped in the hole, and covered with a foot." All the farmer had to do was to chop out the "mutton cane" and thin the corn as it grew.[25] So fertile was the soil that even with such minimal cultivation a farmer could expect his land to yield "seventy-five bushels of corn" or "from a bale to a bale and a half of cotton to the acre."[26]

The Bobos prospered. By his second year in Coahoma County, Fincher was able to afford a hand operated mill for grinding the family corn into meal, a sure sign of affluence among the Delta pioneers. Less prosperous settlers made their meal with a crude grater fashioned by punching holes in a tin pan.[27]

Despite the agricultural bounty that could await the hardy soul with the energy and discipline to carve a farm out of the wilderness, the first Delta settlers faced one very serious obstacle: the high water that attended the seasonal rains. "To those who dwell here," wrote Memphian George Phelan of the Delta in 1882, "there are two seasons more sharply defined than the four divisions of the almanacs. These are wet and dry."

From early summer through most of autumn, when rainfall was sparse, travel was not a problem. Then the Delta byways were "the best roads in the world without exception." To tour the Delta at those times by "carriage beneath the interlocked trees" and "smell the fragrant odors breathed lavishly by the swamp," George Phelan insisted, was "one of the most delightful experiences" the world had to offer. Once the winter rains set in around mid-December, "however," he added, "it only require[d] forty-eight hours to make [that] beautiful country one sea of nasty, villainous, sticky mud" that rendered wheeled conveyances "almost impracticable."[28]

Floods regularly accompanied the rains. While the almost annual winter and spring[29] overflows that inundated much of the Delta replenished the land with water-borne nutrients, during their duration they rendered life exceedingly difficult for humans, livestock, and wildlife. They also made having a boat of some kind a necessity for the Delta pioneer.

Certainly skiffs and yawls—boats that required saws and planks and hammers and nails for their construction—were used in the Delta during such floods and at other times. The common conveyance on the waterways of the lower Mississippi valley in the nineteenth century, however, was the native canoe, or dugout, as it generally was known in the South. "There is nothing," wrote woodsman and journalist D. B. Weir, "in which a man can get from place to place, in the great overflows covered thickly with timber, brush, vines and floating logs, as a finely modeled light canoe...." Carved with ax and adz from a log in a manner adapted from the canoes of the southern Indian tribes,[30] the long, narrow, shallow draft dugout made the ideal craft for threading through flooded timber. Its relatively light weight made carrying the canoes across dry ridges from one body of water to another a simple matter, as well. Even so, such portages were rare, for, as one astute observer of nineteenth century Delta ways noted, "your true Swamper has no longing for that sort of labor."[31]

D. B. Weir, a man of extensive experience with dugouts in the Arkansas Delta's White River bottom, described one boat he believed to be a prime specimen of the type. This exemplary canoe, he said, was "about fourteen feet long [with a] twenty-four inch beam...." Hewn from a "[black] walnut log," the dugout was "nowhere except perhaps at the ends, over two-thirds of an inch thick...." Weir believed black walnut to be among the choicest woods for dugout construction but thought sassafras, cypress, ash, the tulip tree,[32] cottonwood, and oak, in that order, to be excellent materials, as well. Weir judged "[t]he catalpa," however, to be "the best of all woods on this continent from which to model the dugout, for it is very light, strong, and well nigh everlasting, so far as decay is concerned; but it is seldom that it can be found large enough."

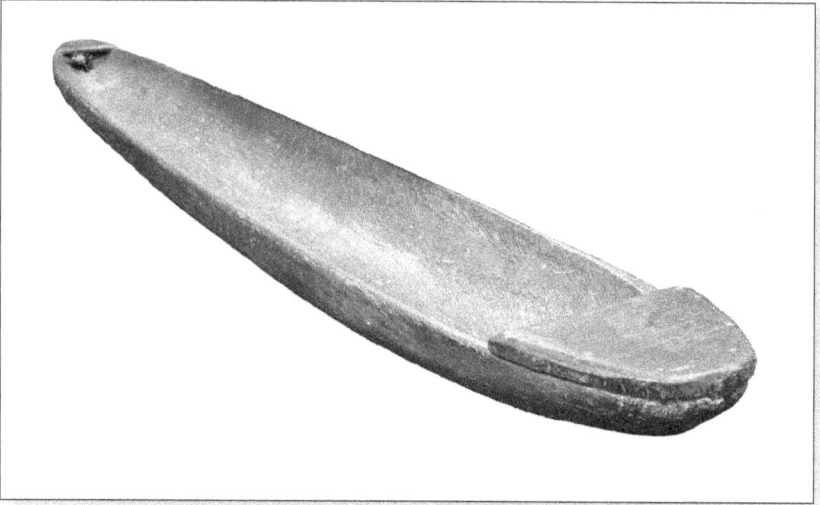

This dugout canoe, part of the collection of the Mississippi Department of Archives and History, was used in the Mississippi Delta from the 1870s into the 1950s. It measures 16 feet, three inches, in length, 21 inches in width, and is ten inches in height. *Photo courtesy of the Collection of the Museum Division, Mississippi Department of Archives and History.*

With each dugout being individually hand crafted, there was no uniformity in the boats. Rather, wide variations characterized their manufacture. "We have these canoes here of all sizes and models," Weir observed, "some for one man scant, and others that will carry a dozen or more."

Weir owned two dugouts: "one a pretty good cypress, large enough to carry three or four; the other of white ash, nicely finished," that he bought for "six bits." The ash canoe would "float two men of medium weight" but was "small enough for one" man to handle alone.

Weir's boats were not, perhaps, the best examples of the dugout when it came to stability. His seventy-five cent canoe, especially, exhibited some unruly behavior. Of that boat, Weir said, "It is continually trying to get on top, or to ride instead of being ridden. It can spill a fellow overboard quickly and gracefully; and, like the 'broncho' of the plains, it is very troublesome to mount, and cuts all kinds of capers when a greenhorn attempts to get into it."[33]

Yet, Weir's undisciplined dugout seems to have represented the rule rather than the exception. "You almost... have to keep your hair parted in the middle to trim such [a] boat," quipped one nineteenth century outdoor scribe.[34]

Given those circumstances one can hardly blame surveyor A. B. Wingfield for his skepticism toward the entire dugout enterprise. Concerning "Uncle" John Randolph Martin's canoe, which its owner called a "perogue,"[35] Wingfield said: "It was nothing on earth but a log hollowed out and sharpened at both ends, and would turn over if you looked at it cross-eyed." While Wingfield "was afraid to sit down in it," old Uncle John would paddle it down the bayou "standing perfectly erect...." There was no danger whatsoever in riding in his dugout, John assured Wingfield. "I hain't paddled this kind of a boat for fifty years and crossed the Mississippi a hundred times in one for nothin', and not learn' something."[36]

Tunica County pioneer Shelby McPeak, among his many other backwoods achievements, built dugouts "to gladden the eye of a connoisseur," according to Memphian George Phelan. McPeak was no ordinary Delta backwoods squatter. Despite a rustic appearance, he was a prosperous planter and local political leader[37] who had dined with Andrew Jackson at the Hermitage, Old Hickory's home just outside of Nashville, Tennessee.[38] McPeak also was a craftsman and a believer in doing things the best way. Probably his dugout ranked a few cuts above the average; still, it is worth considering as an example—if not the typical one—of the art. McPeak's prize canoe, according to Phelan, was the product of "all of his ingenuity and experience," and was "fairly as perfect as that style of boat can be."

D. B. Weir's faith in catalpa as the most durable wood of the Delta forests notwithstanding, McPeak, like other Delta backwoodsmen,[39] apparently ranked the sassafras as the superior tree for dugout stock. The pioneer had crafted his canoe from "an enormous sassafras he found somewhere in the woods." Phelan estimated the original log "must have been over four feet in diameter high up from the roots." After "carefully shaping and hollowing" the log where he found it, McPeak sunk "the embryo boat... in water for a year, to season [the wood against] splitting." Only after the year of soaking was "she… drawn out and set up in his front yard, where he could put the final and lingering touches on her."[40]

The end product "was about twenty feet long," two feet across the beam, and about "eighteen inches deep, with… the bow and stern rather raised…." McPeak then painted his vessel "a dull color between lead and copper, impossible to describe, but as much like an old log as possible," no doubt in an effort to camouflage the boat for stealth in hunting and fishing. It probably served to hide the boat from would-be thieves, as well.

McPeak decked the bow and stern of his dugout "for about a foot" and "bound" it "with iron, screwed on to prevent cracking where the fibers of the wood ran out." Small boxes, "about the size of a big brick," served as seats. McPeak's paddles, in contrast to the very narrow ones preferred by Indian canoe builders, were "very thin and broad" and made of "the lightest bottle ash**…."[41] McPeak also equipped his dugout with wooden forks on one side to hold his rifle and a canvas flap to cover it. Similar pegs held his handmade fishing rod. "A stout setting pole, some ten feet long, with a fork at the end to catch a hold with when pushing through flags[42] and grass, and a big sponge to bail with, finished the equipment of the boat proper," wrote Phelan.[43]

Whether they had highly crafted canoes like McPeak's or six-bit "broncho" dugouts like Weir's, the human residents of the Delta at least had recourse to boats during high water times. Animals, especially wildlife, had little or no means by which to escape the floods.

Without diminishing the horrible suffering afflicting men and women caught in flood zones in the early Delta days, Vicksburg hunting and fishing writer Burr H. Polk expressed his special sympathy for the wild animal victims of the overflows. Human beings, Polk observed during the Mississippi River floods of 1884, generally could take care of themselves and their livestock. Game animals, on the other hand, were at the mercy of men and the elements. By way of example he noted that deer were forced to gather on whatever unflooded ground they could find. There, they were easy "prey to

---

** Probably the "pumpkin ash," a species native to the Mississippi Delta, so called for the buttressing along its lower trunk common among some bottomland tree species, which gives the tree a bottle-like or pumpkin-like silhouette. The wood from the "bottled" portion of the tree tends to be strong but lighter than ordinary ash lumber.

any woodman who owned a dugout" or to starvation, whichever came first. Others would drown in their efforts to reach high ground.[44]

One correspondent for *Forest and Stream* saw some 50 dead deer floating in the flood waters of the lower Mississippi during the spring of 1882. He and a companion also spied a herd of deer swimming through the overflow. The animals were so weak that the men were able to lasso two and pull them onto a skiff. The exhausted animals "struggled but little," being so near starvation that they "soon accepted food from the hand...."[45]

During the overflows of 1880 a Capt. Bell of Yazoo County, Mississippi, supposedly a reliable gentleman, reported finding six panthers crowded together on a spot of dry land rising inches above the surrounding flood. So close together were the cats, according to Bell, that he was able to kill or disable all six of them with a single bullet.[46]

Bears, which usually could climb trees and find food among the branches until the overflows subsided, generally fared better.[47] Still, they, too, were susceptible to hunters crafty enough to find their refuges.[48]

Rising waters sometimes forced animals into places they normally would not go. "Occasionally there was great excitement in some country neighborhood over a report that somebody had seen a bear or a panther which the overflow had driven out of the 'swamp'" and into a settled area, even a town. When that happened, "the farmers of the community would generally get together with their guns and dogs and chase the intruding panther or bear to his death."[49]

Every now and then such a displaced predator would venture into areas so civilized that hardly a backwoodsman could be found to handle it. As late as 1880 rising waters from the bottoms near Memphis, at the top of the Delta, caused a panther to wander into the Bluff City in the early hours of the day. By chance, "Walter Ganong, a Coahoma County boy who was accustomed to panthers and not afraid of bear," happened to be in town. Young Walter, 15,[50] shot the cat as it "perched on a lamp post in the city... at day break...."[51]

4   Bears Before Breakfast

Regular floods notwithstanding, the Delta woods were "full of bears"[1] in pioneer times, according to George F. Maynard, Sr. Born about 1853, Mr. Maynard was certainly among the oldest, if not the oldest, of the persons interviewed for the Works Progress Administration's (WPA) Coahoma County history project in the 1930s.[2] His oral history provided many details about early days in the Delta that otherwise might have been lost. So ubiquitous was the bear in the Coahoma County of his youth, he told an interviewer, that when farmers felled oaks to make room for crops, sow bears and their cubs would appear almost immediately "to devour the tender twigs of the fallen monarchs."[3] "It was almost impossible to make a corn crop in some parts of the county on account of the depredations of that famous animal," he said. "People would go out in the corn patch early in the morning and kill a bear before breakfast."

Besides raiding cornfields the bears also preyed on farmers' hogs to the extent that maintaining any sizable number of swine was almost impossible.[4] Consequently, some of the old timers substituted bear meat for pork in their diets. One pioneer said he had known several "old bear hunters who never had a pound of bacon in the house. They would kill a bear and cure it like bacon and make and save oil by the barrel which was fine for cooking purposes."[5]

Bear hunting thus became a major pastime of many of those settlers, as much from necessity as from love of sport, and Fincher Bobo was reputed to have been one of the best bear hunters of the pre-War days. While little is known about Fincher's hunting adventures, Mr. Maynard's memories from his boyhood supply us with a few interesting details. As a child Maynard was the frequent companion and hunting partner of his grandfather, Col. George N. Saunders,[6] a veteran of the War of 1812[7] who sometimes hunted with Fincher.[8] No doubt Maynard heard the tales of Fincher Bobo from old Col. Saunders.

Maynard's oral history reported, among other things, that Fincher once killed six bears in one day. Maynard also said that Fincher kept a pack of 30 bear dogs. Even in those days maintaining that many dogs could be a costly enterprise: Fincher's dogs once dug up and ate his family's entire cache of butter.[9]

At least one hunting story from Fincher's time has been preserved in the Maynard history, although it focuses more on Bobo's hunting companions than upon Fincher himself.

Fincher Bobo, Col. George N. Saunders (Maynard's grandfather), and several others, including a "fat Methodist preacher," were bear hunting. The pack of about 20 dogs jumped a big one. Col. Saunders stayed on the dogs' heels and was first to reach the bear when he treed. Saunders dismounted and shot the beast, which fell limp to the ground. The Colonel rushed to slit the bear's throat to bleed it as was the custom of the day.

As Saunders stood astride what he thought was a dead bear, preparing to cut its jugular, the animal, without warning, took to its feet with Saunders on its back. The bear's resurrection so startled the Colonel that he dropped his knife and grabbed the animal's ears in an effort to keep it from biting him. The excitement of their master riding a bear was more than the dogs could stand. As one body they charged, jaws snapping, nipping the Colonel as often as the bear. Saunders shouted for help, but the scene was so outlandish that the fat Methodist preacher, the only other human present, was paralyzed with laughter. Finally, Bobo and the rest of the hunting party arrived and put the bear, the Colonel, and the pudgy parson out of their respective miseries. Saunders soundly cursed the preacher and went home.[10]

Exactly what type of bear those woodsmen were hunting is up for debate. The only species of bear found naturally east of the Mississippi River is the American black bear, scientifically called *Ursus americanus*. For 150 years or more, however, naturalists have sought to distinguish the black bear of the Deep South as a special form of that animal, if not an entirely separate species.

Forest and Stream founder, Charles Hallock, writing in 1899, for example, wrote that "there is in Louisiana, Mississippi and sometimes in the southern Arkansas…swamps a big, perfectly black bear" that Hallock believed to be a unique species. This "swamp bear," as he called it, was "much above the average weight of black bears" and often "marked by a white horseshoe on its breast...."[11]

Perhaps because of the unsurpassed fertility of the region's soil and the Deep South's short, mild winters, those Delta animals regularly reached, as Hallock noted, extremely large sizes and weights by black bear standards. Such bears, Hallock wrote, typically "weigh[ed] from 400 to 680 lbs.," with even larger ones reported. One Coahoma County bear killed in the 1840s supposedly weighed 886 pounds after being field dressed (eviscerated).[12] Even by a conservative estimate, such a bear would have had a live weight of some 975 pounds, making it among the heaviest black bears ever killed.[13] One might suspect that such reported weights were mere guesses; that hunters surely had no means of weighing bears killed in the nineteenth century Delta wilderness. Hallock rejected that supposition. According to his argument, heavy, bulky items were probably more easily weighed in the old Delta than in most places today. There typically was, he pointed out to his readers, an "accurate set of scales, made for weighing bales of cotton, to be found at [the many] steam-boat landings"[14] common along major Delta streams.

Interestingly, as early as 1800, naturalists were identifying a "yellow bear" in the same approximate parts of the South in which Hallock placed his "perfectly black bear"—northwestern Louisiana, and the Mississippi Delta—and also in the great swamps of coastal North Carolina and Virginia. Professor Edward Griffith, writing in 1821, designated this bear, which he described as ranging from a reddish brown "cinnamon" to blond, or yellow, as a separate species from *Ursus americanus* and named it *Ursus luteolus*, which, of course, is Latin for "yellow bear."[15] In 1895 Dr. Hart Merriam determined that "certain cranial and dental peculiarities" he had observed in skulls from bears taken around Prairie Mer Rouge, Louisiana, justified classification of the so-called "yellow bear" as a species distinct from *Ursus americanus*, and concurred with Griffith.[16] There is no evidence that the skull specimens Merriam examined were from bears that were anything other than black in color.

While a blond phase black bear is not uncommon west of the Mississippi, particularly in mountain meadows or areas of sparse or open timber, *Ursus americanus* in any phase other than black is almost unheard of east of the Mississippi today.[17] The historical record generally indicates that Delta bears of earlier times were black, as well. There are exceptions, though. The name of the Delta village of Nitta Yuma, which at least one source says is a corruption of *nitta homa*, Choctaw for "red bear,"[18] may hint that cinnamon colored bears once were seen at least occasionally in the Delta. A 1909 story for the *Saturday Evening Post* by Vicksburg jurist and writer Harris Dickson reports the killing of a "huge brown bear" in the Delta woods by a party that included the famed Washington County, Mississippi, bear hunter, Holt Collier.[19] Such rare examples, however, seem to establish the general rule that Delta bears were almost all, if not entirely, of the black phase.

Finally, in the 1950s, biologists determined that the so-called "yellow bear," whatever its true color, was not in fact distinct enough to warrant a separate species designation. It was, the scientific world decided, a subspecies of the ordinary black bear, which has since been nominated *Ursus americanus luteolus* and is commonly called the Louisiana black bear.[20] Biologists today generally consider the Louisiana black bear to be one of 16 subspecies of *Ursus americanus* and believe that it is found currently in parts of the states of Louisiana, Texas, and Mississippi.[21]

Whether *luteolus* is the bear that predominated in the Coahoma County of the nineteenth century cannot be known with certainty. What we can know is that whatever its scientific classification, the Delta black bear made Bob Bobo a celebrated figure among nineteenth century American sportsmen.

5 Young Bob Bobo

Even for families with luxuries like hand powered grist mills, the Delta wilderness was hard on settlers. Fincher Bobo died in 1856 at the young age of 41. His son, Bob, was but nine years old. The family buried Fincher in Fredonia Cemetery near the present day town of Como in Panola County, Mississippi.[1]

Fincher's wife, Sarah, subsequently married Dr. Samuel Clark, a widower. Dr. Clark's son, Curt, from his marriage to the late Mrs. Clark, was close to Bob's age. Bob and Curt would become the closest of friends and practically grow up in the Delta woods.[2] Though he might not have killed a bear "when he was only three," as the song says of Davy Crockett, Bob Bobo almost certainly was hunting the fanged and clawed predators of the Delta at an early age.

Although the Delta pioneer experience in and of itself offered ample adversity to forge and try a man's character, Bob's mettle was destined to be tempered and tested in the drama of battle, as well. On December 20, 1860, following the election of Abraham Lincoln, South Carolina seceded from the Union. Mississippi did the same on January 9, 1861. The world turned upside down for many in the U. S. over the following weeks. By February, Florida, Alabama, Georgia, Louisiana, and Texas had left the Union, as well, and a meeting to organize the Confederacy had begun in Montgomery, Alabama. After Confederate troops fired on Fort Sumter on April 12, 1861, Virginia, Arkansas, North Carolina, and Tennessee also seceded. With the First Battle of Manassas Junction on July 21, 1861, the Civil War was underway.[3]

A year and a half later, 16 year old Bob Bobo no longer could be constrained from joining the fight. He ran away from home[4] to enlist with Company B of the 18th Mississippi Cavalry Regiment on February 1, 1863,[5] shortly after that unit was organized.[6] Attached to Nathan Bedford Forrest's Cavalry Corps, the 18th saw service in battles in Tennessee and Mississippi and sustained heavy losses. At an age when boys today are thinking about the next football game or wondering if they will pass their driver's license tests, Bobo was fighting Yankees with rifle and sword. Despite his tender years, Bobo, through it all, proved "one of the boldest followers of a bold leader."

Shortly after General Robert E. Lee's surrender, a battle-hardened Bobo, still a teenager, was mustered out of the service on May 1, 1865. He returned to Coahoma County with little more than the clothes on his back and "the scars of several wounds."[7] It was late spring, the Mississippi River was at flood stage, and almost the entire county was inundated. Bobo and a friend—most likely his step-brother, Curt Clark—paddled about the countryside in a dugout canoe until they reached a ridge that was slightly higher than the prevailing water level. Game fleeing the surrounding flood had flocked to the high ground, the only dry land for miles. "We tied up and went out a little way from the boat," Bobo recalled in an interview. "My friend saw a deer and killed it, and then we killed two more in a few minutes. I walked down the ridge and saw a small bear, and I shot it, and then I saw another, a very large one, and I killed it, too, and a moment after I killed a third. We hunted about fifteen minutes and had to stop, for our boat would hold no more meat."[8]

The high ground they found already had a name—Anise Ridge—apparently so called for an anise scented weed that grew there in abundance.[9] Bobo returned to Anise Ridge the following year and settled on an especially promising piece of that land. His first week in residence on his new property he killed 13 bears. In another five day hunt he garnered more than a ton of bear meat. On yet another day on Anise Ridge he killed game yielding 1,200 pounds of meat in two and a quarter hours.[10] The area today is still known as Anise Brake[11] or Bobo Brake.

Bob Bobo quickly developed a reputation as a bear hunter exceeding that of his father, Fincher. In the process Bob "did not neglect his material interests." He set to work clearing land and planting cotton. Managing his holdings with "energy and thrift," he eventually developed a plantation of some 2000 acres, 900 of which were in cultivation and the rest containing some of the best hunting cover in the state in those days.[12]

Such an industrious young man would not go long without a wife. On November 24, 1868, Bob married Anna E. Prince of Memphis, Tennessee, at the home of her mother. The attendants included Bob's brother-in-law, Richard Nelson "Nels" Harris,[13] and Bob's little sister, Katherine "Kate" Rivers Bobo Harris, who had married Nels some seven months earlier.[14] "A truly worthy and deserving gentleman," read the announcement in the *Memphis Daily Avalanche*, "never wooed and won a fairer, sweeter prize."[15]

In 1869 Bob and his step-brother and farming partner, Curt Clark, discovered that it was sometimes easier to make money by renting one's land to others than by farming it oneself. The landlord approach to farming, they also learned, had the additional advantage of leaving more time for bear hunting. With their croplands let to tenants and finding themselves with no real work to do, Bobo and Clark entered into a project not exactly calculated to warm the heart of Bob's new bride: they took some of the plantation hands and spent almost an entire year "in the swamp. We didn't come out for three months at a time." If they needed supplies they simply sent one of the hired men back for them.[16]

During that time Bobo and Clark kept a record of the game they killed. By the end of the year they tallied "304 bear, 54 deer, 47 wildcats, and 9 panthers." Bobo credited their many bear kills to the tenacity of his pack. If his dogs discovered fresh scent, they almost always brought the bear to bay. "One season," for example, Bobo "lost only two runs," killing 150 of the 152 bears chased by his dogs. As many as nine bears were killed in one day that year in front of the Bobo pack.[17]

There is no known record of Anna Prince Bobo's thoughts about her newly acquired spouse running off to the woods with his hunting buddy for the better part of a year. She must not have held it much against her young husband, however, for not too many months after Bob's return from his prolonged bear hunt the couple welcomed their firstborn son into the world. They named the baby boy Fincher Gist Bobo after his paternal grandfather.[18]

6   The Bandits' Bear Hunt

The year Bobo and Clark spent so much time in the woods—1869— an event took place at an obscure Louisiana horseracing track that resulted in Bob Bobo playing host to one of the most famous—and infamous—characters of his day: Jesse James.

Few personalities in American history are more enshrouded in myth and legend than James. Rightly or wrongly, much of the South, struggling with post-bellum poverty and mourning the lost cause of the Confederacy, saw in Jesse and his brother Frank, their cohorts the Younger brothers, and all their outlaw comrades, men who, like themselves, had suffered at the hands of northern aggression. Unlike most former Confederates, the Jameses, the Youngers, and their fellow outlaws had not surrendered, but had continued the fight by robbing Yankee controlled banks and railroads. Such was the myth, in any event. Less romantic minds in the North and the South alike, however, viewed the James-Younger Gang as thugs who even during the Civil War had ridden outside the bounds of the law and, at least in the post war period, were vicious criminals.

His admirers and detractors alike, however, found James's notoriety exhilarating. Many in the South and Midwest, in fact, cherished and clung to their local stories about the James-Younger Gang robbing this local bank or that business establishment, even when the hard evidence proved the outlaws were nowhere near such vicinities at the times of the crimes in question.

The Mississippi Delta was not immune to the fascination with Jesse James. Local tradition has long associated Jesse James with Coahoma County. Perhaps the most interesting story connecting the James Gang with the Delta comes from an account by one Capt. Kit Dalton, a self-professed former Confederate guerrilla and a claimant to membership in the James Gang.[1]

According to Dalton, he and Jesse had drifted into Louisiana hoping "to buy a small farm for each of us and settle down to the quiet and prosaic life," apparently in the northeastern part of the state, either in East Carroll Parish, near Lake Providence, or in the Bayou Macon country around the city of Monroe in Ouachita Parish.[2] Other members of the gang, including Jesse's brother Frank, Wood Hite (a cousin to the James brothers), and Cole Younger (and, probably, his brothers Jim and Bob, as well) soon joined Jesse and Kit in the Pelican State.[3] "I can assure you our intentions were good...," Dalton wrote.

The Youngers and the Jameses were racehorse fanciers. They owned thoroughbreds and raced them from Texas to Saratoga Springs, New York. Once in Louisiana they quickly located a racetrack. One of the gang—the press later would identify the man as Cole Younger—had a saddle horse he believed could outrun almost anything on four legs. Younger entered the animal in a race with himself—at almost six feet and two hundred plus pounds[4]—as the jockey. So confident was he that his horse was the best that he bet $700—about all he had—that he would win the race. Since photographs or drawings of the gang members had not been widely circulated in those days the local turf enthusiasts had no idea that the out-of-town racer and his companions were the infamous James and Younger Gang.

Frank James (l.) and Kit Dalton, Confederate
Veterans Reunion, Summit, Mississippi, 1910.

The race began and looked to be no contest. Younger and his horse led the way through the last curve and had a strong lead down the final stretch. Seeing a strange horse about to beat a local favorite and win the pot of local money was more than one Louisiana man could bear. He rushed to the track and waved a blanket in the face of the lead horse. Younger's mount shied and swerved, slowing its pace just enough to cause it to lose the race.

Younger was furious. He rode to the judges' stand and lodged with the three men who refereed the races "a vigorous protest against such trickery." The judges and the crowd alike responded with jeers. According to Dalton's version of the event, one of the judges shouted, "Cut it out. You have lost. Take your medicine like a man."[5]

Younger responded, "It's an outrage! Do you, sir, think I am going to stand for an outrage like that?"

"Say, clear out from this," the judge responded, "before I have you pinched."

The horseman continued: "But, justice, man; justice is all I want."

The judge, having no idea how dangerous was the man he had rebuked, threatened him again: "You'll get that and a d— sight more if you open your head again."

Cole Younger determined to tolerate no further such abuse. "Hand my money here, you d— vampire, or by the eternals I'll blow your infernal brains out," Younger shouted, unholstering a Colt's dragoon revolver as he spoke. Instantly, one of the other judges loosed a shot in the rider's direction and to his great misfortune, missed. He did not live to fire a second round.

At that point, recalled Dalton, "the ball now opened in good earnest."

As the surviving judges reached for their guns the other gang members rode to their friend's aid. In seconds, the two remaining officials lay dead beside the first. One of the "nimblest of our boys," wrote Dalton, mounted "the judge's stand and collect[ed] back the stolen money with compound interest…."[6]

According to the *Chicago Tribune*, besides the three judges, two more Louisiana men died later from wounds received in that melee.[7]

Dalton did not identify the outraged rider as Cole Younger but simply as a member of the James-Younger Gang. The *Tribune*, however, positively named Cole Younger as the angry horseman. Younger himself denied any role in the killings. In his 1902 autobiography he wrote: "One of the lies that had been… broadcast concerning me is that I killed five men and shot five others in a row over a 'jobbed' horse race in Louisiana. There is this much truth about it—there was a jobbed race, and after it I fought a duel, but not over the race."

In his book, though, Cole Younger denied just about every illegal act of which he ever was accused except for his role in the Youngers' disastrous Northfield, Minnesota, bank robbery attempt. Younger hardly could have denied taking part in that crime, for he was caught in the act, tried, convicted, and imprisoned for it. In all probability, Younger was not telling the truth about his involvement in the racetrack incident, just as he obviously was lying in denying his participation in so many other crimes.[8]

Whether or not Younger was the chief perpetrator in the Louisiana racetrack shootings, and regardless of the number slain, the outlaws, according to Dalton, "made a clean-cut getaway without the slightest injury to ourselves or horses and… headed north for Mississippi." Three weeks later the Jameses and Youngers and their entourage were in Coahoma County "visiting relatives of the James boys," wrote Dalton, "who received them most cordially" and introduced them under assumed names to "a Mr. Bobo, a famous bear hunter…." That Mr. Bobo, of course, was Bob Bobo, who extended his customary hospitality and, according to Kit Dalton, "arranged a bear hunt in our honor."

The outlaws had never experienced such a thing. "[W]e enjoyed listening to the yelping pack," Dalton would later write, but found little pleasure in "trying to keep up with it through the terrible forests of canes and bamboo." Bobo, the outlaws quickly realized, relished crashing through the brakes as much as they loved robbing Yankee trains. Not "a bear in all Mississippi jungle-land," recalled Dalton, "could get through one of those almost impenetrable canebrakes easier and with less damage to himself than our honorable host."

The bear that Bobo and the outlaws were pursuing came to bay against the root end of a fallen tree. Although Dalton recognized that Bobo could have brought the bear to a quick end himself, the planter "had taken us out for the chase and wanted one of us to have the pleasure of bagging" the beast. The Jameses' cousin, Wood Hite, was accorded the honor. He "dispatched [the bear] with one shot from his big pistol."

Whether they believed the heat had died down enough from the Louisiana troubles to permit them to move about freely again, or whether they feared being invited on another bear hunt, the outlaws quit Coahoma County shortly after their outing with Bobo. Whatever their reason for leaving, Dalton called the gang's time in the Delta "one of our most delightful vacations."

In his 1914 memoir, *Under the Black Flag*, Dalton wrote: "should [this book] fall into [the Bobo family's] hands, it will more than likely be a surprise to [them] to know how cordially they entertained a band of outlaws…."[9]

Maybe Bobo would have been surprised to have learned the identity of his guests and maybe not. Other Coahoma County traditions regarding the Jameses and the Youngers in the Delta suggest that at least some persons in the area well knew the gang's identity.

In 1938, when he was 73 years old, Wilbur T. Gibson told WPA interviewer Florence F. Montroy that when he was a boy of 13 or so (around 1878)—almost a decade after the Jameses' bear hunt with Bobo—"Jesse and Frank James made a very dashing entrance" into Coahoma County. The brothers were driving "a carry all," Gibson said, a rig he described as "somewhat like a surrey" and, in the Jameses' case, drawn by "two very handsome horses, one a black and one a gray…." According to Gibson, Jesse and Frank had come to the Delta for the "express business" of robbing "a certain man" whom they believed to be "a Dam Yankee" of "his, supposedly, fabulous fortune."

While in Coahoma County the outlaws lodged with some Delta kin, a family that not only was friendly with the intended victim of the James boys but had benefited from the man's generosity: the wealthy gentleman had lent them a sizable amount of money. The Jameses' host, upon learning his guests' plan, sought to dissuade Frank and Jesse from their designs. The highwaymen finally abandoned the plot upon learning their intended victim was no kind of Yankee at all, but, in fact, a true son of the South; so went the story, anyway. The crime thus averted, the host kept the identity of his guests secret for the remainder of their stay. It was only after the James outfit left the Delta that neighbors learned the visitors were in fact the notorious James brothers.[10]

The James-Younger Gang apparently was in Mississippi close to the "about 1878" date given by Gibson in his account of the outlaws' visit. According to the recollections of Judge Jefferson Snyder, which appeared in a 1938 issue of the New Orleans *Times-Picayune*, the outlaws in 1879 robbed some stores in the southwestern Mississippi towns of Washington and Fayette before escaping to a hideout just across the river near St. Joseph, Louisiana.[11] Snyder's account does not say whether they also were in Coahoma County during that same approximate time period indicated by Wilbur Gibson.

Mrs. John Bell Hood, daughter-in-law of Confederate General John Bell Hood, as well as a local history writer for the WPA, dramatized what appears to have been the Wilbur Gibson Jesse James story in a 1936 pageant presented at a schoolhouse in Jonestown, a plantation village in the northern end of the county. In Mrs. Hood's version of the legend, set in 1882, the D. M. Russell family was "entertain[ing] unawares" Jesse James at their Matagorda Plantation house following the outlaw's "failed attempt to hold up [a] Mr. Dickerson," a wealthy landowner who resided in the Friars Point area, ten or twelve miles northwest of Jonestown.[12] While the Russells and James were seated at the breakfast table, "Maj. T. G. Dabney, chief engineer of the Levee Board," interrupted "the breakfast by the tragic announcement of the breaking of the levee at Delta," a landing on the Mississippi about four miles north of Friars Point. Existing accounts of the play fail to report anything further about James's activities at that time.

Mrs. Hood's story made for colorful local pageantry, perhaps, but it is unlikely any such combination of persons ever gathered at Matagorda. The levee broke in Coahoma County in February of 1882. Jesse James had rented a house in St. Joseph, Missouri, in November 1881 and was murdered there by Bob Ford on April 3, 1882.[13] It seems improbable that James was in Coahoma County during the interim period, especially given the fact that the Mississippi River and many Delta streams were at flood stage from December 1881 until spring 1882.[14] Moreover, historical evidence places Jesse James in and around St. Joseph in February of that year.[15]

A different story about a James Gang visit comes down to us from an old timer identified only as "Old Citizen." When interviewed in 1936 for the WPA's Coahoma County History project, the Old Citizen told writer Mrs. J. L. McKeown of a time in "the 80s" when "Jesse James breezed into Friars Point [then the county seat] and spent the night in the home of a Protestant preacher."[16] According to the Old Citizen, Jesse "went up town" and joined in the poker games "and enter[ed] into all forms of their enjoyment." The locals believed the parson knew exactly who his guest was all along, but the outlaw's identity was not "leaked out," said the old timer, "until James had had ample time to reach parts unknown."

If the Jameses or any of their cohorts returned to Coahoma County in the 1870s or 80s, there is no sure proof of it. Quite likely the outlaws so enjoyed the Delta hospitality shown them by Bobo and his neighbors in 1869 that they did return in 1878 or later for another visit. If so, they almost certainly did not join Bob Bobo for a second bear hunt. For as Dalton wrote in his memoir, despite their years of experience as Confederate guerrillas and train and bank robbers, he and his companions in outlawry "had never encountered a Mississippi jungle before" their hunt with Bob Bobo. They had found the Delta canebrakes so intimidating, Dalton assured his readers, that they would "never tackle one of them again unless that were the sentence passed" upon the outlaws for their "misdeeds of the long ago."[17]

7 Bobo's Reputation Expands

While Bobo might not have entertained wanted bandits again, over the next two decades he would host many bear hunters from many backgrounds and many places.

Just how and when Bob Bobo's reputation first spread beyond the borders of Coahoma County cannot be known for certain. As early as 1871 the *Urbana Union* newspaper in the small town of Urbana, Ohio, some 650 miles to the northeast, published what was certainly one of the earliest out-of-state articles noting Bobo's prowess as a bear slayer. The short news item in the *Union* noted that R. E. Bobo of "Coahoma County, Tennessee," had killed six bears the preceding week.[1] Although the *Union* got the state wrong, it spelled Bobo's name correctly.

The year 1874 was eventful for another reason: the Bobos had another son. This one they named Robert Eager Bobo, Jr. Like his brother Fincher, he was destined to follow his father into the bear woods.

At some point, probably between Fincher and Bob, Jr.'s, births, the Bobos also had a baby girl, Sara Clara, who, Bobo family tradition says, died as an infant. Nothing else is known of her. While the Bear Hunter, perhaps, could submerge his sorrows at the loss of a child in the excitement of the chase, Anna was left alone with her grief during Bob's long absences with only the plantation hands and household servants for company. Not surprisingly, Mrs. Bobo eventually would seek solace from outside her home.[2]

The press, though, was more concerned with Bob, Sr.'s, hunting exploits than with his family life, and the Bobo stories continued to flow into and out of the newspaper offices. In November 1876, for example, James G. Chism of the Coahoma County Mississippi River village of Friars Point sent the editor of the Memphis *Daily Appeal* a foot from a panther "killed by

Mr. R. E. Bobo and Mr. R. N. Harris" not far from Chism's home that fall. The editor dutifully related Chism's story to the paper's readers.[3]

It would be the 1880s, however, before Bob Bobo's reputation would reach truly national, if not international, proportions. Perhaps what was the first nationally circulated piece on Bobo appeared in 1882 in the sporting journal *The American Field,* published in Chicago but read throughout the United States and even in Great Britain and Europe. Written from Crockett's Bluff, Arkansas, by "Byrne," the pen name of writer D. B. Weir, the article painted a picture of the Mississippi Delta designed to excite any would-be bear hunter. Bears were so pervasive in the Delta, Weir told his readers, that their predations, if left unchecked, would ruin the Delta farmers and planters. Hunting the beasts, he explained, was not merely a sporting pastime, but a necessity.

As proof "of how plentiful bears are in that section, and how many an expert can kill," he cited a letter written to him by "Major Bobo" in care of the *American Field*. While extensive quotations attributed to Bob Bobo by others exist today, the letter to "Byrne" is one of the few surviving examples of Bobo's own words as written by the Bear Hunter himself:

> Mr. Byrne, Dear Sir: Yours of October 27 is at hand. You are right in saying that "sportsmen are not strangers," therefore no excuses are necessary. I will be glad to have the gentlemen take a hunt with me provided they bring some good dogs* and leave them with me when they go home. I have a pack of twelve fine dogs, and can kill a bear at any time that I wish, but the bears are not fat yet, and will not be in full flesh until about December 1, after which will be the time to hunt them. As you are in one sense a stranger to me, I of course, feel some delicacy in giving you the facts as to my life as a hunter, therefore I will only say,—and I can give good reference as to its truth—that I killed 304 bears, 47 cats (wildcats), 21 deer and 17 panthers in one season, and that I kill from 75 to 200 bears, etc., every season. I have killed 32 bears since August first, but am not hunting much this year. A fine crop of cotton is seriously in the way of sport. So soon as that is safe I hope to see your "tender foots," and I will guarantee them some fine sport, and the best in the shop. There is no game in this locality except bears, and plenty of them. The high water last Spring drove the deer all out. As you say, there are no strangers among

sportsmen, you will please excuse me, and let me hear from
you again. I will close by saying there is nothing small about
me when there is a chance for sport.

> Respectfully yours,
> Rob. E. Bobo

*The Major means by this, that any kind of common dogs that have
any hunting in them, will be an acceptable addition to his pack, for
bear hunting is rough on dogs, and to keep up his pack, one must be
continually adding to it.[4]

Despite Weir's use of the title "major" in reference to Bobo, as far
as can be determined, the Bear Hunter never held a military commission. Surviving records indicate he enlisted in the Confederate forces and
mustered out as a private. Military titles, however, were commonly used
as signs of respect by Southern men in referring to other Southern men.
While to outsiders it seemed as if every man in the South was "a colonel,"
in reality, other ranks—"captain," for example—were at least as common,
maybe more so, with the exact title apparently determined by local custom. In Mississippi, factors such as the individual's age, wealth, whether
he was a large landholder, and his perceived status in the community seem
to have been the determining considerations. To Weir, who did not live
in Coahoma County but was writing from across the Mississippi River in
Arkansas, Bobo appeared to have the standing of a major, so "Major Bobo"
he was to Mr. Weir.

Men like "Major" Bobo, Weir told *The American Field's* subscribers,
"are, as a natural consequence on their large plantations, somewhat isolated,
and love good, intelligent genial, company…." Consequently, Weir felt no
qualms in assuring his readers that "any gentleman sportsman wishing to
join in the most exciting sport left to us on this continent, will be warmly
welcomed by Mr. Bobo and other bear hunters in the Mississippi and White
River Bottoms."[5]

Besides being the years that saw Bob Bobo heralded for the first time
in the national press by writers like D. B. Weir, the 1880s also were the
decade of the railroad in the Delta. The locomotive and train brought
swift change to the Mississippi bottoms. Formerly inaccessible areas were
open to settlement, and settlers already in the Delta backwoods no longer

suffered the isolation experienced by those of Fincher Bobo's generation. Transportation of timber cut in the Delta had once been a matter of rafting logs down bayous and rivers. With the construction of railroads, loggers were no longer hostage to water levels and limited to waterfront markets downstream. Steam locomotives could haul their logs directly to the saw mill. Most importantly, cotton—the staple crop of the Delta planter— could be transported swiftly to the markets and textile mills of the north and east.[6] A new prosperity was on the way.

As the railroads stretched their ways into the recesses of the great swamp, the "gentlemen sportsmen" spoken of by D. B. Weir did indeed come. One of the earliest of them, however, came first, not as a hunter, but as a representative of the Louisville, New Orleans and Texas Railroad. The L. N. O. & T. had plans for the Delta that called for tracks directly through Bob Bobo's property. Almost exactly a year after Weir's article in the *American Field* the company dispatched a surveying crew to Coahoma County to shoot the lines for their proposed road. Along with it traveled a Memphis-based company agent by the name of Thomas A. Divine, known as Tom to his many friends.

It was October 25, 1883, and the railroad men were relaxing in their camp located within 200 yards of where Bobo would soon build the home that would become the seat of his plantation. All around thickets "of vines and cane" rose over "the most magnificent gum, ash and hickory man ever looked upon," much of it hung with garlands of wild grape. Not a sound was heard "save the woodpecker's tune on [a] dead limb above…." Through this autumn stillness, beneath the festoons of muscadine and creeper, came a lone rider upon "a little country-raised horse, with a bear's leg dangling down on either side of his flank": Bob Bobo. Bobo "deposited the bear in [the railroad] camp," sat with the men a while, then took his leave.

Within another year's time, the L. N. O. & T. would be providing ready transportation across the Delta and would have a stop on Bobo's property appropriately named "Bobo Station." Sportsmen, quite literally, would be able to ride the train right to the planter's doorstep,[7] a development that would be the source of much change for Bobo and the Delta. Unbeknownst to Divine and Bobo at that time, Divine would play a significant role in making Bob Bobo's name nothing short of famous among nineteenth century American sportsmen. That, though, was yet a few years off.

Change was coming for the Delta and Bobo from yet another quarter about that same time. In 1884 the World's Industrial and Cotton Centennial Exposition, the South's first world's fair, opened in New Orleans. Mississippi, a state hardly on the nation's mind since the close of the War Between the States, played a prominent role in that event: all the lumber used in construction of the exposition's buildings originated in the Magnolia State. Mississippi's state exhibit also showcased the state's forest products, not the least of which was the magnificent timber from the Yazoo-Mississippi Delta and the adjacent hills.[8]

While lumbering already was an active industry in Mississippi, the New Orleans world's fair brought the state's extensive forest resources before an entirely new audience, creating a demand for the state's "timber lands at prices unknown prior to the Exposition."[9] White oak staves for barrel-making were much desired by brewers and vintners in those days. Within five years of the New Orleans world's fair, staves from Mississippi were bringing the premium prices of from $75 to $140 per thousand at the port of New Orleans,[10] from whence they were shipped to Europe to become barrels for, among other beverages, French and Spanish wines.[11] It did not require a prophet to predict what the introduction of railroads combined with the heavy demand for Delta timber eventually would mean for Bobo's woodlands.

In May1886 Bob Bobo made another international press appearance, this time on the pages of the popular sporting weekly, *Forest and Stream*. In that publication a correspondent writing under the pseudonym Cavalier and reporting on the abundance of game in the Arkansas Delta's Cache River bottom told his readers: "Mr. Bobo, who lives opposite here in Mississippi killed forty black bears last winter....Mr. Bobo does his hunting with a .44 repeating rifle."[12]

Perhaps prompted by Cavalier's article, Thomas Gregory Dabney, also a correspondent for *Forest and Stream*, made several efforts to communicate with Bobo by mail concerning his hunting adventures. When he received no response to his letters Dabney decided to call upon the Bear Hunter in person. In the fall of 1886 Dabney traveled to the Bobo plantation hoping to interview the master of the house. To his disappointment he found that the "genial host was 20 miles away in the Hushpuckana swamp, with a party of gentlemen from the North, whom he was... initiating into the mysteries of bear hunting in the Mississippi canebrakes." He was received cordially, however, by Mrs. Bobo, whom he described as "a charming matron" who dispensed "the hospitalities of her home with a graceful and bounteous hand."

Dabney, the chief engineer for the then nascent Yazoo-Mississippi Delta Levee District and the dean of levee builders of his day, had ample opportunity to visit Bobo's vicinity of Coahoma County. In the winter of 1887 he returned to the Bobo plantation, this time specifically for the purpose of extracting from Bobo some tales of his exploits in the Delta woods.[13] To his delight, Dabney found the great hunter at home. Having learned of Bobo's supposed reputation for being somewhat tight-lipped with his hunting stories,[14] the engineer had come prepared with a generous quantity of what he called "Nelson County," no doubt a reference to the chief product of that district of Kentucky, which is known as the bourbon capital of the Blue Grass State. "Under the relaxing influence of a moderate horn" of that elixir, Dabney told *Forest and Stream* readers, Bobo happily reminisced to the engineer's satisfaction.

With the publication of Dabney's article, Bobo's reputation expanded further. The curious, including newspaper reporters, began to appear on his doorstep with greater and greater frequency, all hoping to hear some exciting stories. Typically, Bobo's visitors wanted to know how many bears he had killed, the most he had killed in a year, the biggest, etc. Sometimes it became a little tiresome, even for a man who liked to talk bear hunting as much as did Bobo. Once a newspaper editor asked Bobo to relate for what must have been the 100th time or more his personal record for one day's bear hunting. A friend standing by whispered, "Tell him anything, say twenty-seven." Bobo did, the editor printed it, and for years it was passed around that Bobo had killed 27 bears in a single day.[15] That, of course, was an exaggeration, even for the great Bobo.

"Country life in the swamps of Mississippi," wrote one chronicler of the early Delta days, "is at best monotonous, but particularly so to the ladies.... [S]ettlements and plantations are too far apart to admit of much social visiting, so their lives are anything but pleasant."[16] That must have been especially true for Anna Bobo. In addition to the general lack of companionship common to backwoods women, she also had a husband who left on hunting trips for extended periods of time and had suffered the loss of her only daughter.

At some point between 1887 and 1890, while Bob and the boys were off hunting, Anna, apparently no longer able to tolerate her lonely life, "ran away to Central or South America with a railroad man" known only as "Mr. Norton." She took with her only a large trunk and whatever she packed into it. Anna would not be heard from for some 20 years.[17]

Anna's desertion surely wounded deeply the strong-willed Bobo's pride. The Bear Hunter refused to accept it, in fact, and identified himself as a widower thereafter. [18]

Bobo would not remarry.[19] He would continue bear hunting. His name appeared once more on the pages of *Forest and Stream* in 1892, this time in a piece by an anonymous hunter from Rushville, Indiana, who called himself only "C. C." The Hoosier, in concluding an account of a hunting trip to the Delta's Sunflower wilderness, wrote of meeting in Mississippi a "Mr. R. E. Bobo" whom he described as "an enthusiastic hunter" who owned a large pack "of the very best bear dogs." C. C. reported that in 1879 Bobo had killed "304 bears, 52 wildcats, 47 panthers, and 66 deer."[20]

8   Mashed up Cattle

In the midst of this rise to fame Bobo suffered some damages occasioned by the newly arrived railroad when a locomotive "mashed up" a few of his cattle. He sent in his claim for the dead cows and the railroad sent Tom Divine down from Memphis to resolve the matter. This Divine, of course, was the very same man who had met Bobo in the railroad camp in the fall of 1883.[1]

Divine was no ordinary railroad man. The Memphis-based claims agent for the Illinois Central Railroad[2] was a prominent Bluff City sportsman who served a number of terms as president of the Memphis Gun Club and was an honorary member of the Beaver Dam Club in Tunica County in northwestern Mississippi,[3] the hunting club made famous some years later by outdoor writing legend Nash Buckingham. Divine's name regularly appeared in the sporting press and was known to hunters and trap shooters across the country. An 1895 issue of *The Sporting Life*, a Philadelphia, Pennsylvania, tabloid, reported that there "is not a more popular man in the South than Tom Devine."[4]

"It was kind of woolly down in the Delta in those days,"[5] as one writer put it. Divine was not fully prepared for just how "woolly" it was. A large portion of that wooliness stemmed from the early Delta settlers' propensity to answer offenses with violence. As Emerson Hough observed in *The Story of the Outlaw*, his classic work on the Wild West's gun-fighting culture, "the West got its hot blood largely from the South." As a case in point he cited a story told by Bobo of a local man who was known for doing some loud and often unwelcomed talking. "My friend," Bobo told the loudmouth, "I have always noticed that when a man goes out hunting for trouble in these bottoms, he almost always finds it." No more than a fortnight later the blowhard threatened a simple man in "jeans pants" who was minding his own business. His insult was met with an immediate and fatal shotgun blast from the offended party.[6] Bobo, himself, while described by a friend as "one of the best living survivors of the old-time Southern type, generous" and "hospitable," was also "ready to resent any wrong upon the instant...." Even so, Hough emphasized, Bobo was "animated by a large sense of fairness and justice."[7]

Bobo proved quite adept at facilitating Divine's understanding of just what a sense of "fairness and justice" required in the matter of the mashed up Bobo cattle. As the tale was later told, the railroad agent offered Bobo $15 for the dead bovines, the standard Divine settlement for every damage loss claim from a couple of cows to a horse and buggy to a wife and children. Bobo, though, demanded $55. The men got out their pocket knives, sat on a log, and began whittling and dickering.[8] They must have presented quite a sight: Bobo, the lean and lank clear-eyed and sinewy country man, tall, with drooping mustache, and, if Hough's fictionalized account of this meeting in his novel, *The Law of the Land*, is historically accurate, the Memphis dude, Divine, "just above middle stature,[9] and of rather spare habit of body, alert, compact and vigorous, [and] smooth-shaven, except for a well-trimmed dark mustache."[10]

Divine, who knew little of Bobo beyond whatever he had learned during their brief meeting in 1883, underestimated his adversary. "Why, those cows are dead now, man," the claims agent argued. "What's more, you've buried 'em. They ain't worth more'n $15 to us, and I'm only offering that because I rather like you."

Bobo dropped his demand to $50, but showed no sign of going any lower. The smoke of the evening train for Memphis appeared in the distance as the sun set. Divine folded his knife. "Well, Mr. Bobo," he said, "I see we can't agree. There's my train coming, so I reckon I'll get aboard and get back to town." At that, Bobo reached somewhere into his clothing and drew out a long and substantial pistol. "I don't reckon that's what you're going to do at all," he told the surprised railroad man. "I reckon you're going to sit down on this log and write me out a check for $50, right now."

"Fifty dollars?" said Divine. "Why that's what I've said all along. Is it possible you have misunderstood me?" Divine wrote out a railroad check for $50 and caught the train for Memphis.

Soon after his settlement with Bobo the railroad sent Tom Divine back to Coahoma County, this time to compromise the claims of a man whose wife and children had been killed by one of his employer's trains.

The incident had also destroyed the wagon in which the woman and her brood were riding and had killed a family hog that was also on board.

Divine offered his standard $15 in settlement of the widower's losses. Like Bobo, the gentleman rejected the offer, but with a little more intensity than was the case with Mr. Bobo. The man's neighbors joined in the settlement discussions, believing, no doubt, as a friend of Divine's would later put it, that "it was a shame, as nice looking a woman as that and several fine children, should go at $15." The locals' particular negotiating technique involved placing Divine on a table with one end of a rope tied around his neck and the other end affixed to a rafter. Bobo arrived on the scene just as the locals were about to close the deal by having Divine jump off the table.

"I know the man," Bob Bobo said, "and he's all right. Turn him loose." That was all the neighbors needed to hear. Tom Divine's sentence was immediately commuted and the Memphis man was freed from the makeshift scaffold. He was subsequently able to convince the widower that "his wife was a bit cross-eyed, and one of the children had warts," and that "the hog wasn't worth over the $15 at the outside on the hoof."

It is almost a certainty that the original teller of those stories exaggerated them a bit. While Divine, no doubt, was a highly skilled settler of claims lodged against his employer, the railroad agent also had the reputation for being "always just, always... kind," and "the friend of every man who met him," hardly the type who would actually try to settle the claim of a husband for the deaths of his wife and children for $15.00. More than likely the characterization of Divine as a sharp dealing, hard-hearted, compromiser-of-any-death-claims-for-$15.00 sort of fellow was for the purpose of eliciting laughter from the man's friends and acquaintances who would have known the stories to have been completely at odds with Divine's nature. For those who did not know the claims agent, the tales at least provided some outlandish amusement very much in the tradition of southwest humor.

Regardless of whether Bobo actually rescued Divine from the noose, the railroad agent may well have saved Bobo's life. Not long after Bobo and Divine first met, a disagreement arose between Bobo and some of his plantation laborers. An armed mob composed of aggrieved farm workers assembled and was en route to Bobo's house with considerable malice afore-thought. Fortunately, Tom Divine once more was in the area on railroad business. He learned of the plot and with four or five friends rode to the

Bobo plantation in advance of the mob. When the leaders of the rabble learned they would be met by half a dozen men well-experienced in the use of weapons, they had a change of heart and canceled their plans.

Bobo and Divine were "like brothers" thereafter.[11] As the man who introduced Bobo to Emerson Hough, Divine also arguably was the man most responsible for the fame Bobo was about to enjoy or, perhaps, suffer.

9   The Writer Down South

As an editor of *Forest and Stream*, Emerson Hough had many opportunities to hunt in many parts of the country. In the summer of 1894 Hough received three invitations for fall hunts in the South: a Dr. W. D. Taylor of Brownsville, Tennessee, invited Hough on a quail hunt to be held not far from Memphis; Cincinnati, Ohio, railroad executive W. W. Peabody, Jr.,[1] requested that Hough join him on a hunt in Texas, with transportation to be by private rail car; and Tom Divine, of Memphis, offered a camp hunt for waterfowl at the mouth of the Mississippi. Hough accepted all three invitations.[2]

The writer boarded a southbound train in Chicago just in time to arrive in the Volunteer State for the opening day of quail season during the first week of November. Dr. Taylor and Mrs. Taylor, his host and hostess for the quail hunt, "put the stranger at home at once." Hough "was soon acquainted with all the youngsters of the" household, and by the time his luggage arrived from the train station, he "was one of the family." Hough called that easy and quick hospitality and familiarity that he encountered on his travels through Dixie "the South of it."

Hough also found in Dr. Taylor's hunting entourage plenty of dogs and horses and good shots, a combination he would encounter everywhere he traveled on his first sporting tour of the South. Southerners, Hough concluded, "shoot more black powder… than they do anywhere else in the world, and they raise more sportsmen to the square inch…." The South, Hough declared, was the only remaining "American part of America."[3] Little wonder a sportsman like Hough immediately fell in love with Dixie. "Oh, I bless the day I first went South," he would later write.[4] For the rest of his life the lower Mississippi country would remain among Hough's favorite destinations for sport or otherwise.

After a couple of days of productive quail shooting (the second day of the hunt saw three hunters bag 47 birds) with Dr. Taylor, Hough prepared to travel to Mr. Divine's Memphis office to discuss his upcoming trip with the railroad agent to the marshes of the Mississippi estuary. Before leaving Brownsville, though, he was treated to a lively discussion with Dr. Taylor and his hunting companion, Dan Miles, concerning the fabled "horn snake," a serpent deriving its name from an alleged horny protrusion said to resemble a rooster's spur and to extend one to two inches from the reptile's tail.[5] The official editorial policy of *Forest and Stream*, Hough said, held that no such creature existed because no naturalist had verified its existence. Hough, though, whether from personal conviction or from a desire to demonstrate solidarity with his host, sided with Dr. Taylor and Mr. Miles, who both contended they had examined such a snake. Having resolved that issue, Hough left for Memphis.[6]

Upon his arrival in the Bluff City Hough quickly discovered Divine's plans for him were more immediate than the previously proffered waterfowl hunt near the Gulf of Mexico. Hough would not be traveling with Divine or the other members of the party going to Louisiana. Instead, he first would proceed by train to a station in Coahoma County, Mississippi, some 75 or 80 miles south of Memphis, for a bear hunt arranged by Divine. The man who would be Hough's host on that hunt, Bob Bobo, was in Divine's office to meet him.

It is hardly surprising that Divine would use Hough's southern visit as an opportunity to introduce the writer to his dear friend, Bob Bobo, and even less surprising that the outdoor journalist would use his initial meeting with the hunter to ask about his past adventures in the Delta. Bobo's unassuming recitation of his bear hunting history amazed Hough. "The Rocky Mountain Hunter," Hough would later tell his readers, "who kills a half a dozen bears in a year is an object of veneration. If he kills twenty in a year he is a grand mogul." Here Hough was, though, in the presence of a man who "spoke of killing a bear as nonchalantly as I ever heard anyone speak of killing a squirrel."

Hough mentioned to Bobo "a certain hunter in West Texas" who a few years before had claimed to have "killed 160 bear in one year. . . ." On that alleged record, which Hough himself doubted, the unnamed Texan styled himself the bear hunting "champion of the world."

Bobo was unimpressed: "That fellow makes me tired," he said.

If Bobo said much else, it was not recorded by Hough. Divine did most of the talking. Hough, Divine told the writer, would leave Memphis on Monday, November 5, 1894. Then, he would stop off in Coahoma County "just long enough to kill a bear," hunting a second day, should it be necessary. The bear hunting party, Divine told Hough, would likely wander far from Bobo Station, Hough's initial destination. Consequently, Hough would need to carry all his gear on the hunt. As soon as he got his bear Hough would board a train for New Orleans at the nearest Delta whistle stop. The whole bear hunt would be accomplished that simply, Divine assured him. Hough easily would be finished in time to rendezvous with Divine and his hunting comrades in New Orleans on Thursday, November 8. Tom Divine, to his employer's good fortune, was a far better settler of claims than a predictor of bear hunts.

The meeting was over quickly and the three men went their separate ways. No doubt they little expected that Hough would soon make Bobo *the* backwoods celebrity of the 1890s and, in the process, would help spell the end of the glory days of Delta bear hunting. They probably had even less of an idea that Hough would become, like Divine, Bobo's fast friend in the bargain.

Notwithstanding his doubts about what he called "this railroad fashion of bear hunting," Hough happily set out for Bobo Station. Along the way he found the Delta to be "a land of luxuriance, of big trees and heavy corn and cotton." Almost nowhere was bare ground visible, so dense was the vegetation. Quoting Memphis newspaper editor Gus Matthews, Hough called the Delta a land "'where the trees grow big and where the wildfowl come' to the lakes among them, and it seemed a country meant for a man to live in without fretting out his heart." It was, Hough concluded, "a country of breadth, not of narrowness; of liberality, not of sordidness; of generosity, not of avarice and selfishness." For the moment Hough "pitied the city dwellers, and rejoiced that for a little while [he] had left the city far away."[7]

10 A Few Dogs

Bobo's plantation manager met Hough at the railroad station and escorted him to Bobo's residence, which Hough described as "long, low, and wide, one storied, with wide galleries all about it, a typical plantation house." Homes of the hired hands, smokehouses, storerooms, barns, and other out-buildings surrounded but did not crowd the main house.[1]

From this headquarters Bob Bobo administered a plantation of "between 800 and 1000 acres";[2] he did not seem to know for sure the exact extent of his holdings. There was, though, he was confident, "no richer soil on earth." Hough was convinced. He described for his readers a loamy soil so lush that after eight weeks of autumn drought "there was not a cake nor a clod visible. You could crumble into fine black flour in your fingers the hardest" lump of dirt you could find.

Bobo leased nearly all his arable "land to a firm of [sweet] potato growers" based in Memphis for the then premium price of $10 per acre. On the remainder Bobo's hired hands raised "cotton and corn, and cattle and hogs, and about everything else" needed to feed his family and the other "100 souls on the place." In addition to his farming operations, Bobo owned a cotton gin and a logging business. Hough, totally unfamiliar with southern agricultural ways, was fascinated by the gin and made a point of photographing it. The plantation hands found it "a most singular and amusing thing… to see a man who had never seen a cotton-gin at work before."

In his Delta wilderness stronghold, Hough concluded, Bobo was "the lord of this manor," living "as a patriarch of old, the protector of many," though unpretentiously so. Leaders such as Bobo, who attained and merited their positions by "nobility of character," Hough determined, were "the only aristocracy America can afford."

After giving Hough a tour of his plantation, Bobo went into his house and came out holding a hunting horn. "I will show you a few dogs," he said, in what was the first of numerous understatements Hough would hear during the course of his Delta sojourn. The planter loosed a blast from the horn "at which there came a great confusion of tongues, and the bear pack came running in from every direction" and from every hole and recess within sound of the horn. Hounds appeared "[f]rom under the house and out of the house and behind the house," wrote an amazed Hough. The barns and the outbuildings likewise poured forth canines, and the yard filled with "a howling, jumping, baying lot of dogs," more than Hough had ever seen "in one pack before."

"This is only a few of them," Bobo told Hough. Bobo, Hough learned, had dogs scattered about the countryside. His friend and hunting partner, Felix Payne, kept a substantial number of the Bobo dogs, as did numerous farm hands throughout the area. All told, Bobo estimated his pack at between 60 and 80 animals.

Descendants of the foxhounds Fincher Bobo had brought to Mississippi far back in the antebellum days formed the nucleus of the Bobo kennel.[3] "We never dare let go of that cold foxhound nose," Bobo told Hough, a "cold nose" being a dog man's term for a hyper-sensitive sense of smell. The Bobo bear pack also contained a large component of redbone and Walker blood,[4] hound breeds that, like the original foxhound strain, possessed exceptionally fine noses. Such cold nose breeds, Bobo explained, were absolutely necessary to "puzzle out the faint trails" often left by bears.[5] (Redbones and Walkers, of course, are used to this day by bear, deer, raccoon, and cougar hunters.) Bobo's great-grandson, the late Robert Eager Bobo,[6] of Clarksdale, Mississippi, once said that his ancestor's dogs were "the finest to be found anywhere."[7] One writer described the hunter's affection for his pack as second only to his love for his family.[8]

A serviceable bear pack required more than just cold noses. A good bear dog, Bobo emphasized, besides a superb olfactory capacity, had to have breeding enough to trail bear and "not trail anything else." Many "cold-nose dogs," Bobo had found, either would not trail a bear or were readily distracted by "deer, or cat, or coons or other such stuff."[9]

Col. James Gordon, of Pontotoc County, Mississippi, wrote at length on the various hunting dog tendencies in his 1885 *Forest and Stream* piece entitled, "Bear Dogs":

> [L]et me say in the language of an old homespun friend
> of mine, now passed away to the happy hunting grounds,

"There are hoof dogs and claw dogs." The hoof dogs are those which prefer trailing an animal with hoofs, such as deer, antelope, wild hogs, etc. The claw dogs, on the other hand, are more zealous in trailing animals that wear claws, such as bears, wildcats, foxes, 'coons, hares, etc. Most dogs will chase deer, and I have had hounds that would go wild after a deer, but would scarcely notice a fox trail. I have also had foxhounds which refused to notice deer at all, even to follow a bloodied trail. Such dogs naturally take to bear hunting, and become so infatuated with the sport they cease to notice any other kind of game and become specialists on b'ar. Such dogs soon become valuable as strikes and test dogs, which a hoof dog never attains to. Dogs that are fond of chasing deer are more difficult to break to bear hunting, and nothing is more provoking than to have a pack quit a bear trail and run off after a deer, which are numerous in localities where we look for bear. For this reason but few hounds make good bear dogs, yet I once saw a pack of hounds that would fight a bear as close as one would wish and never notice a deer track. These hounds would chase a man with little training, and such packs are now kept in our State penitentiaries for recapturing escaped convicts. Such things are shocking to humanity, but it is an evil which grows out of the system of leasing convicts to work on farms; but whenever you find a hound which loves to run a man's track you find a claw dog, and one that will take to bear.

Gordon also believed that dogs with noses that were *too good* made poor additions to a bear pack. A decade before Hough's Mississippi visit, Gordon had observed on the pages of *Forest and Stream*: "I … do not want a dog with a very cold nose… ." It is preferable, he explained, "to hunt a fresh trail than [to] follow one" on which the game "has passed along twenty-four hours before you struck it."[10]

A good bear dog, in order to live beyond its first encounter with a bear, also had to have enough sense to stay alive, which entailed the instinct to know when to advance and when to retreat. In his piece for the *Spirit of the Times* styled "Bears and Bear Hunting," veteran hunter Henry J. Peck, a Sicily Island, Louisiana, physician and planter, wrote that an "old he" bear "weighs about five hundred pounds [and] has the strength of an ox… . [A] dog in a bear's reach," he noted, "stands no more chance than a mouse in the claws of a cat… ."

Consequently, the overly game dog that knew no fear would quickly find itself seriously outmatched. "[I]n bear-hunting," Dr. Peck emphasized, "the old adage holds remarkably true—that

> He that fights and runs away.
>> May live to fight another day;
> But he that is in battle slain,
>> Can never live to fight again."[11]

What a pack required, hunter George D. Alexander wrote in 1890, were dogs that would "snap and spring back, and never give up fighting in that manner until the bear was killed."[12] James Gordon held a similar view. Bear hunting necessitated "hang-on but not hold-fast dogs," Gordon said. "I want my pack to cling to a bear fighting close, and nipping his hams at every chance, until he is forced to tree; then to bay until I find them, no matter how long it may be. I want dogs that snap, not dogs that hold."[13]

Mississippi born Texas bear hunter Warren Brown got a somewhat humorous lesson in what can become of a bear dog that "holds on" instead of "snaps" when his prized dogs, Clint and Guard, jumped a 400 pounder in the Big Thicket country of southeast Texas. Just as the big bear started up a tree, Guard locked his vise-like jaws onto the bear's hind foot while Clint clamped down on the beast's abbreviated tail. They slowed the big bear down not a whit.

Brown watched in amazement as his quarry proceeded some 20 feet up the tree, both dogs in tow. Brown was in a quandary: if he shot the bear might fall on the dogs and kill or severely injure them. Such was a very real possibility: one of Delta hunter Lyman Webster's pack was crippled when a freshly shot bear fell on it from a tree.[14] On the other hand, if Brown did nothing, the bear might climb so high that when the dogs eventually opened their mouths they would suffer serious injury or death from their resulting falls. Fortunately, the bear quickly reversed his course and backed down the tree. Brown shot the beast when it was within four feet of the ground. The dogs leaped away in time to avoid being struck by 400 pounds of tumbling black bear.[15]

W. W. Titus, of Clay County, Mississippi, a nationally known bird dog trainer of the late nineteenth century, provided another example of the dangers of excessive canine zeal in his memoirs published in the

American Field. Two Mississippi pointers named Dick and Fannie, reported Titus, had enthusiastically joined in with a pack of foxhounds baying a bear against a thicket called the "Briar Patch Swamp." The hounds, said Titus, "were standing off a respectable distance barking...." The bird dogs, rushing in where the main pack feared to tread, jumped "right on top of the bear...." Unfortunately, "[t]he fight was a short one," recalled Titus, "for the bear with a slap disposed of Dick, ripping nearly half of his hide off him." Fannie somehow managed to escape the bear's grasp relatively unscathed. Miraculously, Dick eventually recovered, though he thereafter bore "a long, unsightly scar on his back and side, reaching the entire length of his body... as a memento" of his bear fight.[16]

Most bear hunters preferred the bulk of their pack to be composed of mixed breed dogs. Pure bred canines were typically specialized to the point of being either uninterested in hunting bear or, like Dick and Fannie, enthusiastic to the point of being suicidal. To Dr. Henry J. Peck's way of thinking, the bloodhound was such a dog. Although it had perhaps the most sensitive nose of the canine world, the bloodhound, he found, would fight a bear so closely that it quickly was killed or injured.[17] On the other hand, according to A. B. Wingfield, one Bolivar County, Mississippi, hunter crossed bloodhounds with "fighting dogs" and beagles to produce "as fine a pack of bear hounds as there was in the State of Mississippi."[18]

Most hunters also agreed that the pure-blooded bulldog or bull terrier made for a poor pack member—and a short-lived one. "The full-bred bulldog," Dr. Peck said, was at best "a very indifferent bear dog; he cannot smell well, and, of course, is no hunter." Further, wrote Dr. Peck, "[h]e is a slow runner and," most problematic, "when he comes up with a bear, he seizes hold of it, and the bear kills him as quick as thought; and, even if... disposed" to dodge a bear's attacks, "he has not sufficient activity to get out of a bear's way... when the bear makes a charge upon the dogs."[19]

Tunica County, Mississippi, bear hunter Shelby McPeak found the bulldog a disastrous bear hound for another reason. A city friend had sent McPeak a pure blooded specimen of that breed to try on bruin. McPeak, unfamiliar with the characteristics of bulldogs, knew only that the dog was too pugnacious to be penned with the rest of his pack. To prevent intra-kennel fighting he separated the new addition to his canine stock from the main group until the day of the hunt. Even then he kept the bulldog tethered until his other dogs bayed a bear in a Delta brake, at which point he unleashed the animal. The bulldog, though, to McPeak's disgust, paid "no manner of attention to the bear, but killed three of my best dogs before I could kill him." Meanwhile, the bear made his getaway.[20]

Outdoor writer and veteran dog breeder George Alexander, writing in 1890, maintained his prejudice against bulldogs even to the point of objecting to the introduction of any significant amount of bulldog blood into a bear pack. Such breeding, he said, "always resulted in the death of the dog"[21] due to the bulldog's reckless ways.

The majority of those weighing in on the subject, however, found that some bulldog blood could be a positive in bear dog stock. Dr. Henry Peck, for example, liked a cross of hound and cur crossed again with bulldog. The term "cur" in those days more so than today was "very vague and indefinite, and [was] applied to many varieties of dogs," Peck noted. The animal to which most old time bear hunters referred by that name was "an active dog, of a yellow color, a pointed nose, and ear that is partially erect and partially dependent," said Peck—"a watchful sprightly" dog. The hound and cur on bulldog mix, Peck believed, produced a dog with the "fine nose and bottom of the hound, with the speed and fierceness of the genuine cur." The bulldog blood added weight, strength, and power that could be of great advantage if bear, dogs, and hunter all found themselves in close quarters.[22]

Like Peck, James Gordon found merit in some degree of bulldog blood in his pack. "I have crossed the greyhound with the bull-dog," he wrote in 1885, and "also the bull terrier and the mastiff; these made fine large, active fighting dogs." Bobo also had seen success crossing such mixed breed fighters with "the foxhound, which made some excellent bear dogs. The finest bear dog I ever saw was a cross of a greyhound and a bull-dog on a foxhound bitch. He was far the best of the litter."[23]

Bobo, like most of his fellow Delta bear hunters, found that crossing various breeds usually was necessary to insure the right combination of cold nose and bear savvy. "I like a cross of staghound pretty well," he said, by way of example. "[S]uch dogs usually will run a bear trail."[24] Bobo also favored "half-breed curs," presumably crossed with foxhounds.[25]

While Col. James Gordon "made many experiments in breeding," he reported fewer successes with his dog crosses than did some of his bear hunting colleagues. Typically, he said, some part of any given litter was "almost sure to be worthless" as hunters. Sometimes he got but "one good bear dog out of a litter of puppies from which" he "had anticipated better results." Gordon believed his "most successful experiments" in "breeding for bear dogs" came from crosses with greyhounds, dogs very similar in fighting style, build, and ancestry to the staghound preferred by Bobo for his crosses. [26]

Most hunters ultimately agreed that heart and aptitude were more important than breeding. As the erudite Hough put it, for Bobo, "almost anything in the way of a dog would do, it seemed, and the Lady Clara Vere de Vere idea was evidently buried in the mist of antiquity which enveloped the history of the [Bobo] bear pack's pedigree,"[27] referring to a Tennyson poem suggesting that character is of more importance than ancestry.[28] James Gordon put it another way: "A bear dog *nascitur non fit*"—a bear dog is born, not made.

Col. Gordon said that his own pack "was composed of quite an assortment of dogs," by which the Colonel meant "every variety of dog I could buy, beg, borrow, and, if it wasn't an ugly word, I would say steal."[29] Gordon "never refused to add to" his bear pack "any kind of dog that chanced to fall" his "way, and often the most 'ornary' looking curs[30] turned out the best bear dogs, while the finest specimens of canine elegance proved most worthless." As an example of the latter, Gordon recalled how once he had "succeeded with much difficulty in procuring the handsomest cur I ever saw, which, when placed in my pack, looked a 'Hyperion among Satyrs.'"[31] The dog "was so belligerent" that Gordon feared the hound would charge the quarry and immediately be killed by the first bear he encountered. "[J]udge my surprise," though, said Gordon, "when I saw this canine warrior tuck his tail between his legs and strike out for camp without having received a scratch, or having been within thirty yards of the bear." Apparently, the mere "sight of [a bear] was enough for the valorous dude.... [S]uch was [the dog's] demoralization," Gordon remembered, "that at night while we were all in camp, he chanced to run against a saddle setting on a black stump, which frightened him so when it fell on him he jumped into the lake by which we were encamped and swam off to the opposite shore and never returned." Gordon concluded from that experience that "it is as hard to judge dogs as men by appearances."

What was really needed in a bear pack, in Gordon's view, was wide diversity: a broad spectrum of canine flesh. "[D]ogs of different sizes,"

Gordon emphasized, "are necessary" for an effective bear pack. Large, strong dogs could be especially useful to the hunter. By example, he cited the case of his favorite bear dog that had borne the name Lawyer "and whose memory is still fondly cherished…." If a bear pursued by Lawyer "ever attempted to cross an open space," said Gordon, the dog "was almost sure to pick up one of [the bear's] hind feet, and by an adroit jerk throw him on his back…." Such a tumble, Gordon noted, "always demoralized a bear and caused him to take a tree." Similarly, he said, if a bear attempted "to jump over a log, a large, active dog, with strength and courage to snatch him back without being dragged over himself, as sometimes happens to a small dog," added "greatly to bringing the bruin to bay."

Early 20th century Delta bear hunters and dogs. Exact location and date unknown. Note the hollowed log used as a makeshift dog trough. Mixed breeding is evident in the pack. The long legs of the dog in the foreground indicate staghound or greyhound in his pedigree. The thick hindquarters and chest of a darker hound in the middle suggest mastiff or bulldog blood. *Photo from author's collection.*

Small dogs, though, were not without their advantages in the bear pack. "[L]ittle dogs are more likely to slip through bruin's arms without serious injury than large dogs," Gordon had learned. He was especially partial to "little rough-coated terriers," whose thick, wiry, fur, combined with their generally loose hides and quickness, were great advantages in a bear fight. When such a canine was caught and bitten by a bear, the dog's skin often would "slip on" its body "under the pressure of bruin's teeth, leaving them to close down on a bunch of hair and [a] roll of skin instead of flesh," saving the dog from crippling injuries. Once free, the dog quickly slipped away from the bear and returned immediately to the fight, wherein its chief role was "to swarm about [the bear's] nose" and "to keep up a din about his ears...." A bear distracted by such an annoyance was less danger to the other dogs and more likely to tree quickly.[32]

Bobo, being of similar mind and experience to James Gordon concerning canines, was no kennel snob and readily accepted any dogs with "any hunt in them" regardless of pedigree.

Identifying the right types of dogs, though, was not all there was to maintaining the Bobo pack. "We are obliged," he said, "to have a great many dogs coming in all the time, for the life of a bear dog in this country is only about four years.... We have to be continually training and trying and selecting." Bobo could only guess at how much turnover there had been in his pack over the years. On the other hand, he was quite certain he had maintained "a long line of good bear dogs."[33] If there was ever any disagreement with Bobo on that point it has escaped the historical record.

11 The Right Place for a Hunt

While still on his initial tour of the Bobo plantation Hough had his first close encounter with a Delta bear. Bobo led Hough to a small out-building, paused, and spoke into it. "Come out here, Miss Alice," he called. Out trotted a yearling female bear. "I nearly always have a pet bear or so around," Bobo told Hough. "We had a mate for this one but it got killed."[1]

Bobo, like many bear hunters, "trained [his] dogs with the aid of a pet bear" such as Alice. Bobo "would put the collar around the bear's neck, tie it to a wagon, and lead it through the woods. Later on, he would turn loose the young puppies that he wanted to train to chase bear." The young dogs, if so disposed by breeding or otherwise, quickly learned that the scent of the bear was the scent to follow.[2]

Alice, Hough said, "was fat, sleek and saucy, [usually] not afraid of the dogs," and would stand and eat from Bobo's hand.[3] She would beat a quick retreat to her house, though, when Bobo, for a little sport, occasionally would tease her by calling the dogs.

While Alice permitted Bob Bobo to feed her and would come when he called, she held most other humans in utter contempt. When Hough reached to stroke her head, for example, she "just barely missed taking off" the writer' leg with "a lightning swipe" of her paw.[4] In reality, Hough observed, Alice merely tolerated Bob Bobo. The only human for whom she was "constantly trustworthy and affectionate" was the planter's son, Bob, Jr.,[5] who could "hustle" Alice "around as he like[d]." No one else dared take liberties with the ursine lady.

Bob Bobo with a pet bear, probably the bear
"Alice" described by Emerson Hough.

Despite Alice's disdain for Hough, the writer was fascinated by the young bear and wrote in detail about her habit of licking the wood around a nail in her house and of the twittering note, which he described as "whickering," that she uttered constantly as she licked, just as a cat purrs when being petted.[6]

Catching a bear like Alice for a pet could prove riskier than trying to kill one, as Bobo's friend John Warren learned the hard way. Warren and Bobo and some others had killed a she bear. Upon examining her they discovered she was milking, which meant that cubs almost certainly were close by. A diligent search located three little bears up an ash tree. Warren "agreed to climb the tree and shake them out" in order to take them alive. Once he neared the diminutive bears Warren had second thoughts. "Look here, boys," he said, "these cubs are a blamed sight bigger than they look down there; that's the way it looks to a man up a tree!"

Bobo, hoping to allay his companion's fears, lied. "I encouraged him to go on and told him that cubs didn't have any teeth until they quit sucking."[7] Really, Bobo was only stretching the truth just a bit. Very small cubs' teeth are so tiny as to render their bites harmless.[8] These bears, though, as Bobo must have known, had grown beyond the harmless stage.

As Warren climbed closer to the bears, they crawled out on limbs to escape him. The limbs were too small to support Warren's weight, but too large for Warren to shake with any effect on the cubs.

Someone had the idea to shoot the limbs off. One at a time the hunters cut the limbs with shots from their weapons. As each cub fell to the woodland floor a hunter would cover it with his body "to keep the dogs from killing him."

When all three bears had been immobilized, Warren descended from his perch. As the men reflected upon the success of their enterprise, Warren reached to pet one of the cubs. In return for his kindly gesture he received a savage bite. "[Y]ou said they didn't have any teeth," shouted an exasperated Warren. Bobo, who by then no doubt had forgotten his prevarication about cubs being toothless, was probably as surprised as his friend.

After putting his pet bear Alice through her paces for Hough, Bobo continued the plantation tour. Hough commented on a bear skin nailed to a nearby shed. In response, "Bobo showed me three more" bear hides as well as the skin "of a very large wolf" from a hunt a few weeks earlier, Hough later wrote. Even though that hunt had netted five bears, Bobo told Hough that the animals were not as plentiful as in previous years. He theorized the bears had moved to another part of the Delta in search of a more bountiful crop of acorns and similar mast.[9] "Still," he said, "I reckon we can get a bear."[10]

In contrast to the diminished bear population, deer were unusually abundant that year. "You could kill a deer this evening if you wanted to, over at the edge of the field, but we don't bother very much with deer."[11] Of course it was never permitted to kill anything but a bear in front of the Bobo dogs.

At dark the men ended the day by sitting down to a plantation supper prepared by the cooks who served the Bobo family. It was a meal, Hough was certain, "as no city club man ever saw.... After all, no cooks surpass the [Black] Southern [cooks], raised in the art," Hough asserted, "and I do think they are the only beings on earth who really know how to make coffee."

Almost the entire meal was the produce of the Bobo plantation: the "many breads, the fowls, the many vegetables—above all the delicious yams," which were rarely available in Hough's Chicago. Only the coffee and the sugar were imported. "And the sugar doesn't come from very far down river," Bobo noted. One could, wrote Hough, "build a wall around the little plantation of Bobo and live like a lord, in defiance of the rest of the world."[12]

Talk swiftly turned to Bobo's hunting exploits. For a few years, Bobo told Hough, he had kept a record of the number of bears he had killed, but that tally was lost in a house fire.[13] As to the total number he had brought to bag over his career, Bobo could not estimate, other than to say, "many hundreds, surely."[14] In earlier years, he explained, "[y]ou could kill bear like hogs. There was good [mast],[15] and the bear were everywhere....I have killed seven bear in one day, and six the day following, and very often three or four in a day. Once I killed in three days fourteen, three, and six bear....Felix Payne and I kept count one year, and we jumped 151 bear and killed every one before" one got away.[16] Bobo and his brother-in-law, Nels Harris, sheriff of Coahoma County at the time of Hough's visit,[17] once bagged thirteen bear on an overnight hunt. On another such brief hunt they "brought in nine, all large ones." Of course, in Bobo's best year, as was often told, the hunter slew "304 bear." Hough reported that Bobo also killed in that same year "52 deer [and] 13 panther."

Those figures, however, deserve some scrutiny and may not have been entirely accurate. An article in the New York based *Fur Trade Review* dated June 1, 1894, stated that in the twelve months from September 1873 to September 1874, 304 bears "were killed by the parties who followed [Bobo's] dogs."[18] Yet, recall Bobo's letter to *American Field* writer D. B. Weir in 1882 stating that in one year *he* had killed "304 bears, 47 cats (wildcats), 21 deer and 17 panthers."[19] Since it is doubtful that Bobo or his dogs were involved in killing exactly 304 bears in three different years, it is reasonable to assume that in each of the three citations the references to 304 bears involved the same year. Yet, there is a discrepancy in the deer and panther numbers—quite a variation. Moreover, it is not clear from the *Forest and Stream* and *American Field* letters whether Bobo meant he himself had pulled the trigger on 304 bears or whether what is described in *Fur Trade Review* is how it happened, i. e., that his guests did some of the shooting but in front of his dogs. Mississippi bear hunting, after all, was first and foremost a communal sport with the kills usually credited to the one for whom the hunt was organized.[20]

Hough, however, definitely reported that Bobo said he killed 304 bears himself in a twelve month period. Hough wrote, quoting Bobo: "So far as I know that is the largest number of bear ever killed in one year by any one man."[21] Whether he actually killed that many, or whether he was crediting himself with bears shot before his pack, or whether Hough misquoted Bobo, we cannot know with certainty. What is plain is that 304 bears is a lot of dead bruins.

What, one must wonder, would one man do with so many large dead animals? Some hunters, like Bobo's boyhood neighbor, Lyman Webster, shot for the market, selling the meat and the oil.[22] Not Bob Bobo. "I never sold any meat," he told Hough.

Hough considered the argument that Bobo "was indulging in too much killing, and that the meat must have been wasted." Hough denied it. As proof he recalled one occasion in the camp of the Bear Hunter. "I asked Captain Bobo for a piece of bear meat" to ship "North to my friends who might like a taste of bear." Despite the fact that eight bears, mostly large ones, had been killed during the preceding week, there was not enough meat in the camp to satisfy Hough's request. The meat and hides had all been claimed by Bobo's guests.[23]

It should be remembered, too, that Bobo had "over 100 souls on the place" and some 60 to 80 dogs to be fed.[24] The human demand for bear flesh was so great, according to Hough, that the dogs rarely got a taste of their quarry except at a kill when the bear was skinned and the dogs were treated to the offal.[25]

Certainly there was occasional waste. "I have killed many a one that I never even skinned," Bobo admitted. His "cold blue shooting eye," so bold and fierce when looking down the sights of a Winchester carbine, quailed at the thought of gutting the quarry. "I have a sort of weak stomach for cleaning a bear," Bobo confessed, "and if no one else was around to do that, very often I would ride away and leave the bear lying."

Bobo made no real use of the hides he did collect. Once a peddler offered to buy all the bear hides Bobo could supply. The hunter gathered up 15 dozen bear skins and struck a deal with the man for three dollars each.[26]

Generally, though, bear hides were tacked up on a wall, rolled up to be saved as proof of the size of the game killed, or simply left in the woods.[27]

Despite Hough's efforts to justify the mass slaughter of bears, the truth is that Mississippi hunters in those days were not especially concerned about wasting bear meat. Bears were so numerous and so destructive of livestock and corn crops that they were considered vermin to be exterminated, not a natural resource to be conserved. Bobo certainly did his part in their eradication. In the end, though, there can be little doubt that the hunters never dreamed the bruin would become so scarce so soon.

As Bobo noted, by the time of Hough's visit, bears were plainly not as numerous as in the first two decades following the War Between the States. Still, during the Christmas season of 1893–94, less than a year before the journalist Hough visited Coahoma County, Bobo killed nine bears in five days.[28] With good reason Hough believed he had come to the right place for a bear hunt.[29]

12 The First Strike

Hough's bear hunt, scheduled to have begun the day of his arrival, did not commence until the next morning (Tuesday, November 6). The writer continued to be a bit nervous about his time constraints, noting that he "had one day in which to kill my bear and catch a train." To make such a schedule work, he believed, required that he leave his baggage, including his press camera, at Bobo Station to be placed on the night train for New Orleans. That, of course, was against the advice of Tom Divine, who had told Hough to keep all his gear with him at all times.

There was nothing to worry about, Bobo assured Hough. The party would strike out in a south-southeasterly direction, hunting along the Sunflower River toward Bobo's logging camp, somewhere between the present community of Bobo [the old Bobo Station] and the current site of the state penitentiary at Parchman. "We will put you on your train," Bobo said, "at the nearest station on the road this evening." Then he added: "If we don't [get a bear today], we'll go on down to the logging camp on the Sunflower, and there we are sure of a bear tomorrow."

Hough was taken aback. "But, my dear sir, what will Mr. Divine do if I don't show up on board that train tonight? I've promised to be there."

Bobo found no problem with such an interruption of the Divine plan. "I reckon Tom Divine knows what sort of man you're with," Bobo said. "[H]e can take care of himself; and you'll be getting plenty to eat yourself." Then Bobo added something that let Hough know precisely "what sort of man" he was with: "Does he think I'm going out after bear and not get any bear? No bear, no train, my boy, so you might just as well be cheerful over it."

Hough, though somewhat concerned that his delay might disrupt the plans of the hunting party that would be waiting in New Orleans, "wanted the bear as badly as anybody." While he would have sacrificed a successful hunt for the sake of keeping his scheduling commitments, Hough admitted that he "was not absolutely filled with grief to see the matter taken out of [his] hands thus decisively."[1]

The law of the hunt established, the participants, each riding a horse or mule, proceeded into the Delta woods. Hough had the good fortune to be mounted on Coleman, an experienced bear hunting horse supplied by one of the locals.[2]

Besides Bob Bobo and Hough, there were Bob's son, Bob, Jr.,[3] and Bob, Sr.'s, nephew, Frank Harris (the sheriff's son). Also along were three of Bobo's plantation hands, Black men and veteran bear hunters, to whom Hough, in the unfortunate manner of his day, referred only by first names: Tom, Pete, and Bill. A pack of 53 bear dogs accompanied this "cavalcade," as Hough described the group. "We might kill more bear," Bobo said, "by taking the six or eight best, but we have to be continually training the young ones to keep up the pack."

Hardly had Bobo uttered those words when an example of the ongoing process of dog conditioning presented itself, affording Hough an opportunity to understand just how intimately familiar Bobo was with his dogs. About half the pack—mostly young dogs—struck scent and veered off the main track, crying out for all they were worth. Hough noticed that "one old ginger-colored, big-headed half-breed, a staghound and foxhound cross, with long white whiskers about his face" and a docked tail, did not "stir from the path."

"That's old Henry," Bobo said, indicating the bobtailed dog, "the best bear dog we've got." If Henry opens, Bobo continued, "you can bet it is bear." Nearby was a second dog, "a slim, slit-eared, peak-nosed foxhound" called "Raphael." He paid the young dogs no more attention than did Henry. Like Henry, Raphael would run nothing but bear. Raphael, though, had a "colder nose than Henry, and Henry" knew it. While a note from Raphael signaled bear, it took confirmation from Henry to assure Bobo that the trail was not too old. "If Raphael opens, and Henry goes to him and opens, too, you can bet all you have that it's bear, and pretty fresh, for old Henry's nose isn't cold enough to run a very faint trail." When both Henry and Raphael agree, he added, "we lay all the dogs on" the trail "and let her roll." This time, though, neither Henry nor Raphael sang out. Raphael briefly "snuff[ed] at the trail the puppies" were following, "then turn[ed] around and came back to the horses," a clear signal to Bobo that the less astute members of the pack were running deer, not bear.

During all this explaining the younger Bob and his cousin, Frank, followed by Tom, Pete, and Bill, chased after the young dogs, whipping them off the deer trail, "using clubs, rifle barrels, and anything at hand, [to] pound the dogs back...." The pups made such a "doleful lamentation" at the punishment that Hough positively felt sorry for them. "I'm afraid we're going to have trouble with the puppies," Bobo said, "but that's part of the game."

About eight miles out from the Bobo home the party entered a stand of "magnificent timber"—oak, ash, hickory, and gum—and came upon the slightest of rises in the landscape of the type that passes for a "ridge" in the Delta country. The first real canebrake Hough had ever seen sprawled across it. He described the growth as "like a million cane fish poles set on end, so densely that it seemed a mouse could not crawl between"[4] them. Trees grew among the cane but not as close together as in the surrounding woods. Thickets of interlocking brush choked the few caneless pockets. It was a "jungle... such as [Hough] had never seen in all" his life. The only path through this botanical hell was an old rotting plank tram road, or dummy line,[5] once used by loggers for hauling felled timber to the mill, and it was fast being obliterated by the advancing cane.

Hough contemplated the living fortress enclosing him and concluded that it was the ideal "harborage of the game" they sought. What hunter could ride through it? Who could even stalk through it on foot? Surely no traps could be set in it. It was indeed a bear paradise. In it a bear could find everything it needed. Why "come out in the open and invite a bullet?" The dog pack, though, observed Hough, was man's invention for rooting the bear out of such redoubts.

A "whimper from a puppy" was the first note to signal the strike of bear scent. Little wonder, given the beating the young dogs received for running the deer earlier, that a pup would be half-hearted in announcing to his pack mates that he had crossed a trail. About twenty other hounds chimed forth in a likewise reluctant chorus. The always dependable Raphael, however, with his "tenore-robusto," immediately and confidently confirmed the trail as that of a bear. The basso-profundo of the equally reliable Henry reinforced Raphael's assertion.

"Come on," shouted Bobo, as he tore off down the dummy line, followed by the others. Within a few moments Bobo reined in his horse, paused, and ordered the others to "keep everything still while I listen to the dogs. That bear ought to come right through here—oh, hang it."

Bobo could tell by the pack's disharmonious song that it had suffered something of a mutiny. The bulk of the pack, made up of young dogs, had charged off after a deer, leaving Raphael alone. Or so Bobo said. Hough could not distinguish any one hound or group of hounds from the half a hundred canine voices he heard coursing through the cane.

Henry, as disgusted with the situation as Bobo, "walked deliberately out of the brake, looked up in his master's face, wagged an intelligent stump of a tail, and… curled himself up for a nap, as if to say that he didn't care a cent what those fool puppies were doing."

Bobo surmised from Henry's reaction that the trail was an old one, unlikely to yield success. "Too cold for your nose, eh, Henry?" Bobo said. The observant Hough concluded that the art of bear hunting consisted as much in reading the dogs as in shooting bears. Bobo proved to be a master at both skills.

Bobo, Hough, and the older hunters sat on their horses on the old dummy line trail for two hours. Finally, the younger Bobo and Frank rode in with some of the pack in their wake. They had seen a fine white-tailed buck hiding within two feet of them but had left it alone as required by the code of the bear hunt. Tom, Pete, and Bill, they reported, had ridden up to the head of the pack to turn the rest of the dogs back.

Bill came in next saying that he had heard "cane a-poppin' ahead of Raphael" and believed the dog was on a bear. Bobo, of course, had never doubted Raphael had scented bear. His only concern had been that the trail might be old, putting the bear too far ahead of the group to be huntable.

Bobo and his party continued to blow their horns to summon the pack. One by one the dogs appeared. Bobo decided that the hounds, acting totally out of character, had lost the bear's trail. Such an event, Bobo assured Hough, was a rarity with his pack, but it had certainly happened. He blamed it on the young dogs splitting off after deer scent.

When it was clear nothing would come of the chase, Bobo and the others sounded their horns to call the dogs back in. Over the next hour, one by one, the pack returned to its master's position on the tramway amidst the cane.[6]

The party regrouped and proceeded through the Delta jungle casting about for a bear trail. To follow the dogs "cross-country" through that wilderness, wrote Hough, was "an impossibility."[7] "The strongest horse," he said, "could not force his way fifty feet into the heaviest cane, and a man on foot would be helpless." Hough supposed that a man walking could not make one mile a day through those brakes unless he had a cane knife.

The cane knife was a ubiquitous implement in the lower Mississippi Valley in the nineteenth century. Many of the old bear hunting stories mention them as if everyone knew what they were. It is no simple matter, today, though, to find someone in the Delta who is familiar with the term. The cane knife—at least the Mississippi version—is now largely a forgotten instrument.

There are occasional descriptions of cane knives in the old stories, though. While the tool's purpose—to cut cane—would seem to have been served best by a machete-like hacking blade, the accounts are clear that most of the knives relied upon by bear hunters of Bobo's day could be used as thrusting, as well as slashing, instruments. Such implements must have had pointed blades and sharp edges, like Bowie knives or even daggers, rather than the relatively blunt ends of machetes and sugar cane knives.

The Bobo cane knife as described by Hough was "a heavy-bladed [tool] about 2 feet long" and weighing about three pounds. Such an implement, at least in Hough's experience, was "used by all brake hunters."[8] Bobo's descendants have until this day a stout blade that family tradition says was the great hunter's "bear knife."[9] The knife, a Dahlgren Navy Bowie-style bayonet from the War Between the States with a blade length of eleven inches, a total length of 16 ½ inches, and a weight of two pounds, is smaller than the cane knife described by Hough. Hough, however, subsequently gave varying descriptions of other knives that he said were very similar to Bobo's. It may be that Hough simply made inaccurate guesses as to the size and weight of Bobo's knife. On the other hand, Bobo very well may have had more than one knife for bear hunting. It is worth noting that the handle of the Dahlgren bayonet owned by Bobo's kin is bent noticeably upward from its original straight lines, suggesting many years of use in cutting cane or other hacking work.

Bob Bobo's bear knife and sheath. *Photo by author.*

George Alexander, writing in 1882 about bear hunting in the Coahoma County of the 1840s, told of a cane knife shorter than the Bobo knife described by Hough, longer than the Dahlgren bayonet owned today by the Bobo family, and substantially heavier than both. According to Alexander, that cane knife, which was carried by a bear-hunting Mississippi Delta plantation slave named Booby McNeil, was 22 inches long and had a heft of about six pounds,[10] a very heavy weight for a knife of that length.

It could be that one writer overestimated the weight and/or length or that the other underestimated, or both. More probably, each writer was correct as to the knife he described. Cane knives, after all, as Dr. J. H. Peck of Catahoula Parish, Louisiana, noted, typically were not mass-produced but were "of domestic manufacture "—homemade. Peck described the knives with which he was familiar as weighing about "two or three pounds—very much larger than the common bowie knife—about two-thirds the length of the Roman short sword, or the artillery sword, now in use [c. 1845[11]]."[12] The artillery sword was 25 inches in total length, including the 19 inch blade,[13] which would make the knives described by Peck approximately 17 inches long with 12 inch blades. Such knives, said Peck, were "frequently made out of a blacksmith's rasp, that has been worn smooth; at least the rasp is preferred, if it can be had, in consequence of its superior temper. The handle is usually of buck's horn. The scabbard is made of sole leather, and is attached to the left side of the hunter by a belt of strong leather."[14]

Having a cane knife was not enough—a man needed the skill to use it. Hough quickly surmised from watching his host that cutting cane was not just a matter of random hacking. "One must know the angle for the knife blade," he learned. "At the right slant the heavy blade of the knife falls straight through the cane and the severed stalk drops straight down and does not" obstruct the trail. Those unused to such work, Hough noted, would be "at sea in this country."

The party worked its way through the dense cane via game trails, dried up bayou courses, and old "hacks," traces arduously cut with cane knives by hunters, loggers, and travelers who had passed that way previously. Fortunately for Hough and the other hunters many portions of the canebrakes in which they were hunting already had been crisscrossed with such hacks.

Even so, finding one's way through the Delta wilds required an almost supernatural sense of navigation. There were no mountains or hilly ridges in the canebrakes that could be climbed for a lookout or used to mark one's bearings—just flat land with only the slightest changes in elevation. Even if one knew his directions and where he was going, unless he could find one of the hacks, which Hough described as mere slits in "the wall of green," that knowledge was useless.[15]

There was no substitute for experience when it came to "riding cane." Bobo, Hough believed, was the sole champion in that class. "Many men have thought they could follow Bobo through the cane," Hough wrote, "but it is said no man ever did it."[16]

Most first timers in the brakes, Bobo told Hough, "were continually getting lost and requiring a search party, to the delay of the hunt." Hough took it as a compliment that Bobo considered him a "deviation from the usual rule." Hough admitted, though, that his sticking close to the chief huntsman was not so much a matter of skill as it was fear. The mere idea of being separated from the party was a harrowing thought. "To be lost in a cane-brake," Hough had decided at the outset, would be "a thousand times more awful than to be lost in the mountains."

Hough's fellow outdoor writer, the scribe of Hazel Creek in the Great Smoky Mountains, Horace Kephart, once related on the pages of *Forest and Stream* his experience of being lost in an Arkansas canebrake. Such thickets, Kephart found, offered

> advantages for getting lost and staying so which no other North American real estate can afford. Once let a man enter blue cane, he is alone with his Maker. The parted reeds close behind him like water over a sinking ship. Before, behind and all about him there is nothing but cane. He cannot lift a finger without pressing cane. Below him is a bed of cane; above him cane; for the leafy tops fairly shut out the light of heaven. In any direction that he may turn his eyes cannot pierce six feet. He moves on; it is cane, cane. His strength is quickly spent against the ever-yielding but ever-rebounding cane. He seeks an altitude, an opening, anything to give him bearings; there is none. There is nothing to climb for an outlook, nothing to escape by detours—nothing but cane. He is lost; and can defy the very powers of a bonding agency ever to find him.[17]

With avoiding such a fate in mind, Hough had resolved at the beginning of the hunt that should he become separated from the others he would not attempt to find them. Rather, he would leave it to Coleman, his experienced mount, to find the way home.[18]

A good bear horse like Coleman was an invaluable commodity in the Delta woods. While some bear hunters, no doubt, rode horses of the finest blood and features, appearances and pedigrees meant little in the canebrakes. Bear horses, like bear dogs and bear hunters, were not judged by ancestry or outward bearing. Valor and fortitude counted far more than lineage.

"What the horses were up against in a bear race" astounded outdoor journalist John Baptiste de Macklot Thompson, also known as Ozark Ripley. Many hunters Thompson had observed in the Arkansas brakes forced their mounts "by the over-liberal application of long cruel spurs" into "close-growing cane that looked impenetrable to man or beast...."

Sometimes the horses would become so wedged into the cane their riders had to dismount to cut for them a way out. Such charging into walls of cane and briar often "drew blood from" some of the bear horses he saw; others "seemed ready to drop from exhaustion." The real bear horses like Coleman, though, "were game animals and did their part well. Apparently the spirit of the hunt enthused them" such that "their wounds were but mere incidents of the chase."

Such a horse was the ancient mare ridden by Tunica County pioneer and bear hunter Shelby McPeak. According to George Phelan, who knew the hunter in his later years, McPeak's horse, once "a bright yellow sorrel," had "long since given way to a grizzly brindle of no color whatever." She was one-eyed—no doubt having lost the missing one to a cane stab—and "the ugliest, rawboned, worst-tempered devil in the state," at least to those other than her master. As far as McPeak was concerned, however, "she [made] up in virtue what she lack[ed] in looks." The old horse would browse contentedly all day, exactly where McPeak left her, and never wander off; no tether was necessary. She could "dodge trees and vines as well as a man," and she could thread her way through the roughest canebrake "like a wild turkey." The mare would come to McPeak's "horn but not budge for another.... [I]n short, she [was] his bosom friend," and McPeak would ride no other horse. When a fellow hunter teased McPeak about the aged boney nag he called his bear horse, he offered to race her against all comers for ten miles through the cane. History records no takers to that challenge.[19]

Like McPeak's mare, Hough's mount, Coleman, knew his way around the woods and was "an expert at taking cane." It was Coleman, Hough assured his readers, who deserved all the credit for not getting lost. "I just staid with the horse,"[20]he later wrote, and the horse stayed with Bobo.

Fortunately, Bob Bobo had an instinct for negotiating canebrakes cultivated by a lifetime in the Mississippi wilderness on par with Coleman's. "The rest of us didn't know where we were going," Hough confessed. The only thing Hough knew for certain was that he "wasn't going to catch any train that night...."[21]

13 Into the Sunflower Wilderness

Shortly past mid-afternoon the hunters came out of the cane "into open woods." To their left threaded "the dark and sluggish waters of the Sunflower River," one of the chief streams of the Delta. Then, as now, the Sunflower was flanked by high banks. Hough estimated the distance down the incline from the crest of the bank to the water's edge to be at least 100 feet. The party proceeded to ford the river.

Hough found the sight of the hunters and hounds crossing that wilderness stream almost rhapsodic. "A more spirited hunting scene would be hard to find," he wrote. "The deep banks, shaded thick with its many tints of green,[1] were lit up by the evening sun which made bright the broken water."

Some of the hounds entered the stream immediately, swimming the river in a long line. The mounted hunters followed, single file, rifles held across their saddles. A few dogs, afraid to swim, lingered, "crying to be carried over," as the "whippers-in"[2] herded them toward the water. Meanwhile, the first dogs across were shaking themselves dry on the opposite side. "It was a pretty picture, that one at the ford," said Hough, and he supposed that the artist who could capture such a scene on canvas "could achieve a lasting fame."

"We are now getting into the wildest country in the Mississippi Valley," Bobo told Hough, once they were across the river. South of the Sunflower, Bobo explained, was "a strip of country 40 miles by 60 or 75 miles, without any house on it, and it is full of game." Bobo predicted that it would one day be cleared and farmed, since it was as rich as any land anywhere. "I hope I will never see that day," he added.

The riders followed the Sunflower for about two hours, Bobo and Hough talking all the while. The value of Delta timber, the Hunter told Hough, was just beginning to be appreciated. "The finest ash timber in the world is in these bottoms," he claimed, "and no better oak ever grew than you see around you in these woods." The latter was in special demand in Europe where it was favored as stock for wine cask staves. An oak bolt four feet by eight inches by four inches, "cut with the proper curve," Bobo said, "is worth $1.80...as it lies here on the ground." The inevitable growth of the timber industry, Bobo knew, would mean the eventual demise of hunting in the Delta. There was yet fine hunting, though, he noted, along the Tallahatchie-Yazoo basin from the Sunflower to Vicksburg.[3]

As they rode on, Bobo regaled Hough with a portion of his store of bear lore. "I suppose you know," he began, "that a bear is bound to go where the feed is. They will travel any distance to get to feed."

Food was usually no problem. The Delta, Bobo emphasized, was the perfect "bear country" in that regard. From the summer until around October, the bears enjoyed the sweet fruits of the woods: pawpaws, pokeberries, and other seasonal offerings.

The bears, of course, continued to plague the Delta's cornfields, often doing serious damage to crops. The big animals loved corn so much, in fact, that they would risk encounters with humans, whom they usually avoided at all costs, if an ample supply of the grain was at hand. One farmer whose fields had been the subject of a bear's depredations was surprised when the hounds trailed the bear, not only through his fields, but through his very barnyard. The bear had been watering at his horses' trough right beside his house![4]

A settler, perhaps, could have forgiven a bear for helping himself to a meal from the corn patch now and then, but that was not the animal's typical habit. As one Arkansas hunter noted in 1886, "[h]e usually tears down and destroys a great deal more than he can eat."[5]

As late as the 1890s a correspondent gave a description of the extent of the bear problem farmers faced on the pages of the *St. Louis Globe-Democrat*. A man named Richardson who owned land along Hushpuckena Creek not far from Bobo became so plagued by bears one August as his corn was ripening "that he was obliged to do something to save his corn crop." The bears were raiding his fields and eating their fill of "the juicy, milky ears." The exasperated planter hired "a man in his neighborhood, who understood the ways and customs of bears, to abate the nuisance if possible. He abated it to some extent," the newspaper reported, "by killing thirty bears in" August "and ten or twelve in September." After "that, the corn became too hard to be longer tempting."

At least bears normally did not eat hard corn. Bobo once found bears feeding heavily late in the fall in "one little field of hard corn. I reckon they couldn't get anything else to eat," he told Hough. Whatever the reason, Bobo and his companions hunted in and around that corn patch for four days and "killed 2,100 pounds of meat," using "that one field for a starting ground" for their dogs.

Typically, though, once the cool weather arrived and the summer foods were gone, the bears switched to mast such as pecans and acorns.[6] "When the nuts get ripe in the fall," Bobo said, "the bear climbs the tree for them." That feeding in the trees was called "lapping," for the bears ensconced themselves in the forks, or "laps," of trees, when eating ripening nuts. Thus situated, the animals pulled the mast-laden branches of the trees toward them, often snapping the limbs in the process. "You can hear the limbs breaking and popping at a great rate" if you are in the woods when it is going on, Bobo told Hough.

Oftentimes nut-seeking bears wandered far from their warm-weather haunts in search of nuts. Consequently, said Bobo, "a good bear hunter puts no dependence on what he hears about plenty of bear in the summer." Rather, "[h]e studies the feed, and knowing the habits of the game, he moves around until he locates the mast."

By way of example, Bobo noted that "[e]arly this year we had a heavy freeze all over northern Mississippi, and this killed down the mast over a good deal of the country…." As a result, he said, "the bear [had] moved out very largely." Had he known earlier that Hough would be visiting Bobo said he could have undertaken a mast scout to locate a better bear feeding ground for his hunt with the writer.

Tomorrow, Bobo promised, "I'll show you the wildest country you ever saw." Had the year been a good one for mast, Bobo said, "we could kill bear like frogs" there. As it was, while he believed they would have no trouble raising a bear, Bobo did not expect anything like the numbers to be found in a normal mast year.

Just before dark the hunters arrived at Bobo's logging camp. Fincher Bobo, the older Bobo son, had charge of the operation, assisted by a foreman named Heide and a "gang of loggers and rafters,"[7] individuals generally not held in high esteem by polite Coahoma County society.[8] There Hough found a little clearing walled in by the dense Delta woods and canebrakes wherein lay what he called "the ideal camp for a hunter." There were "three shacks, or cabins," made of rough planks: two were bunk houses, and the third served as a kitchen and mess hall. Bear hides were tacked to the walls of the shacks, and the foreman, Heide, showed the party a skin taken from a panther he had killed a short time before. It measured eight feet, nine inches, from nose to tail tip, almost as long as the biggest panther Bobo's contemporary, predator hunter Ben Lilly, had ever seen.[9]

Bobo (r.) and unidentified hunters with horse and hounds.

Bobo, though, was not interested in cats. He immediately inquired concerning the presence of any bear sign about the place. In response Heide displayed a poor quality skin taken from a bear he had killed some days before while deer hunting. One of the camp laborers reported having seen bear tracks at a waterhole about two miles away. Reassured that not all bears had left the vicinity, Bobo, who was at that time not very familiar with the country along that side of the Sunflower, gathered from the loggers such information as they had on the waterholes and stream courses, places bears were sure to frequent during the dry days of early November.

That night the hunters gathered between the cabins around a great fire built of massive hardwood logs. Bobo held forth again on the subject of bears. "It is a mistake," he assured Hough, "to think that the black bear of this country is a small and timid animal." Bobo said he had "killed them to weigh 700 pounds dressed."[10] Eighteen years earlier Bobo had given a more precise weight for his heaviest bear to another *Forest and Stream* writer. "I killed one," he had told T. G. Dabney, that, "without the entrails, weighed 711 lbs." Bobo killed that monster one night in a cornfield "about half a mile from the house." Bobo and three others tried to load the animal onto the plantation express wagon but found that four men could not manage to lift the beast into the bed of the vehicle. They finally managed to get the bear back to the house by tying it to the wagon's rear axle and dragging it.[11] Bears of that size, though not unheard of, certainly were not typical. Three to four hundred pounds was a more common weight.[12]

A Delta bear, Hough learned, typically would flee from dogs and men just as bears anywhere would.[13] "The kind of bears that inhabit New York, Chicago and other large cities and are hunted (on paper) by fancy sportsmen, may be awfully savage beasts," an Arkansas hunter who called himself "Backwoodsman" told the readers of *American Field*, but "the black bear of Arkansas and the Southwest generally is… the most… cowardly brute, in proportion to his size and strength, that roams the woods. …I have yet to hear of an authenticated instance in this country (Arkansas) of a bear *voluntarily* attacking a man." Still, even Backwoodsman admitted that under the right (or, perhaps, wrong) conditions, a black bear would make a "lively fight,"[14] as many a dog and not a few hunters had learned to their misfortunes.

Certainly under most circumstances a man had nothing whatsoever to fear from a bear. As Col. James Gordon noted in one of his bear hunting stories published in *Scribner's Monthly*, the typical black bear would "fac[e] a score of dogs rather than one hunter."[15] Still, the size of the animals and the tales told about them rendered some men absolutely phobic in a bear's presence. Bobo told a story of a neighboring man and a boy "building a wire fence" one fall day along nearby Black Bayou. "The boy," as Bobo told it, was doing the work and the man was standing up near the house…." The boy looked up to see "a big bear begin to climb over the wire fence, trying to get through to where it was used to watering." The boy "dropped his tools and made a running jump for a tree near there." From his position the man saw everything. He took "his gun and started around the corner of the house," apparently intent on shooting the interloper. Simultaneously, the bear cleared the fence and began trotting at an angle across the yard, uncomfortably close for the man with the gun. Instead of shooting, Bobo said, "[t]he fellow drops his gun right there and makes a flying leap" for the tree the youngster had climbed seconds before. "[H]e went plum to the top of it in about two seconds," according to Bobo, "and says he to the boy, who was above him up the tree…, 'Move up! Move up!'" The boy must have thought the man's behavior as funny as did Bobo, for he "told the story on him, and the fellow didn't like it any too well."[16]

Though rarely a danger to humans, a grown bear was not the least bit reluctant to turn and fight the dogs when the opportunity arose, Bobo said. Adult bears were fearless enough not to arise to run from a pack until the dogs were almost in their beds with them. The smaller bears, if pressed hard by the pack, he said, would take to a tree. A heavier one would be more likely to stay on the ground, fighting if the dogs got too close, usually with his back against a tree.

The danger posed to dogs on such occasions can hardly be overstated, for the bear, whatever his reluctance may be to fight, is a formidable opponent and deadly on dogs when pressed into combat. "If a bear is surrounded by hounds and starts to fight," wrote Paul Rainey, who often hunted in Panola County, Mississippi, during the first two decades of the twentieth century, "he generally goes through the pack after one hound; once he catches him, he kills him outright."[17] Then, with the same deliberation and determination, the bear turns his attention toward another specific dog.

Bob Bobo had a similar observation: "If [a bear] gets a hold of a dog," he said, "he will bite his whole head in" if he can. Accordingly, the best bear dogs did not allow themselves to be drawn in too closely when fighting a bear thus bayed.

Occasionally, Bobo said, a Delta bear would even attack a man. "I have had two or three come at me," he said, including, "one, an old she bear which I shot almost up against me."

Bobo acknowledged "that he had been bitten a couple of times by bears, but never seriously…. " He also said he knew of "one case where a man was knocked down by a bear and pretty badly chewed up."[18] Such a thing was a rarity and most likely to happen with a wounded bear. Typically, the dogs would pull down, or at least distract, a bear before it could get to the hunter.

Shelby McPeak had a close call with a Delta bear that easily could have ended in tragedy. Shelby's nephew, William McPeak, who had served with Shelby as a Confederate scout during the War Between the States, was Shelby's regular hunting partner and accompanied him on that nearly disastrous bear outing. William, 20 years Shelby's junior, could neither hear nor speak. The two communicated by means of a slate and a piece of chalk that William carried for that purpose.

On the day in question the McPeak pack struck scent and the bear, an old sow, seeking refuge from the dogs, burrowed her way into the densest of cane patches creating something of a cavern in the thicket connected to the outside world by a short, narrow tunnel through the brake. The dogs followed the old she into the passageway. The McPeaks reached the brake shortly thereafter.

Unseen by but very audible to Shelby, a horrendous fight between bear and canines was underway within the recesses of the brake. Shelby knew he had to kill the bear before it killed all his dogs. The only way to the fray was through the tunnel created by the bear. The resilient cane had closed up so much since the bear broke through it, however, that Shelby could not negotiate the thicket by his own strength alone. By means of the slate and chalk, Shelby laid out his plan to his hunting partner: Shelby would burrow head first into the brake toward the bear fight. William would assist by pushing his feet and legs. William agreed, and Shelby, armed with pistol and knife, crawled into the cane as William shoved.

The short tunnel quickly opened up into the small cave carved out of the thicket by the combat of bear and dogs. An unhappy sight greeted Shelby: almost all his pack was dead. The two dogs left alive cowered against the cane, the fight totally whipped out of them. The bear, fight in her yet, moved toward Shelby. The hunter screamed to William to pull him out, but to no avail. Shelby's shouts quite literally fell on deaf ears. In fact, operating on his written instructions, William pushed even harder. Shelby had no choice but to fight with the weapons at hand. Somehow, with pistol and knife, he managed to kill the bear before it was able to get its jaws on him. Shelby resolved never again to go bear hunting without the company of a man with a set of "patent ears."[19]

There are plenty of old stories from the lower Mississippi Valley of bear hunters who were not as fortunate as McPeak. Dr. Henry J. Peck once wrote of an Arkansas hunter who met his end at the jaws of a bear. The man "was creeping through" a "tangled cane-brake to shoot a wounded bear, when the bear suddenly jumped upon him, and, with a bite through the muscles of the inner part of the thigh, cut the femoral artery and caused immediate death."[20]

The *Yazoo Whig's* January 21, 1848, edition carried the account of a deadly encounter between Dr. Isaac Hamberlin and a large black bear near the Mississippi Delta village of Satartia. Hamberlin's party was hunting along the shores of Lake George when the dogs bayed a big bear in a thick stand of cane. Hamberlin reached the bear first and fired, but the ball entered the bear's head at the wrong angle and did little more than enrage the animal.

With no time to recharge his muzzleloader, Hamberlin attempted a retreat, but the furious beast overtook him, seized him by the thigh, and threw him on the ground, tearing all the muscle from his femur in the process. The dogs rallied and pulled the bear off the doctor, but only momentarily. The bear quickly fought them off and turned back to Hamberlin. The doctor, too crippled to stand, managed to draw his knife and make one or two cuts across the bear's neck. The slashes, unfortunately, were too shallow to do any real damage. The dogs once more engaged the bear and, once more, the bear repelled them. A third time the bear attacked Hamberlin, who again struck with his knife. This time the bear caught the knife in his jaws, shook his head, hurled the blade off into the cane, and then bit the doctor's arm, crushing it to "jelly." Before the bear could bite Dr. Hamberlin again, another member of the party arrived and shot the bear in the neck. Though the shot did not stop the bear, it caused it to run into the cane where it encountered a third hunter who fired the shot that finally killed the bruin.

The hunters placed the doctor in their boat and prepared to return to Satartia to seek medical care for their friend. The gravely injured Hamberlin insisted that the bear be brought back with the party. The doctor succumbed to his injuries after three days of excruciating pain. The bear, though lean, weighed 310 pounds, field dressed.[21]

14 The Right Weapon

Dr. Hamberlin's use of the knife in his situation was the act of a desperate man. Some old time bear hunters, however, intentionally relied on their blades to kill their game. For such a man, wrote one Delta scribe, to "shoot the bear" was simply "too crude. His purpose was to kill the animal by means of a knife held in his hand."[1]

The concept of intentionally attempting to kill a bear with a knife is understandably difficult for many twenty-first century readers to accept. Even some nineteenth century Southern bear hunters discounted such reports calling them more the stuff of "dime novels" than of real life. Among that group of skeptics was an Arkansas woodsman named Barnes who hosted Horace Kephart on his 1895 Arkansas bear hunt. "I've never seen it done, and never met a reliable man in Arkansas who claimed to have seen it," he told Kephart. Still, he did not rule out entirely the idea of bear slaying with the knife: "I won't say that nobody hunts bear with a knife, for sometimes one of these planters finds time hanging on his hands and might be capable of anything, from riding a cyclone to signing the pledge…," [2] the "pledge" being a reference to the promise to abstain from alcoholic beverages promoted by "temperance" groups in the nineteenth century.[3]

It is hard to believe that the planter Bobo ever saddled a tornado and, perhaps, even harder to believe that he ever took the pledge. It is hardly contestable, though, that Bobo and a number of other Mississippi hunters regularly killed bears with knives, however rare such a feat may have been in Barnes's part of Arkansas. South Carolinian Wade Hampton, III, who frequently hunted on and around his lower Mississippi Delta plantations, reportedly slew some 80 bears with the blade.[4] Ben Lilly, who began his bear hunting adventures in the Mississippi Delta and who would serve as "chief huntsman" for Theodore Roosevelt's 1907 Louisiana bear hunt, is reputed to have gone through a "knife phase" in his hunting career when he did not carry a firearm on his hunts at all.[5]

The penchant for the knife as a hunting weapon, no doubt, had deep roots in the culture of the lower Mississippi Valley, where, historically, it was the weapon of choice in individual combat. While under Spanish Rule in the eighteenth century, the Mississippi River town of Natchez experienced such a plague of killings by knife that the colonial government outlawed steel-bladed weapons in that city and the associated territories. The local subjects did not let such a law prevent them from going about armed with knives—they simply began to make their stilettos from wood.[6]

James Bowie, of Alamo fame, made his reputation fighting with the knife in the famous Vidalia Sandbar duel and brawl near that same riverfront town of Natchez. His favored blade style, supposedly first forged by his brother, Rezin, became known as the Bowie knife and was the standard weapon carried by frontiersmen and hunters of the South and West throughout much of the nineteenth century.[7]

Knifing a bear, as practiced by the old Delta hunters, was not simply a matter of random stabbing and slashing, but "required skill and daring no less than bull fighting."[8] The knife wielding hunter did his best to strike the bear in the heart. "[O]ne good stab does the work," Col. James Gordon told would-be bear slayers in an1870s piece for *The Turf, Field, and Farm*. "[B]ut be careful to reach over and stab…the opposite side [from] which you stand," he warned, "for the bear invariably turns to the place last hurt."[9] A hunter who failed to properly direct his knife the first time might not get a second chance.

The favoring of knife over firearm by many in the old South certainly involved then current notions of bravado and machismo. Memphis lawyer Col. James Goodloe[10] admitted as much in his recollection of his first bear hunt as a boy in antebellum Washington County, Mississippi. As the young Goodloe stood admiring the sizable bear he had just killed with a single shot from his ten gauge muzzle loading shotgun, his dogs charged off on a second trail. After a short run, the boy "came up to the whole pack, covering a two hundred pounder, a two year old bear." Flush with victory from the kill he had left only seconds before, the youngster saw in the struggle before him only the "opportunity for more glory!" Goodloe "hauled out" his "heavy knife, about a foot long and sharp on both edges, made by our blacksmith, pushed the dogs aside, and kneeled to stick the struggling bear to the heart…."[11]

The dogs, Goodloe later wrote, "evidently thought I had him and loosed their holds." At that point the young bear turned his attention toward the young man and charged. The boy instinctively shoved his booted foot at the animal, which bit the heel and began to claw the leather legs of the boot. The young Goodloe, taken totally aback by the turn of events, began to scream, which caused the dogs to pile back on the bear, saving the boy from an almost certain and severe mauling. Goodloe finished the young bear with his knife as the dogs held it down. "[A]nd I feel sorry for it to this day," Goodloe confessed in his 1917 recollection.

For most, however, the use of the blade was not a matter of machismo. Rather, the type of cover in which bear, hounds, and hunter typically met necessitated the use of steel. The Delta bear tended to make his stand in close quarters.[12] In the tight recesses of the canebrake where thick vegetation inhibited evasive movements, even the savviest bear dogs were often at the mercy of their quarry. The bear might kill them all if the hunter did not swiftly end the fight.[13] In such confines, however, the hunter could not shoot the bear without risking killing or crippling his dogs. Under such circumstances a knife posed far less danger to the pack than did a gun and, consequently, was frequently the preferred option for killing the game.

The knife also served as a backup weapon, especially in the days of one and two shot muzzleloaders. "A cane-knife, from eighteen to twenty inches long, of the best metal, and weighing not less than four to five pounds," according to hunter and writer George Alexander, "was a *vade mecum*—an indispensable weapon for a bear hunter. The double-barrel gun... might snap [i.e., misfire], but there was no discount on a good cane-knife...."[14]

Hunters used other blades besides the *de rigueur* cane knife as hunting weapons. As mentioned above, Bob Bobo's "bear knife," according to family tradition, was a Civil War bayonet.[15] United States Senator and former Confederate general Wade Hampton's descendants still have the weapon reputed to have been his bear knife: a double-edged dagger with a 8 ¼ inch blade.[16].

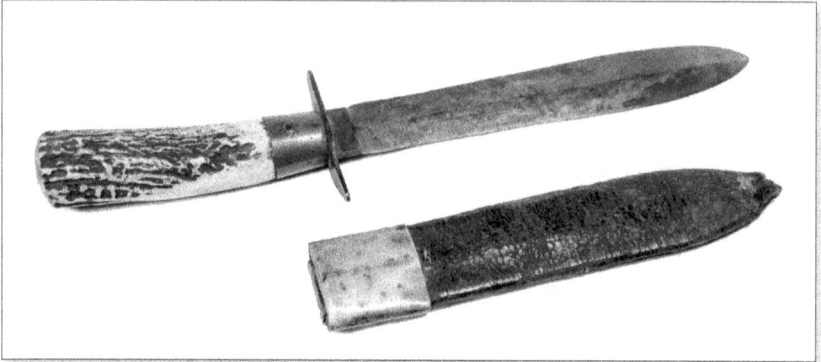

Wade Hampton III's bear knife. *Photo by Jay Haas courtesy of Hampton Ford.*

Only once did Bobo intentionally undertake a gunless hunt for bear. He told writer T. G. Dabney about it during their 1887 interview. It happened during his youthful hunting years with his stepbrother, Curt Clark. Bobo and Curt had taken two of the hands with them with the intent of "blaz[ing] a hack through a cane thicket." Knowing that the presence of firearms would tempt them to abandon their project at the first sign of game, they had agreed to leave their guns at home. Bob's dogs, however, while left behind, had been neither penned nor tethered. In a short time a half dozen of the pack had found Bobo and were following him and Curt through the woods.

As the young men began their hacking work the dogs struck "a fresh bear track,... gave chase, and... treed the bear" close by. It was more than the two young planters could stand. They went straight to the dogs and discovered a sizable bear up a tree.

"Curt Clark," Bobo recalled, "was a regular dare-devil."

"Bob," the stepbrother said, "let's kill him with our knives."

"I was a much younger man then, and equal to anything," Bobo recalled, "so I agreed."

After securing promises from the two plantation hands "to stand by with their axes" in case the knives weren't enough, the young men proceeded. Using a trick still practiced by squirrel hunters in Mississippi to flush their game, Bobo yanked a grapevine that ran up the tree trunk to where the bear was holding. The vibration of the vine had the desired effect: the startled animal quickly shinnied down the tree trunk.

Bobo, positioned to strike a death blow with his knife just as the bear touched the ground, stuck the beast as planned, "[b]ut my knife struck a rib and did not penetrate." Pandemonium erupted. "Instantly we were all in a promiscuous pile. Curt and I, the dogs and bear, in a rough-and-tumble fight." The hands, who had promised backup, were nowhere to be seen, having run for their lives as soon as the first knife thrust had failed in its intended effect.

"Curt and I used our knives for all that was in them," Bobo said. Then, "Curt tripped and fell on his back," and "[t]he bear was on top of him." Curt knew that unless Bobo intervened, he had fought his last bear. "He gave me a look," remembered Bobo, "which said, 'it all depends on you, now.'"

"I would rather the bear had killed me than Curt," Bobo told Dabney. Bob channeled all his mental and physical strength into one "desperate lunge and struck" the bruin's "heart with [his cane] knife." The bear fell dead on Curt.[17]

While that may have been the only bear Bobo set out to tackle with a blade alone, he killed many others with the knife when circumstances required it. Generally, though, Bobo reserved his knife for cutting cane.

Judge Harris Dickson wrote of one Delta hunter who used a less formidable blade than Bobo's or Hampton's when he somewhat accidentally knifed a bear. Delta bear hunter Holt Collier and his hunting companion, one Capt. Blake, had teamed up for an autumn bear hunt with a sometime farm laborer called Long Ike. Ike and the Captain took their stand on the high side of an embankment in a small clearing adjoining a dense canebrake. Holt mounted his horse and struck out into the woods with his pack bent upon driving a particularly large old he bear toward Ike and Capt. Blake. The Captain and Ike sat waiting and listening to the hound music as the pack followed a hot trail. Ike amused himself by carving on a log with the rather long-bladed folding knife he habitually carried.

An hour or more had passed when the calm was abruptly interrupted by a commotion off in the brake: the bear Holt was driving had taken a stand and was fighting the dogs. The sound of thrashing cane grew louder—the pack was pushing the bear toward Ike and the Captain.

The woods suddenly were awash with the sounds of dogs and bear, but the cane was so thick and the fight so mobile that it was impossible for

Ike and the Captain to tell at any given moment exactly where the pack and its opponent were. As the Captain strained his eyes and ears to locate the contestants, the bear suddenly appeared, backing out of the canebrake. Preoccupied with the hounds, the bear took no notice of the Captain, but backed right into him, bowling him over.

Ike, a yet unseasoned bear hunter armed only with his folding knife, leaped out of the way, diving into the depression on the other side of the embankment. The Captain, regaining his feet and his composure, quickly loosed both slugs from his shotgun in the bear's direction. The bear, believed by the Captain to be mortally wounded, disappeared over the embankment in the direction of Long Ike.

The Captain shouted for Ike to administer the coup de grace with his knife. "Stick 'im, Ike! Don't let him get away! I've shot two holes clean through him!"

Ike reflexively complied, stabbing the bear half a dozen times or more with his knife. The shaggy beast collapsed at his feet.

Just then Holt appeared. As the Captain told Holt how he had shot the bear in the chest and how "Ike [had] finished him with the knife," Ike was examining the dead bear, running his hands over the animal's hide. Ike suddenly went pale. "Captain, lemme have a drink." Blake handed over his flask and Ike took a long slug of whiskey. "Captain," Ike said, "You ain't never shot this bear!"

"What?" responded an indignant Blake.

Holt gave the bear a once over. "He's right, Captain. There's seven stab holes. Ike cut him pretty nigh all to pieces, but 'tain't no bullet ever touched *this* bear yet."

"Well, Holt," said the Captain, wryly, "the joke's on me."

Ike turned and walked toward his mount. "Me and my mule are going home," he said. "I'm too good a field hand to be a projeckin' around killing bears with a pocket knife."[18]

Hunting bears with a knife, as addictive as it seems to have been for some, obviously was not for everybody.

Bobo's occasional use of the knife notwithstanding, he took the vast majority of his bears with firearms, with his choice in guns dictated by the environment in which he hunted. Given the short visibility in the dense cane and Delta undergrowth, Bobo, like most bear hunters, preferred carbines. The longer barrels of full-sized rifles rendered them unwieldy in the thickets.[19]

Others, like Col. James Gordon, used neither long nor short rifle, finding that "after the labors of a bear-chase the nerves are apt to be a little shaky for drawing a fine bead with" such a weapon. For that reason hunters of Gordon's school preferred "short, double-barrel shot-guns, loaded with buck and ball,"[20] that is, a spherical projectile large enough to fit tightly in the barrel—around .71 caliber in the case of a 12 gauge—topped with three or more large—.30 caliber (no. 1) or bigger—buckshot.

Some hunters found even the abbreviated shotguns and carbines difficult to manage in the cane and opted for handguns. Tunica County hunter Shelby McPeak had for "his weapons [only] the army revolver and [a] long bear knife."[21] Likewise, "Alf." Daniels, who hunted regularly at the confluence of the White and Cache Rivers in Arkansas, not far across the Mississippi from Bobo, used only a pair of ".44 Colts revolvers," believing anything longer to be "unhandy getting through the thick, heavy canebrakes." Alf. Daniels, incidentally, must have been quite a character. In the 1880 census report for Monroe County, Arkansas, the divorced Daniels gave his marital status as "grass widower" and his "profession, occupation, or trade" as "bear hunter and a curiosity."[22]

Bobo, too, in his younger days had "killed many a bear"[23] with a handgun when he, like Daniels and McPeak, had often hunted with only a "Colt's army pistol." Bobo, though, had learned the hard way that use of the revolver in bear hunting could be "very demoralizing to the dogs" and, as a result, demoralizing—or worse—for the hunter. A man had to move in so close to a bear to kill it with a pistol, Bobo explained, that any dogs fighting the bear were likely to experience substantial shock from the discharge of the weapon. Once exposed at close range to an ear-splitting revolver blast hounds often became pistol shy. Thereafter, they tended to back away whenever a hunter exhibited a handgun. In making their retreat the dogs necessarily would release their holds on the bear, a turn of events with potentially nasty results for the hunter. For that reason Bobo preferred the knife to the revolver if closing with a bear under circumstances in which a long gun could not be used.

Despite the handgun's shortcomings as a bear hunting weapon, having a pistol, specifically a Colt's six shooter, at his side had once saved Bobo's life when the use of his knife did not turn out as planned. Bobo had approached a bear held by his pack with the intent of dispatching it by knife when the animal suddenly seized his knife hand with its mouth. The hilt of the knife was perpendicular to the bear's jaws, preventing the animal from closing its mouth completely and crushing Bobo's hand.

Bobo's fist, nonetheless, was in the grip of the beast's teeth. Stuck to the bear as fast as Brer Rabbit to the Tar Baby, he could not get away. The prospect of being mauled or bitten to death by the bear was, quite literally, at hand. Instinctively, Bobo reached for his Colt's Army Model with his free hand and drew it. With his other hand still tight in the bear's mouth, he pushed the revolver's muzzle against the bear's head, pulled the trigger, and sent a pistol ball through the beast's brain. The bear fell dead in its tracks and disaster was averted thereby.[24]

A Louisiana man whose hand was similarly caught in a bear's jaws about 40 years earlier was not so lucky. According to the *Spirit of the Times*, which reported the story, the bear's jaws crushed the man's hand such that he never recovered the use of it.[25]

15 The Life of the Bear Dog

While the hunters in the Bobo entourage enjoyed fireside fellowship their first night in the Sunflower Wilderness, the camp laborers were tending to the dogs. There being no Purina® Dog Chow® in the canebrakes in those days, hunting dogs were generally fed a homemade concoction called "dog bread," the recipe for which varied from hunter to hunter. Typically, the base was cornbread with meat broth, meat scraps, or other additives. The hired hands were unaccustomed to feeding 53 hungry hunting dogs at one time, and the dog bread cooking was running way behind the hounds' appetites. Consequently, as the food was dished out, the pack's pecking order decided who ate first. The bear dogs, being by nature and nurture a pugnacious lot, did not always agree as to what the pecking order was, and it was generally determined on an ad hoc basis. As a result, there were groups of dogs fighting for a propitious place in the chow line all over the camp. The scrapping hounds, Hough wrote, would fight anywhere they happened to be—by the fire, under the horses, or "between someone's legs." The hunters, whenever possible, broke up the fights, often with stout cudgels from the firewood stack.[1]

The dogs generally feared nothing, Hough observed, except men, for whom, he said, they bore "the odd foxhound reverence." Hough found it ironic that "[s]ome of the best bear dogs in the pack would yell the most dolefully if" a man "but reached for a long cane" and merely "threatened [the hound] with it."[2]

Hough did not conceal his sympathy and admiration for the bear hounds. He would later pen something of a tribute to the bear dog in general and to Bobo's dogs in particular:

> The life of the bear dog is one of war and tumult. His training is of the rudest, consisting mostly of a half-killing with a club when he is caught running anything but bear, and an entire killing when he is afraid to run that. In the

bear chase it is his duty to fight the bear, and if he be not wary as well as bold he gets killed or crippled there. After the bear is dead he gets his reward—if he can lick all the other dogs which jump on him as soon as he gets a mouthful of liver or other tidbits in his jaws. At the camp his wounds have small attention and he must fight in spite of wounds. He will not be fed too highly there, be sure, for cornmeal bread is thought enough for him to run on. For this also he must fight and for place at the fire he must fight, being ware the whiles that he escape a swift and nimble foot if he gets in the road of the human beings who engineer his destinies for him. There are few such caresses for the bear dog as there are for the bird dog.[3] He knows no kindnesses and no comforts. He grows up rough, unkempt, shaggy, surly, suspicious and highly belligerent. He will fight anything on earth with the greatest of pleasure, from a buzz saw up, and if he gets a grueling you never will hear him complain. His life is short, but full of action, as that of the warrior should be, and while he lives he walks through his daily round of activity with a continual chip on his shoulder.[4]

Not only did a bear dog face almost inevitable death at the jaws or claws of a bear, it also ran a very real risk of being killed by a bear hunter. In the chaos and close quarters of the hunt, when man, dog, and bear often quite literally were colliding with each other, a bear dog could easily be struck by a bullet or blade intended for a bear.[5] Early Coahoma settler Asa Bell Edwards lost one of his favorite dogs, "Old Rapid," to the "unlucky knife" of a hunting companion who was "blindly striking" at a wounded, attacking bear.[6] One of Bobo's pack intercepted a bullet intended for a bear.[7]

While on an extended hunting outing in 1888 with the settlers along Jones Bayou, which runs through the present city of Cleveland, Mississippi, in Bolivar County, surveyor A. B. Wingfield learned an unfortunate lesson in the dangers a bear dog faced from the hunter as well as from the bear. Wingfield had been invited on a bear hunt with one John Jones, John's Uncle Zack Jones, and some of the other residents of the Jones Bayou country. Uncle Zack, one of the patriarchs of the vicinity, and his wife were the proud parents of "four grown sons and a yard full of [nine] sandy-haired girls," one or more of whom Wingfield was "sparking."[8]

Along on the hunt and essential to it was the old man's pack of 27 bear dogs, most of whom were the progeny of Uncle Zack's favorite hound, old Mark Anthony, a "registered, pedigreed beagle," and his equally noble consort, "Cleopatra." Uncle Zack, on his own, could never have afforded such well-bred canines as Mark Anthony and his mate, which, even in those days, were worth hundreds of dollars. Wingfield joked that, had the opportunity presented itself, Uncle Zack would have been willing to swap all nine of his "sandy-haired gals" to acquire such hounds, "and he would almost have been willing to have thrown in his old woman for good measure."

Fortunately such a trade had not been necessary. The beagles were gifts from a wealthy and appreciative St. Louis cotton factor Uncle Zack once had hosted for a bear hunt.

No doubt Mark Anthony, like his owner, had gotten a bit gray about the muzzle in the time since he made his first appearance in the canebrakes of Bolivar County. Uncle Zack's love for the old dog, however, had not lessened one whit, but, in fact, had increased following Cleopatra's death in a bear fight the preceding year. However Mark Anthony's coloring may have changed over the years, he was no less game in a hunting scrap.

At the outset of the hunt, Jim Pyron, one of the neighbors of the Jones clan, gave Wingfield some advice. The Jones boys, Pyron told him, "were young and strong and knew every trail and short cut through the cane and would beat [Wingfield] to the bear invariably." If the surveyor wanted to kill a bear on this trip, Pyron said, he would need to get with "one of the Jones boys and tip him pretty heavy...." Otherwise, Pyron continued, "one of the Jones boys was sure to kill" any bear the dogs brought to bay. Wingfield, flush with confidence after having killed a Delta bear elsewhere some weeks before, boasted that he "was something of a woods-man" himself and would take his chances with the Jones boys.

The pack struck scent and in short order had a bear backed up in the thick cane. Pyron and Wingfield raced their mounts toward the sounds of the fray, but were too late. Before they could even get to the dogs, a gunshot announced the end of the fight. "Jim brought out an oath that would make Pluto blush," Wingfield wrote, "and said, 'I told you so.... Them durn Jones boys [are bear] hogs every one of them!'"

Another bear, though, was started within minutes. Again, one of the Jones boys killed the quarry before anyone else could get to the scene of the

action. Wingfield finally admitted he was outclassed and realized he would
have to take Pyron's advice if he hoped to kill a bear in Bolivar County.

The party spent the night at Uncle Zack's place. To maintain good
relations with the Jones clan, Wingfield, over the previous weeks of his Delta
stay, had given John and his kin "many a hundred of Winchester cartridges
and many a fancy hunting knife or drinking cup or cartridge belt" that one
of them had taken "a fancy to."[9] Before they started into the woods for the
next morning's hunt Wingfield "quietly slipped a five-dollar bill into John
Jones's hand with a hint that if he wanted any future favors" Wingfield
would need to "kill the bear that day." Jones valued Wingfield's patronage
and did not want to lose it. The deal thus made, "John went off and held a
consultation with his three brothers."

The dogs quickly struck scent and bounded away in full cry, old Mark
Anthony in the lead. John told Wingfield to stick close to him if he wanted
to kill the bear, and off they went.

Wingfield and Jones were tight on the heels of the pack, quite a bit
ahead of the other hunters, when they "heard just ahead... the awfulest,
most blood-curdling row that man's ears ever listened to." Fearing the worst,
John, picked up his pace. "Come quick," he told Wingfield, "they have got
him cornered, and he is mad as a Mexican bull.... [He] will kill every dog
in the pack if we don't git thar in a hurry."

Wingfield "instinctively stuffed two or three more cartridges into the
magazine" of his Winchester and followed, satisfied that his five dollars
had been well spent, for "John was big and strong and broke the way
through the cane," making the going much smoother than it otherwise
might have been. The young Delta man was "the best bear hunter"
Wingfield had "ever seen."

The trail to the bear fight quickly led to a "thick and stiff and matted"
canebrake that even the strapping John scarcely could have penetrated had
not the bear and pack bulldozed something of a path before him. As it was,
the hunters could only get through the brake by crawling.

After about a hundred yards on their hands and knees the two men
came to an opening wherein the large cane had been burned out by fire
and replaced by smaller, new growth "switch cane." Circular in shape,
and not 30 yards across, the clearing formed a sort of natural arena in
which the dogs and the bear were contending like warriors in some ancient

gladiatorial contest. John, who had promised Wingfield the bear, shouted to the surveyor to take his shot and to "not shoot the dogs."

Wingfield waited for an open shot. When it came, in hopes of stopping the bear's "terrible forepaws" and protecting the pack, he "planted a ball in the [bear's] foreshoulders." The bruin loosed "a howl of rage,... bit his shoulder several times, then turned" his attention in Wingfield's direction. Both hunters knew a charge was imminent. "Look out! Look out!" Jones shouted.

Wingfield realized it would take only "about three seconds for [the charging bear] to cover the 30 ft. intervening between" himself and the enraged beast. He began to shoot and lever and shoot as fast as he could, no longer concerning himself about hitting the dogs, but simply trying to save his own hide. Jones, who was not the immediate object of the bear's attention, thought it something of a joke to let Wingfield, who previously had staked his claim to this bear, handle the furious bruin on his own. The younger man held his fire and laughed. Wingfield levered yet another shell into the chamber of his Winchester and shouted across the opening: "Shoot, you infernal fool! Are you going to stand there and see him eat me up?" Apparently, he was.

"After my rifle had belched fire four times," wrote Wingfield, "there were two hounds dead on the ground from the bullets...." The bear, hit by "at least three of the balls... but still full of fight," rose up on his hind legs and again started for Wingfield. "My jaws closed like a steel trap. I have never had my nerve tried quite so hard since that time," said Wingfield. "I was like a person drowning. I thought of everything mean I had ever done since I was born."

Just when Wingfield was certain he was done for, old Mark Anthony, Uncle Zack's highly prized pet, "sprang in front of" the bear "and grabbed him by the throat." Now John quit laughing. He "sprang forward like a tiger to save old Mark, but he was not quick enough.... [W]ith a quick slap of his powerful forepaw," the bear "sent old Mark a bleeding, mangled mass into the edge of the cane."

At that very instant, John and Wingfield leaned into the bear and fired simultaneously, their rifle barrels almost touching the bruin's head. "The bear," shot in the skull and neck, "rolled over as dead as Hector, after Achilles had dragged him four times around the walls of Troy." It was, though, said Wingfield, "a dear bear," having cost five dogs—two killed by Wingfield's

Winchester, and the venerable Mark Anthony and two others slain by the bruin.[10]

Old Uncle Zack quickly arrived at the scene of the deaths. "The sight of old man Jones bending over the dead body of Mark crying like a child" was a sad one indeed for Wingfield, who felt more than a little responsible for all the canine destruction. "I hed a powerful sight sooner a give the whole balance o' the pack an' a kept this one dog," the old hunter said.

"I did not until then know," confessed Wingfield, "that a man ever formed such an attachment as that for a dog."

Wingfield "offered to pay Uncle [Zack] right on the spot for the two dogs [he] had killed" and explained that it had been "necessary to save [his] life." Uncle Zack would not take so much as a penny from his guest. He did give "John a terrible abusing," Wingfield wrote, with some obvious satisfaction, "for not trying to save the dogs and not taking a hand in the row sooner." John tried to blame Wingfield, saying the surveyor "hed gi'n him a bran new $5 bill for the 'tunity to kill that bar and he wanted me to get my money's wuf." The backswoodsman "wanted to get the laugh on me," said Wingfield, "but he didn't get it and lost five hounds trying it."

Problems for the bear dog were not limited to those encountered during the hunt. They also could come from quite unexpected quarters. In camp Emerson Hough got an object lesson in the random perils faced by the bear dog when, during the endless fighting that went on among the dogs when they were not hunting, one particular hound went for another right at Bobo's feet. The planter reacted in a manner that not only "[i]llustrated the headlong and impetuous character of our hunt and hunter in chief," Hough said, but demonstrated the man's impatience with dogs (and, no doubt, humans, too) that forgot their station. Without a second's hesitation, Bobo reflexively kicked the offending dogs, catching one hapless hound "just right" to lift "him clear off the ground and [send him] back downward right in the middle of the big log fire!" Fortunately for the dog, he landed in a burned down area of the bonfire and escaped with only his dignity wounded and his fur singed. Unfortunately, he raced up under one of the cabins where the foul smell from the burnt hair so irritated the hounds already there that immediately another fight ensued. For a short time, Hough said, "we had the biggest and most universal and loudest dog fight I ever heard or witnessed."

The empathetic Hough felt sorry for the singed hound. Although "[t]he dog was not hurt much…," Hough later wrote, "I did not envy him his lot. To be kicked about in two, roasted alive, and then jumped on by your neighbors is what you might call hard luck, especially when it all happens in less than fifteen seconds, and right when you're not expecting it.

The cold-eyed Bobo betrayed not a hint of concern, but continued his narratives without "changing a muscle of his face."[11]

16 Wolves, Panthers, and Squirrel Hunting at Night

Bobo's talk was not only about bears. "There are some wolves in these bottoms," too, he told those around the fireside. He recalled a man in the Delta he had known who had been treed by a pack of the canine predators. The man managed to kill a few of them but ran out of ammunition. He broke his gunstock clubbing the wolves before he was finally rescued by other hunters.[1]

There were panthers in the woods, as well, as the cat skin exhibited by Bobo's logging foreman earlier had demonstrated. The locals loved to talk about them and the visitors liked to hear about them. Recall the Indiana hunting party Bobo met in 1892. A Delta saloon keeper told that group of nonresident hunters of a panther killing a man in the Sunflower Swamp sometime before. According to the story, the cat had leaped upon a hunter from an overhead limb and killed him with a crushing bite to the neck. Was the bartender simply having some fun at the Hoosiers' expense? Perhaps, but he did show them a panther skin purported to have been nine feet long. While it is doubtful the hide was that big, it was certainly large enough to convince the hunters of the veracity of the barman's tale.[2]

The saloonkeeper's story may or may not have been true, for panthers, perhaps even more than bears, were often the subjects of exaggeration and prevarication in the Delta. For example, remember the panther foot James G. Chism sent to the editor of the Memphis *Daily Appeal* in 1876— the one he said was from a cat killed by Bob Bobo and his brother-in-law, Nels Harris? Chism told the newspaper that the panther had "measured eleven feet four inches from tip to tip." The cat's foot, Chism assured the editor, had "measured 8 inches across" when the animal was first killed.[3]

It is doubtful in the extreme that the true measurements were anything like that large. The celebrated bear hunter Ben Lilly, who spent his boyhood in Mississippi and who had killed panthers[4] from "the Mississippi River to the Continental Divide," once wrote that the big cat's habits and measurements varied little throughout that area. The biggest panther he reported was taken in Mexico and measured "8 feet, 9 ½ inches" from the tip of its nose to the tip of its tail.[5] That was an exceptionally large specimen, according to Lilly. Mature male panthers, he said, averaged "from 7 to 7 ½ feet." That is more in keeping with other historic records of Mississippi cats. The *Spirit of the Times*, for example, reported in November 1843 the killing of a seven foot, eight inch, panther in Warren County, Mississippi, near the southern terminus of the Delta country.[6]

"The fresh hide of a full-grown male" panther, Lilly noted, will stretch out about three feet" beyond the live length of the cat. That elasticity accounted for the exaggerated size of many panthers, Lilly believed,[7] and very well could have been responsible for Chism's description of Bobo's and Harris's cat.

The supposed eight inch breadth of the foot of the cat killed by Bobo—as reported by Mr. Chism—must have been an exaggeration, as well. Perhaps, it, too, was stretched for measuring. The typical panther track is only about four inches wide.[8] That Chism qualified his statement by saying the foot measured eight inches "when killed" certainly indicates it was not that large when he sent it to the *Daily Appeal*'s editor.

Whatever the Friars Point cat's actual size it had done large damage around that river front village. According to Chism the panther had "killed four grown horses" in the area prior to its death.[9]

While panther predations on stock were not uncommon in the Delta in those days, Bobo said he personally had never known of a cougar attacking a human. He added, however, that the big cats would occasionally follow a man in the woods. One night, in fact, a panther stalked Bobo and a companion for six miles though the Delta swamps. The cat left them only after they swam their horses across a bayou.[10]

The campfire talk turned to what sounds, if any, panthers made. Conventional wisdom then, as now, held that a panther's call was a blood-curdling thing like the "scream of a woman." Col. James Gordon, who certainly was not ignorant on the subject, once described the Delta panther's vocalizing as "not altogether unlike the shriek of a woman in distress." It was, he said, "a sound that pierces the senses rather than the ear alone, and makes a chill creep over the frame, and the heart beat fast."[11]

Hough, playing devil's advocate, observed that many experienced woodsmen had contended that the big cat not only did not scream like a woman, but, in fact, uttered no sounds that could be heard more than a few steps away. Bobo's contemporary, Ben Lilly, said much the same thing: "I have heard [a panther] squall and spit like a tomcat. I have never heard anything like a woman's scream from a panther."[12]

"Well, maybe they never heard one holler," said Bobo. "They do, just the same. Their call is a sort of scream." Bobo, too, said he had heard panthers "give a sort of coarse, rumbling purr or whine, like a big cat…. The panther that followed us was crying out every once in while. It sometimes came up within a few feet of us in the dark."

Despite his close encounter and the stories told to visiting hunters about the supposed ferocity of panthers, Bobo believed there was nothing to fear from the cats. "I think a good willow switch would do to scare away about any panther in the country," he told Hough.[13]

Besides hearing the wolf and panther lore, Hough also met an especially interesting character by Bobo's campfire, who, oddly enough, or, perhaps, not so oddly, was not mentioned by Hough in his subsequent narratives of his time with Bobo. His name was Lamar Fontaine, and to call him merely a fascinating man would be the grossest of understatements. Slightly more than six feet tall with a beard and a head of hair as thick as any bear's fur, he was an impressive man by his looks alone. His story, if he can be believed, and many think he cannot be, is amazing. He claimed to have been born in a tent on the prairies of Texas in 1829, to have lived four years with the Comanches, sailed to the arctic on a naval vessel, traveled throughout China, served as a Texas Ranger, and fought the British as a Russian soldier during the Crimean War, all before his 27th birthday.

When the Civil War erupted, Fontaine enlisted in the Mississippi Rifles, Jefferson Davis's former regiment that had distinguished itself at Buena Vista during the Mexican War. Despite suffering horrendous wounds early in the Civil War, Fontaine served throughout the conflict as a scout and sharpshooter. He also made a name for himself as the author of the lyrics to "All Quiet Along the Potomac," one of the most popular of Civil War era songs (this, too, was disputed).

By the 1880s Fontaine had settled in Coahoma County where he worked as a surveyor[14] and became fast friends with Bob Bobo. "Not too many moons" before Hough's 1894 visit, in fact, Fontaine may well have saved Bobo's life.

One morning while Bobo and Fontaine were hunting from a back-woods camp the pack, led by Bobo's then premier dog, Dublin, jumped an exceptionally large he bear—the biggest Fontaine had seen. As the bruin broke from a canebrake and crossed an open glade, Fontaine "sent a Winchester bullet into the great beast," slowing him down enough for the dogs to catch up. The old boar fought the pack off but not before Fontaine "staggered him" with a second shot, which caused the bear to turn to engage the dogs once more. Bobo arrived at the fight just as the bear caught "two of Bobo's favorites" in his grip.

The Bear Hunter would not risk killing his dogs by firing his carbine. He charged the bear, knife drawn, to put an end to the contest. The remainder of the pack, "encouraged by his presence, made a fresh attack." In response, the bear rose and with one swipe of a powerful paw "knocked Bobo's knife away,…splitting the back of his hand severely" in the process. As Fontaine later told the story to the newspapers, the bear, still erect, "drew Bobo toward him." As the big animal's "huge jaws flew open to grasp" the Bear Hunter's head, Fontaine said, "I raised my rifle and sent a ball crashing into [the bear's] mouth. Bobo's head was not more than three feet from the muzzle of my gun and in a line with the bear's head."

The bear and Bobo collapsed to the ground. As the sound of the shot died away, for a moment, even the dogs were quiet and still. Fontaine was sure he had killed both Bobo and the bear. To Fontaine's great relief, however, Bobo rose almost immediately, dazed from the concussion of the blast and with "his normal ruddy complexion…pale," but otherwise in good shape except for some singed whiskers, powder burns on his face, and a hand badly cut from the bear's blow. Since that close call, Fontaine later wrote, "I have cared little to join in the sport" of bear hunting.[15]

Fontaine's presence in camp during Hough's hunt with Bobo, however, proved the Confederate veteran continued to enjoy the company of bear hunters. At the time of Hough's 1894 visit Fontaine was 65 years old, still a master of the rifle, and "famous throughout the South as soldier, jurist, sportsman and poet." What is more, as Hough would learn, as a "practical joker" Fontaine had "no superior in the world."[16]

As Hough, Fontaine, and the others sat together by the fire that chilly November evening, Bobo appeared to drift off into sleep. The rest of the party, perhaps full of adrenalin after "a hard day's hunting for bear," stayed awake, but in a "contemplative and reminiscent mood...." During a lull in the conversation "Fontaine arose from his seat, donned his hat, and then with the most nonchalant air picked up a .22 cal. rifle...." After testing the gun's action and appearing to find it satisfactory, Fontaine moved away from the fire toward the darkness. Though no one else seemed to notice, Hough, all the while, watched with unconcealed interest. Finally, his curiosity overcame him, and Hough asked Fontaine what he planned to do with the .22.

"Going squirrel hunting," came the reply.

Hough must have thought he misunderstood something crucial. "Squirrel hunting! What, this dark night?"

Fontaine, with a "tone of indulgent tolerance," as if "informing another [gentleman] of facts [he] should know," replied, "Of course. Our very best squirrel hunting is in the darkness of the nighttime at this season of the year...." Fontaine further explained that "the best weapon, in fact the only successful one for night hunting, is the rifle." Then he added, "Don't you really know anything of this lovely sport?"

Hough could not quite take in all he was hearing. "But how do you see to shoot?"

"Oh, it has to be learned by experience," Fontaine answered, the terse nature of the reply betraying, perhaps, growing impatience with the Chicago writer's inexperience.

With that, Fontaine walked off into the blackness of the Delta night.

The other hunters said nothing. They merely continued their contented gazing into the blazing campfire.

Within a few minutes the sharp crack of a .22 broke the silence. "That's a dead squirrel," said one of the men. Another short while went by and, again, the rifle sounded, this time with three quick reports from a different quarter of the woods. That squirrel "was running," piped up one of Hough's companions. "It's dead now, anyway," a third hunter said. "Wonderful gift for a man to have," chimed in another. "It is no wonder he was so famous for night work in the army."

The sporadic shooting continued out in the dark woods for another thirty minutes. Then the group heard footsteps coming toward the fire. "Mr. Fontaine, bunch of squirrels in hand, walked in with the matter-of-fact bearing of the man who has done the deed so many times that he has ceased to think of it with any warmth." Except for Hough, none of the hunters appeared surprised or even very much interested.

Hough, on the other hand, was amazed. He "praised [Fontaine's] skill and commended his success." When his fellows failed to marvel at Fontaine's incredible feat, Hough roused the sleeping Bobo to discuss Fontaine's night time hunting. The great bear hunter "woke suspiciously easy, and said, 'Sonny, you have told us that you killed grizzly bears in the Rocky Mountains, shot all over Louisiana, and yet you break in on my slumbers to have me admire a bunch of squirrels which are cold and stiff and perhaps fly-blown, for they were killed three days ago with a shotgun.'"

"A singular merriment thereupon pervaded the party."[17] Hough knew he had been had. Meanwhile, "the New Orleans express was speeding southward," and Hough "had quite forgotten it."[18]

17 Riding Cane

The next morning (Wednesday, November 7), with the sun "hardly over the edge of the earth," the hunters rode out of camp and into the woods sounding mellow notes from their horns to assemble the pack. The hunting horn, in writer Hough's estimation, constituted "a large factor in the science of bear hunting." Made from "the horn of the humble cow,"[1] the instrument provided not only a means for calling the dogs, but served the hunters as a practical, if limited, method of communication while separated in the woods.

Bobo personalized his horn by stretching the raw skin from the lower part of a deer's rear leg, including the dewclaws,[2] over it. When the skin dried it became for all practical purposes glued to the horn. Such an addition to a hunting horn must have been common in Mississippi in Bobo's time. James G. Norwood, who was born in northern Mississippi in 1847, the same year as Bobo, also had a hunting horn covered with the skin from a deer's leg. The hide on Norwood's horn, however, did not include the dewclaws.[3] Why these hunters bound their horns with rawhide cannot be known for certain. It may have been purely for decoration, but, in all probability, the deer skin helped protect the horn from cracking. A long rawhide strip, attached to either end of Bobo's horn, served as a carrying strap for the instrument.

There was, of course, an art to blowing the hunting horn. It was a skill that required training and practice as surely as playing a bugle. The hunter unaccustomed to the horn could not always sound it.[4]

Just as the experienced hunter knows the individual voices of his pack, so could the members of the Bobo hunting party recognize the sounds of the others' horns. Everyone also knew the code for communicating by horn: two shorts and a long summoned the dogs; a single long note requested the others' positions; three longs meant "come to me"; and repeated and continuous blowing signaled "a kill and assemblage after the chase." Hunting etiquette dictated that horns should be used sparingly so as not to interfere with the notes of the huntmaster—in this case, Bobo—whose prerogative it was to call and "lay on" the dogs.

In open country, Hough speculated, this woodsman's telegraph could be heard as much as a mile away. In the dense Delta woods and canebrakes, however, its practical range was substantially less—at best, probably no more than half a mile. Heavy cane especially muffled the horn's notes. A note sounded but 200 or 300 yards away from the listener in the brakes could sound like it was three or four times that far in the distance.[5]

Bobo's hunting horn. *Photo by author.*

The hunters' destination that morning was a water hole in "thick cane country" Hough called Surveyor's[6] Lake.* The men traveled by way of "Tom's Hack," a narrow trail named for the hired hand who cut it and who was among the hunting party. Even with such an improved trail to follow, negotiating the cane was an ordeal. At best, the hack was the tightest of defiles through a great mass of living matter. On either side the

---

* Probably Sevier's Lake. See the endnote for a more detailed explanation.

cane stems and leaves, "like a thousand malicious fingers, pluck[ed] at the horsemen. ... The shaking and switching and cutting of the cane on the face and body [was] continuous and painful...."[7]

It is difficult to exaggerate just how much the cane, brush, and growth of the brake could rip and tear at someone trying to pass through it, especially one on horseback and in a hurry. On one of his hunts with Uncle Zack Jones of Bolivar County, Mississippi, A. B. Wingfield had "all my clothes torn off of me, and nearly had my eyes jabbed out a dozen times" by the briars and cane. So shredded were Wingfield's garments from riding, running, and crawling through the canebrakes that all he had left of his pants were "the waistband and pockets and a ruffle around each leg at the top of my boots." At the end of the hunt he had to remain in the woods until a companion could bring him another pair of trousers lest his pants-less appearance at Uncle Zack's home scandalize the old gentleman's wife and their nine "sandy-haired" daughters.[8]

Besides the risk the Delta canebrakes posed to one's clothes, they also limited the hunters' vision to a very short range. It was "impossible to see twenty feet ahead" in such cover, according to Hough, "even on the line of the 'hack.'"[9] Consequently, in the brake the hunter was utterly dependent upon his horse and had to be prepared at all times to adapt to the animal's movements, even when unexpected. One's mount, for instance, might suddenly leap over a log invisible to the rider. In such a circumstance a slow-to-react hunter might easily find his head or shoulder battered by a tree limb he had assumed only a split second before would pass harmlessly overhead.

The practiced cane horse rarely tried to bulldoze a path through the brakes. Rather, by ducking and dodging, it sought to thread its way through the thicket. The rider, leaning in against his horse's neck, hung on tightly as his mount forged ahead. Such was the Bear Hunter's riding style as described by Hough—at least until a trail was struck and the dogs were hot on a bear. Then, "[t]he hunting horses, under spur, plunged at the thicket full speed, and we had to sit fast and fight the vines and branches as best we could." Under such conditions, said Hough, "you just ride—you forget how."

Carrying a gun through such cover presented definite problems for the cane rider. A hunter typically held his carbine across the saddle when traveling in open woods. That position was unworkable in the brakes—the dense growth would quickly rip the gun from hunter's grasp as his horse forged its way through the thicket. Rather, the firearm had to be held at the horseman's "side or before the face." Typically, when moving quickly through cane, the rider kept his gun parallel to and flush against his mount.

Bobo, always the innovator in bear hunting, naturally developed his own style of holding his weapon in heavy cane. He "had a trick of carrying his rifle stock upward in his" hand that held the reins. That way, if the gun became entangled with cane or vines that Bobo could not break through, the carbine, held in the same hand as the reins, would force back the reins and bring the horse to a halt before the gun could be wrenched from its owner's hand.[10] Bobo also had perfected the art of clearing a path ahead of his horse as he rode. By stretching his knife hand out before his mount, Bobo could cut cane "as fast as the horse would want to walk."[11]

Carrying a firearm through the Delta woods and brakes, especially on horse- or mule-back, presented ample opportunities for tragic accidents. Switches of cane, briar stalks, and tree branches could easily hang inside a trigger guard and cause an accidental discharge of a cocked and loaded weapon.

In 1886 veteran bear hunter, former Confederate cavalry general, and sitting United States senator, Wade Hampton III, learned that lesson in an all too practical way. According to a *New York Times* report, the South Carolina man, who probably owned more land in Mississippi than in his home state, was hunting near his plantation in Issaquena County, Mississippi, "when his gun was caught by a twig and fired off. The charge entered his horse's head, instantly killing him, and throwing him back upon the Senator, who was pinned to the earth." After much struggle, Hampton, who was 68 at the time, "succeeded in extricating himself" and began the long trek back "to the plantation, nearly five miles away." Hampton required a number of days in bed to recuperate from the incident.[12]

Bobo had seen much worse results from carelessness with firearms. Once, while "out in a dugout, with a friend, hunting in the overflow," he noticed that his companion (most likely Napoleon L. "Boney" Leavell[13]) "had his gun pointing right toward me." Bobo immediately told the friend to point the barrel in another direction. "Wait till I get around this cypress knee," the friend said, "and I will."

As the men paddled around the cypress knee, "the gun caught on it... and bang she went," Bobo told Hough. Bobo was "shot... square in the hip with a load of 16 buckshot at a distance of about two or three inches." The entire "load... went into the fleshy part of the hip and thigh" and ranged down his entire leg, with two or three pieces coming out of the sole of his foot. The closest settlement was a 15 hour paddle upstream on the Sunflower River at flood stage.

That Bobo survived such a wound so far from medical help is little short of a miracle. Bobo attributed his good fortune to the fact that his companion, Boney Leavell, "had learned something of surgery" during his time as a Confederate soldier. Boney "had been shot up a good deal" during the War and in fact had lost a foot and ankle in the conflict. Most likely his medical knowledge came from observing battlefield physicians tending his wounds and those of his comrades. Whatever the source of Leavell's skills, his attention to the wound certainly "saved Bobo a leg" and, probably, his life. Nonetheless, Bobo carried several pieces of buckshot "scattered up and down his leg" for the rest of his days.

On another occasion Bobo and some of his hired men "had a good chase after a bear, and we were getting ready to head off the chase at a little open slough." Sam, one of the hands, had his gun at full cock, half cock being the safety position, resting on his shoulder, pointed backwards. Bobo called Sam's attention to the unsafe position of the firearm. Hardly had the words left Bobo's mouth, when, "whang! She went, and he shot Pete, another [hired] man who was just coming up behind, crossing the slough, square in the forehead, and killed him dead."

Yet another time Bobo witnessed sloppy firearm handling end in near disaster. Bobo was on a bear hunt "with a right oldish gentleman" who carried "a double-barreled shotgun charged with bear loads" and "both barrels full cocked." Bobo cautioned the man not to handle the piece in such a manner, but to no avail. The man "said he had carried a gun that way all his life and thought he knew how to carry one as well as anybody."

About that same time Bobo heard a bear coming toward the hunters. Simultaneously, the old man suffered an attack of epilepsy, "to which he was sometimes subject." As the old man's friends tried to assist their companion, Bobo shot the bear. He "hadn't gotten more than a few yards away before whang! went" the old man's gun and "shot a hole in the ground." Then, the second barrel fired, this time blowing "his horse's foot off." As often is the case in such accidents, no one knew how the gun discharged. "No one ever knows how it happens," Bobo said, "but it sometimes does happen."[14]

To avoid such unintended shootings of horses, hounds, or hunters, Bobo maintained an inviolable rule on his hunts: absolutely no weapon was to be carried with a round in the chamber.

On one of the "narrow, choked-up, hacks" Hough witnessed another danger common to what he described as the "rather stern sort of sport" that was bear hunting. Bob, Jr.,[15] the planter's son, riding lead, suddenly stopped and dismounted, his hand against his head. "Tell Papa to come here," he said, blood pouring from his nose. The other hunters parted as best they could in the thicket to let the elder Bobo through.

"What is it, son? Have you got a cane in your nose?"

"Yes," replied the boy.

"Have you got the piece out?"

"I don't know." The youngster showed his father a sizable stick of cane. "Here's a piece of it." Felix Payne gave the boy a leaf of his tobacco. Bob, Jr., rolled it up and stuck it in his nose to stanch the bleeding.

"Well, jump up and go ahead, son," the elder Bobo said. "I've had a hundred canes in my nose, I expect." In the Spartan way of the Bobos the young man re-mounted and the hunt proceeded.

The next day Bob, Jr., coughed up a piece of the cane about as big around as a pencil and half an inch long. Hough surmised that "it had been driven entirely through the nasal passages into the throat."

Hough and the elder Bobo rode a mile or so from camp and struck Tom's Hack again. They followed it about half a mile into thick cane, their ride complicated by the difficulty of keeping the young dogs together until a bear trail could be verified. The big woods must have been a veritable smorgasbord of game scent; the pups were constantly opening up and striking out after deer or raccoon or possum or whatever happened to tickle their olfactories. The old bear dogs, though, the ones Bobo could bank on, sounded not a note.

After some while had passed, one of the dogs—a foxhound—jumped upon "a log, snuffed, whimpered and gave voice to a loud, deep cry." Solid old Henry bayed his approval. The other dogs within earshot converged on the log and joined in the chorus. "That's bear, this time, for a thousand dollars!" Bobo shouted, and the chase was on.

The sound of the pack in full cry after bear was orders of magnitude greater than the sounds of the same dogs running a fox, coon, or other smaller animal. The bayings and howls of the pack, Hough wrote, combined as "a savage, roaring chaos of fierce and angry voices.... [A] man cannot hear it and sit still. The dogs of war are loose in the air and he must ride, he must act."

Bobo shouted directions to the hunters, then crashed his horse "through the cane" and "over the trail, every horse following, as eager as the dogs."[16]

"I often laughed to myself, though Bobo didn't know it," Hough later confessed, "to see him riding through the cane-brake. It was like a wild bull of Bashan[17] broken loose."[18]

Bobo and Hough rode down one hack; the other hunters dashed off in other directions. The pack was split at least three ways: Old Henry and the reliable hounds on the actual bear track; another bunch on the same trail, but running the backtrack—the direction from whence the bear had come; and the rest running a deer or other game. Bobo, for once, seemed confused. He had no idea where the other hunters were or where the bear and the pursuing dogs were.

The writer and the planter sat on their mounts at the dead end of the hack, listening. Between the baffling effect of the dense canebrake and the clattering of dead leaves in the gusting wind, they could hear nothing of the pack. Bobo, losing patience, charged into the wall of cane and pushed his way to a nearby dry bayou bed. There he blew a long blast on his horn. Hough thought he heard a responsive note ever so faint and far away. The men rode in the direction of the supposed reply. They heard the horn again and, this time, men's voices with it. Then, riding single file out of the cane, came Bob, Jr., and Frank Harris. Behind them rode Tom and Pete, the hired men. Fixed to the rear of Pete's saddle, flopping cross-wise on the horse, was the bear. To the party's disappointment, though, it was a small one: at 150 pounds, hardly more than a cub by Bobo standards.

The bear had been taken less than half a mile from Hough and the elder Bobo. Bob, Jr., Frank, Tom, and Pete had heard the dogs tree off in the cane thicket and had crept in to shoot. The bear, though, had detected their advance and dropped from the white oak to which it was clinging to make its escape, just as the hunters approached. Young Bob and Frank both had fired at the fleeing bear but apparently had missed.

The five dogs present, however, did not. They each latched on to the yearling and "strung him out," immobilizing the bruin by pulling on him from opposite directions. Bob, Jr., wanted to capture the bear alive, but Tom was concerned that the dogs might get injured in the process. The hired man rushed in and put two quick bullets into the bear's skull, ending the contest immediately. The wind had been rattling so much in the autumn woods, though, that Hough and the elder Bobo had heard neither the shots that had slain the bear nor the repeated firing and horn blasts signaling the kill to the other hunters.

The elder Bobo and Felix Payne suspected that the young bear's mother was about the woods somewhere. The sow and her offspring must have parted earlier, they deduced, with five dogs following the cub's track and the remainder following the dam. Whatever had happened, the rest of the dogs somehow sensed that the hunt had concluded and a kill had been made. They began to drift in from the cane in hopes of claiming a generous share of bear offal. The game was eviscerated in short order.

After the field dressing and the dog fights over the innards the hunters again tied the dead beast to a saddle mule. The ordinary horse or mule, as Hough later wrote, "is deathly afraid of the mere smell of bear." The horses and mules in the Bobo entourage, though, showed no fear of a bear skin or even a whole dead bear. Hough concluded that these animals "must have had many a bear about them." Hough also observed that the joints of the bruin's front feet had been severed with a knife. The reason for that, Hough learned, was to allow the dead bear's claws to hang loosely and to prevent them from digging into the mule's flanks during the homeward jostle through the brakes. How many bears must a man kill and transport by horse or mule to learn such a procedure? "Surely," concluded Hough, "the art of bear hunting was done fine here."

It was not yet 1:00 p.m. and the hunters maintained hopes of a more substantial bear in the afternoon. Bobo, Hough, and the others mounted up and struck out down the great dried-up river run called Black Bayou, which was timbered with cypress and bordered by stands of ancient oak and gum. The dry wind would not subside, though, and the pack, despite one or two eruptions into full cry, could make out no trail. Then, the unmistakable smell of smoke on the wind and the distinct popping of burning cane conveyed to the practiced Delta woodsmen a clear message: the brakes between the hunters and the Sunflower were afire. The party abandoned their quest for the day and hurried back to the logging camp.[19]

Bobo must have known well the terror and the beauty of the canebrake fire. A writer for the early nineteenth century *Farmer's Register* thought "the terrific magnificence" of a cane fire "unequalled." The hurricane-like roaring of the flames could be heard and the thick black smoke it emitted could be seen up to six to eight miles away. The explosions of the super-heated air in the joints of the cane gave the impression of gun fire from a not too distant battle. The rapid on-rushing of the "tumultuous ocean of flame," leaping "ahead in long tongues with the speed of a courser" would make "the brain reel," he wrote. Occasionally the conflagration would erupt into fountains of fire sending columns of flames "among the topmost limbs of the forest." Despite the tremendous destruction such an event left in its wake, the woodland holocaust provided an unparalleled sensory spectacle. The canebrake fire, wrote the author of the *Farmer's Register* piece, was, "with the deafening noise—the vaulting flame—the dense clouds of black smoke—and the cinders which [fell] in showers behind it—one of the most sublime exhibitions of the power of the great element, fire, which we ever beheld."[20]

One Ned Casteel of southern Louisiana no doubt lacked that writer's appreciation for the aesthetic aspects of a fire in the brakes. He and his hunting party were nearly roasted alive by such a blaze. With not a moment to spare they managed to save themselves by lighting a back fire that gave them enough time to cross a bayou to a green cane patch too wet to burn. The much feared prairie fires of the west, Casteel's party determined, "could not hold a candle to" a fire in a dry canebrake when it came to inspiring fear and awe.[21]

Nightfall found the Bobo party by its roaring, but unthreatening, camp fire. "Well, you didn't get your shot, did you?" Bobo said to Hough. "But you keep close to me tomorrow and you won't be far off at the finish. I want you to kill the bear tomorrow."

"Tomorrow?" replied the befuddled Hough. "I thought I was going to take the train south tonight somewhere down here."[22]

"Well, you're not," Bobo responded, matter-of-factly. "You'd have to ride 15 miles through the dark now by way of the upper ford to the nearest station.... If you swam the Sunflower here you'd have to go ten miles, and you'd have to hurry then, for the train is due there about nine o'clock. You are going to stay right here and go bear hunting some more."

"So I was a prisoner," mused Hough, "and a very philosophical one…..." Hough figured that Divine and his hunting companions would not wait for him in New Orleans at this point, anyway. Hough resolved "to take the world as it came; which is a pretty good way to do, if you can only do it."

Like many a practical prisoner, Hough used his time as a captive to learn a profitable skill. That night Hough, with the help of the others and in hopes of taking a bear robe back to Chicago if and when Bobo released him, skinned the young bear Tom had killed. Hough knew that unless the hide was meticulously cleaned of any bits of fat and meat that clung to it during the skinning process, the robe would spoil and be unfit for preservation and display by the time he returned home. Bobo showed him how to use a mixture of salt and cornmeal to dry the greasy residue in order to more easily strip it from the bearskin.

Hough, who enjoyed the work of preserving a skin as a hunting trophy—"fooling over a hide," he called it—spent much of the evening applying the meal and salt and scraping and pulling away from the robe anything that was neither hair nor hide. His companions seemed mystified that anyone would spend so much time and energy on such a piddling bear. They could not understand, wrote Hough, "how prized such a gift is to one who doesn't live in bear country."[23]

18 Fresh Tracks

Early the next morning (Thursday, November 8) the hunters breakfasted on bear steaks and bear liver from the preceding day's kill. Then each hunter "made himself a bear sandwich for lunch." The bear meat meals, Hough quipped, "made our hearts strong, but [were] hard on the bear." Once the men had eaten and set aside their noon rations the remainder of the cub was given to the dogs who devoured the carcass in a matter of minutes. "When you have along a pack of fifty-three bear dogs," Hough wrote, "there is little danger of any meat going to waste."

The hunters, in hopes of striking a fresh trail, planned to scout the rims of waterholes where they had seen bear tracks the day before. The pack was more cohesive that morning than during the previous day's hunt. There was none of the ranging and running of false trails by subcommittees. Not far from the camp one of Bobo's logging employees approached via a woodland trail. He wanted the hunters to kill a panther he believed he had heard back in the brake. Bobo never veered from his course. He suspected what the hunter actually had heard had been the calling of the old she bear whose cub the hunters had killed the previous morning. "We'll get a bear easy enough where we are going," Bobo said.

Not much later the group spied fresh tracks by a small watering spot. Simultaneously, the pack broke into full cry. Once more the "magnificently savage music" of the baying pack brought a tidal wave of excitement crashing over the writer. "No man," he wrote, "can sit in his saddle unmoved by" the sound of a bear pack in pursuit. "It thrills and tingles and insists that we yell and ride."

Yell and ride they did. When the pack split left and right, Bobo, Payne, and Hough took the left track, which Bobo believed to be "the natural course of the bear."

Bobo spurred his horse and ran out through a dry bayou channel filled with trees and vines and brush. Mounted on the trusty Coleman, Hough did his best to keep up, but Bobo quickly dashed out at least a quarter mile ahead of the others. There was no more "walking or even trotting, but full gallop."

Bobo and Hough stopped on a caney rise on the bank of the old bayou run and listened. No dogs, no tell-tale popping of cane, could be heard. The bear and the pack apparently had turned off to one side and Bobo had missed it. The men pushed further into the cane and listened again: the faintest sounds of baying hounds fell upon their ears.

The bear, deduced Bobo, had smelled the smoke from the burning cane off in the brake, spooked, and reversed his course to get away from the fire. "We must get back," Bobo shouted. The men retraced their course through the dried streambed. It was a brutal, punishing run, "smashing and tearing through the vine-knit," shins and knees and thighs and elbows pounding against limbs, saplings, and the occasional tree trunk. All the while the rider knew that at any moment his horse could trip over a hidden cypress knee and break the necks of man and mount alike. By the end of the day Hough's legs would be black and blue.

Bobo again paused to listen for the pack, this time on a slight rise of the type that passed for a hillock in the Delta swamp. They heard two groups of hounds trailing in opposite directions. Payne declared that he would chase one half of the pack. "Come on with me, now," Bobo shouted to Hough, and tore off through the woods in the other direction, following a dry water course.

Hough followed "as best I could, through an hour or more of the worst riding I ever had in my life" as Bobo "raged" back and forth through "that awful ravine." From one end of the bayou bed to the other and back they galloped, looking for the places Bobo was convinced the bear would cross, but with no sign of bear or hound or hunters.

"Great governor!" Bobo cried. "Can it be that I've lost the pack again today, right when I wanted you to be in at the fight?" The frustrated huntsman rode and sounded his horn, but no one responded.

For two hours Hough and Bobo neither saw nor heard any sign of the other hunters. At last, the tiniest remnant of a note drifted through the woods. Bobo recognized its timbre: it was the horn of his son, Bob, Jr. "And he's coming up Black Bayou," Bobo said. Hough found himself once more pushing Coleman to keep up with Bobo through the hellish terrain of the dry stream bed.

Shortly they saw Bob, Jr., Frank, and Bill riding toward them. The three had not a clue as to where the remainder of the hunting party was. "Well, you're a good lot to let the dogs run plum away from you," Bobo said. "Where are all the dogs, anyhow?"

The young men said they had seen two dogs by themselves about a half mile back. "Why didn't you shoot them?" asked an indignant Bobo. "I don't want any dogs that leave the trail when it gets hot." Bobo asked for the names of the offending deserters.

The little intelligence Bobo received from the boys convinced him of what had happened "as well as if [he] had seen it" himself. The dogs Payne had followed were the hounds that had the true trail. The others were running the back track. The pair the boys saw were coming from "that thick cane, and that's right where the bear went, too." Bobo figured the bear had been killed, for, "Pete and Tom would get him if Mr. Payne didn't." A dead bear also would have explained the two hounds the boys saw leaving the trail.

The group, testing Bobo's theory, struck out for the cane "at a gallop." They heard a horn, and upon their responding, a repetition of notes that signaled a kill answered in reply, sounds that made Hough's "heart sink." Bobo had figured correctly. Hough's hopes of making the shot that would have ended that chase had been in vain.

After a brief push through a few dozen yards of cane, the "hardy Coleman burst through the last of" it into a clearing in which stood a massive white oak. Again, Hough imagined the scene as a painting, this one with horses idle by the great oak, while two score or more of dogs lay "panting, or fighting or sneaking about...." Payne leaned against a tree while Tom and Pete bent over the remains of 350 pounds of black bear, the second they had killed in two days, already skinned and butchered, on the woodland floor.

The two hands had sneaked into the cane and caught the bruin treed about 60 feet up the oak. To keep the bear from sliding down and killing or wounding the dogs, they shot immediately. "We double-fired him, sir," Tom said to Bobo, indicating he and Pete had shot simultaneously. Both bullets had found the bear's heart. He was dead before he hit the ground. Hough figured the fall should have broken every bone in the beast's body.

Bobo relaxed on his mount, hooking one leg around the saddle horn. "Well, there's your bear, and I reckon you got a rug this time, but I would have given twenty dollars for you to have had the shot."

Yes, "[t]his was the bear I should have killed," Hough would later write, "which everybody wanted me to kill, and which it was a ten to one wager I would kill if I kept close to Mr. Bobo." Bad luck had ruled the hunt for Hough, though. He replayed the day and imagined how things might have turned out differently if only "had we turned back with Mr. Payne" instead of taking what Bobo thought was the true trail. Hough did not report whether Bobo granted the two wandering hounds seen by his son a reprieve from the firing squad after he found the bear was dead.

The meat was sacked and, along with the hide, secured to horses. The hunters began the short ride—about a mile—back to the logging camp. That night the members of the party happily stayed up very late, "told bear stories, boiled bear heads,* and scraped bear hides.... And once more the New Orleans express went south through the brakes and forests of the Delta," Hough later wrote, "and I let it go. And Providence alone knew where Tom Divine and the others were by that time," Hough mused.

"We'll kill another bear tomorrow," said Bobo.[1]

---

* Probably to clean the skulls for trophies, but possibly for some game recipe.

19 Bear Hunt Looking Up

"The bear hunting business," Hough concluded, "was looking up." The hunters understood the country and where to look for bear and the hounds had developed into a highly effective pack. Hough had a renewed faith that he would get a shot at a bear and truly did not want to leave without one. He did have a prior commitment in the Bayou State, though, and "felt obliged to tell Mr. Bobo" that he could hunt but one more day. Bobo agreed to release Hough after the morning's hunt. At the conclusion of their final effort the two would ride the 20 miles back to Bobo Station where Hough could catch the 9:20 p.m. train for New Orleans. With that in mind the men planned their hunt to move in the general direction of the Bobo plantation. They followed a trail through occasionally dense cane between the Sunflower River and its former channel, now dry except for isolated cypress-shaded pools. Almost immediately they came upon bear tracks in the mud of just such a waterhole.

The dogs cast about the bank of the old river run, broke into full cry, and ran off into the cane. Bobo, satisfied the dogs were on a bear, told Hough to follow him. The two took up positions in an "open glade along the edge of the heavy cane." The dogs immediately split into two groups, as on previous races. Within minutes, there were other schisms in the pack.

To the inexperienced hunter there would have seemed to have been a dozen different hunts going on. Hough was no longer such a novice. He had learned from his brief time in the Delta woods that some of the dogs would take the back track and run the opposite way from the bear due to their ignorance. Other dogs, especially the younger ones, would abandon the main trail altogether for more interesting or stronger scents encountered along the way: wildcat, coon, or deer, for example. Even the best of hounds would occasionally overrun and lose a trail, especially under warm, dry, windy conditions, such as they were experiencing during their November hunt. Meanwhile, other dogs, whether or not they smelled any game, simply would be "hollering for luck," as Hough put it.

Bobo for once sat peacefully upon his horse, fully aware of which dogs were on the game and which were not. One piece of the pack treed hardly more than a pistol shot or two away. Bobo didn't move. "It's only a coon. The bear has gone the other way." One of the party immediately rushed to thrash "the dogs away from the coon tree."

After a long wait in the glade Bobo and Hough heard the dogs change course. Bobo announced he would "just go over and see which way they turn." Hough stayed with Felix Payne, thinking Bobo would be returning. Payne's success at finding the bear the day before may have been the true reason Hough stayed behind with him.

Bobo shouted something to Hough and Payne that sounded like, "Ride over to the Old River,"[1] the "Old River" being the former channel of the Sunflower dried up but for intermittent pools. Actually, what he said was, "I think [the dogs have] gone over to the Old River," a distinction that would make a difference in the outcome of the day's hunt.

The men, thinking they were acting on the chief huntsman's directions, struck out in "hot haste" for Old River. Bobo actually had intended for Hough and Payne to remain with him to wait to see where the dogs would move next.

Hough and Payne proceeded to Old River and waited there about an hour, hearing the noise of the pack only a few times, and then only distantly and faintly. Still, based on the instructions they thought they had received from the huntmaster, they "waited in confidence that the chase had not passed that point." Periodically they wondered if perhaps they should return to the glade but were afraid to "lest the bear might cross where [they] were."

Noon arrived and it was time for Hough to leave to catch his train. He "hated the thought of leaving the bear country without getting a shot," but the time had come. Hough comforted himself by remembering that during his sojourn in the Delta he "had come to think less and less of killing the bear, and more and more of the consummate skill of the chase, which is the main feature of this sort of sport." Hadn't Bobo told him that the "killing is the least part of the business?" Such statements were somewhat unconvincing, however, coming from a man like Bobo, who, despite having killed over 300 bears in a single year, still had a reputation for always trying to be the one to bag the quarry.[2]

Payne gathered together all the hunters except the elder Bobo and the hands, Tom and Pete, and began the ride back to Bobo Station. As Payne led the party over "mysterious winding hacks" through the cane, Hough felt certain they must be lost. Half an hour later, however, the party came out of the brakes at the ford of the Sunflower.

Payne scrawled out a note, cut a cane, split one end, stuck the note in the split, and jammed the other end of the cane into the river bank at the ford. "This is our post-office," Payne said, "and many a note have Mr. Bobo and I left here for each other." The note named the hunters in Payne's contingent and advised Bobo that their entourage was crossing the Sunflower at 1:30 p.m. with 19 of the dogs. The group plodded along for about three more hours, reaching the Bobo plantation house about 4:00 p.m.

Felix Payne rode on to his place. With the train station at hand, there was no need for further hurry on Hough's part. Hough enjoyed a leisurely supper and was sitting by the fire when Bobo's horn sounded about half a mile down the road. The 19 dogs already home immediately raised a welcoming chorus as the lord of the manor rode onto his castle grounds.

"You missed it by not staying with me today, young man," he said. Hough agreed, but noted in his own defense that it was "pretty hard to tell where the best place was to stay in a bear hunt" with Bobo. Bobo explained that he had gone "back in the thick cane" looking for the dogs after Hough had departed, and that he had had a much rougher ride than the day before with Hough. The pack eventually had broken "back and headed for the open glade where" Bobo had left Hough and Payne.

Bobo reacted to the hounds' course reversal, he told Hough, by racing back for the glade "along a narrow hack through the thick cane there, and at last heard the bear breaking cane about 200 yards ahead of the dogs." Bobo could not yet see the bear but from the sounds in the brake he assumed the animal had either heard or winded him for the bear turned, then stopped. Bobo slipped off his horse, grabbed his rifle, and crept into the brake. "He was half standing up when I saw him, about ten or twelve yards from me," Bobo later told Hough. He killed the bear with a single shot behind the ear from his .44-40. "If you and Mr. Payne had stayed right there in that open place, where I left you,"

Bobo told Hough, "you'd have got that bear. I killed it not 100 yards from where you were."

Hough explained to Bobo about the miscommunication, but that was small comfort to the writer. Three bears missed in as many days. Hough had struck out—but perhaps he could have the skin.

"Skin?" said Bobo, with obvious disdain. "I didn't bring the skin. It was too heavy, and I just threw it over the limb of a tree... for Tom or Pete to take into camp."

"I have been mourning over that fine bear skin that I didn't get—which Mr. Bobo said was bigger than either of the other—ever since...," Hough wrote during the following winter months. He hated the thought of that premium hide "nailed up on a shanty wall" in a logging camp when he "could have made such a good rug out of it for [his] office floor!"

Hough felt even worse when Bobo told him that he had "found a little lake back in that thick cane" after Hough's return to camp. "The bears are using it like hogs," Bobo said. They've got mud splashed clear up the bank to the trees, ten yards from the water." With a concentration of bears located, Bobo said, "the hard part of the hunt" was accomplished. "We could kill a bear or two now every day very easy, especially since the dogs are getting worked into shape. But if you must go, you must, I suppose, and the only thing is for you to come down again next year and get that bear you lost. We'll get him sure."[3]

Hough continued his sporting tour with hunts in south Louisiana and Texas before returning to Chicago to resume his duties with the western office of *Forest and Stream*. His affection for the South, first acquired at Dr. Taylor's home some days before in Tennessee, had grown in Coahoma County to what would be a life-long love affair with Dixie. "Any man from the South is welcome at the *Forest and Stream* office," Hough would later write, "and the only trouble is that too few of them come."[4]

20 The Great Delta Bear Rush

During the months of February and March 1895 Hough published a series of stories about his Dixie hunting outings entitled, "In the Sunny South." Four of those articles described his November adventures with Bobo in the Mississippi Delta,[1] which he called "the best bear country in America."[2]

Hough's praises of Bobo and his environs were sincere, no doubt. On the other hand, celebratory descriptions of hunters and hunting trips were the everyday grist of the *Forest and Stream* mill. In writing his glowing reviews of "the Bobo Bear Country" Hough was simply doing what Hough did. He was back to his normal routine. Life would never be normal again for Bob Bobo, though.[3] As surely as the discovery of precious metal in the Klondike would launch the Yukon Gold Rush in 1897,[4] Hough's *Forest and Stream* coverage of his bear hunts with Bobo would precipitate something of a Mississippi Delta *bear rush* in 1895.

Hough must have suspected his articles on Bobo would result in many out-of-state hunters planning trips to the Delta. Certainly his past articles had generated sporting tourism to the locales about which he had written. While it was always Hough's pleasure to direct the readers of *Forest and Stream* to good hunting grounds, he realized there could be negative results from increased interest in a particular area. It was an unfortunate fact of modern life, Hough knew, that once the northern city sportsmen discovered a locale with an abundance of game they would organize trips there. Local men would offer their services as guides. After that it was only a matter of time before the innkeepers would begin erecting hotels. Then, Hough said, the game was done for. He had seen it happen before.

"My once famous 'game pocket' in Minnesota," Hough wrote, "is a game pocket no more" due to the mob of hunters that had descended upon the area, largely as a result of his own writing. "Once," lamented Hough, "there were deer and bear in the Adirondacks, but when hotels and guides made their killing easy, they disappeared." Similarly, he added, "Dakota is shot out; Wisconsin is fished out."

The guides and the hotels were not the only factors in the destruction of hunting grounds. The railroads played a significant role in that cycle, as well. Hough noted that Mr. A. H. Hanson, the general passenger agent for the Illinois Central Railroad in Chicago, had compiled "a mass of data" regarding "hunting localities, guides, etc.," along the company's passenger routes. The railroads knew the hunters would buy railroad tickets to travel to those sporting destinations. For the railroads, promoting hunting was promoting profits.

Hanson, however, had enjoyed comparatively little success acquiring such information in the Deep South. "Those people," he told Hough, referring to Southerners, "have no idea of business. Here's one letter after another all saying the same thing. 'Mr. So and So is quite a hunter in this place, and he says he will be glad to take out any visiting sportsmen. He has dogs, horses, and everything needed. But he would not take any pay for this, and he would not like to agree to go out at just any time he might be asked.' That's it; that's the same story! They don't know anything about business!"[5] Those Delta hunters were, as was said of one of their chief scribes, Col. James Gordon, "as far removed from this world of chicanery and commerce as the knights of King Arthur's Round Table."[6]

Thus, Hough hoped that Bobo's hunting grounds would avoid the fate of so many other "game countries" ruined by publicity and trade. In the South, explained Hough, "the commercial way of looking at sport has not yet had any growth. … [N]either game nor sport is held generally as matter for barter or sale. Both are held as the privileges of gentlemen, and this is the right way to look at it, too." For that reason Hough considered the South the home of the truest sportsmen in the country. "You can get guides for any part of the Rockies, for the Wisconsin pine woods, for Maine, New Brunswick, the Adirondacks. But for the Delta of Mississippi, I am almost glad to state, you cannot get a guide, and I hope, with all courtesy to gentlemen who love to travel, you never may."[7]

The great hunting country of the Delta, Hough noted, was available only to those fortunate enough to be graced with the "unasked and unpurchaseable hospitality" of its residents. Many Mississippi counties at that time, in fact, prohibited non-residents from hunting "except on the invitation of a landowner." That was the trade-off. Those who came with the permission or upon the invitation of a Delta landowner could expect unparalleled sport and hospitality. For those who didn't, there was simply no decent (or legal) hunting to be had.

For hunters with the right invitation, however, the strip of wilderness between Memphis and Vicksburg that was the Delta in the 1890s offered a chance to experience a last vestige of frontier life. There remained in that region "bear and deer enough for any decent northern hunters," Hough reported. The patient, polite hunter, Hough believed, could soon enough come by an invitation for a Delta adventure. Accordingly, Hough maintained a hope that "a more sensible day in sportsmanship than that which [had] ruined the fields of the North" would protect the Delta from the fate of so many other parts of the country that were once hunters' paradises.

At the same time, Hough tried his best—within the limits of his obligations to write his hunting stories—to steer his readers away from Bobo's woods and brakes. He told his readers that the Illinois Central Railroad split below Memphis into two lines that both ran between Memphis and Vicksburg: the western line, running through Bobo station and the Sunflower country, and the eastern route, hugging the hills that formed the Delta's eastern boundary and running through the Tallahatchie River country. Hough emphasized to his readers that the eastern leg of the I.C.R.R. was wilder and that sportsmen who followed that route could "tap the same game country to much better advantage" than in Bobo's part of the Delta. Hough even named specific locales in the eastern Delta and provided the names of men who would host visiting hunters there. "The best place to head for," he wrote, "is the country between Minter City and Dodd's Ferry. The railway point is Parsons. Mr. Clay, at Tutweiler station, has a pack of dogs. Captain James Dinkins, passenger agent of the Yazoo and Mississippi Valley road at Memphis, can give full advice about this pack and the bear and deer country above referred to."[8]

It was Bobo, however, who had captured the imaginations of *Forest and Stream* readers. Hough's efforts at deflection notwithstanding, Bobo was deluged with letters from would-be bear hunters from all over the U. S. and "almost every country in Europe" after Hough's articles appeared. The letters came by the bushel. Some writers simply wanted advice on bear hunting in the Delta; some wanted to hire Bobo; still others wanted an invitation to hunt with Bobo. Hough himself had complete strangers in various parts of the nation ask him to have them "'put into' that country with Capt. Bobo."

"[I]t never occurred to me," wrote Hough, "that strangers would write to Capt. Bobo and ask to be invited to his house, any more than they would write and ask Mr. Vanderbilt to invite them to his house." Hough said he would prefer an invitation from Bobo, thinking "he sets a better table than Mr. Vanderbilt, does…." On the other hand, were he not likely to be invited by either, Hough indicated he would feel less trepidation in asking Mr. Vanderbilt for an invitation than Mr. Bobo.

Many, of course, would come without an invitation. The problem with such trespassers was not that they posed a threat to the local big game. "I will take a stranger into the woods," Bobo told Hough, "and give him my horse and all my dogs, and I will bet him he can't kill a bear in a month." Hough believed Bobo could collect on such a wager. No, the problem was not that mobs of novice out-of-state bear hunters would decimate the Delta game but that they would frighten it away. Southern bears were great wanderers. If there were too many hunters in the woods they would simply relocate to areas with fewer humans about.

Accordingly, Hough took great "pains to say that the [Delta] country was not open country for the public [and] that non-residents could not hunt without invitation in Coahoma County…." He emphasized to the point of repetition that Bobo and his fellow hunters were not guides for hire.[9] Plainly, Hough very much wanted to protect what he called the "Bobo Bear Country"[10] from the onslaught of hunters suffered by other regions he had publicized in his columns.

Nonetheless, trespassing non-resident hunters showed up in Coahoma County in droves after Hough's pieces went to press. In making a pre-hunting trip scout of the Sunflower country he had hunted with Hough the preceding fall Bobo found more than 100 non-Mississippi hunters camped in the woods, including five different groups from Illinois and two from Kentucky.

Only a few of the non-resident parties had dogs, Bobo told Hough. True to Bobo's prediction, not one of the trespassers had killed a bear, but they had shot at a lot of deer and squirrels and set fires that had burned a sizable part of the area. Also, as Bobo had feared, they had driven the bears almost completely out of his vicinity. In a part of the Delta once teeming with the big predators, Bobo found neither bear nor bear sign. As a result, in his own search for bear, Bobo was forced to ride south of his usual hunting grounds in hopes of finding an area not yet discovered by the out-of-state interlopers.

After experiencing the trouble the *Forest and Stream* publicity had wrought, Bobo, in Hough's words, "consigned all newspapers to perdition" and told the writer, "I wish I had killed you last fall instead of the bear."

Hough lamented on the pages of *Forest and Stream* that his articles had caused such consternation for his newfound friend. It was the irony of being an outdoor writer, he mused, that one's work could ruin the very country one loved. Next to market hunting, he said, "a great sporting journal is the greatest of all factors in the destruction of game." He did not fault his readers for wanting to spend their precious vacation time on hunts in good game country, but he gave this warning as a preface to a call for game conservation and restoration: "Here is the news. You can't always be running a little further and a little further away from your own homes to get at the good game countries. The game countries do not last, they will soon be gone. You must begin to improve your own game countries."[11]

Hough, though, was not yet ready to take his own advice. He would bear hunt again in Mississippi.

21 Hough's Return

A year passed. Tom Divine, now dubbed "Colonel" by Hough, and Bobo had a bear hunt planned to begin Sunday, November 17, 1895.[1] Bobo and Divine were together in Memphis the preceding Wednesday, November 13, and Divine prevailed upon Bobo to sit for a photographic portrait at the Bingham studio, the then most prominent photography business in the Bluff City.[2] While at least two other photos give us a glimpse of Bob Bobo's appearance, the Bingham photograph is the only studio portrait and by far the best depiction of the man extant. Bobo must have worn his wide-brimmed, high-crowned slouch hat almost constantly, for he did not remove it for the indoor studio sitting. He sports a long, flowing mustache trained into a downward handlebar shape. Forty-eight at the time of the photograph, Bobo displays a full face with no noticeable creases or wrinkles. His brow is smooth and unfurrowed. His jaw is strong, and his eyes, deep set and pensive. The hair that can be seen at his temples is relatively dark with no evidence of gray. His face is poised at an angle, the left side forward, such that his "cold blue shooting eye" lies almost in the middle of the photograph, seemingly slightly askew from the right one, as if focused on something the other does not see.

Bobo, by this time, was well-known enough that the *Commercial Appeal*, the premier newspaper of Memphis, wrote that "a mention of his name is to almost give his biography...." It is also indicative of the celebrity, at least in the Memphis area, of Divine and the others who would be involved in the hunt that the event was deemed worthy of a three column article, half news, half humor, in that same paper announcing the gathering:

> A party of bold and distinguished huntsmen left Memphis last evening for Shelby, Miss., where they will be joined by other sportsmen, and then plunge into the interior, taking wagons, mules, burros, camels and elephants and making their way as rapidly as possible to a point within the jungle fifteen miles, about one hundred and twenty stadia,

or four parasangs from nowhere. There they will camp and give their attention ten days to the extinction of large game, turkeys, deer, bear, wildcats, cougars, panthers, hyenas, ichthyosauri, plesiosauri, pterodactyls and chipmunks. ...

The party's personnel is sufficient in itself to make the more intelligent class of the large game—these species which read the papers and sporting journals—extinct from fright could they only know of the purpose of the famous sporting men to invade their territory.... [3]

A line cut portrait of Bobo made from his Bingham studio photograph accompanied the *Commercial Appeal* article.

Despite Bobo's unhappiness with the flood of out-of-state hunters on his turf as a result of the *Forest and Stream* pieces, the Bear Hunter once more invited Hough to join his hunting party. Clearly, Bobo liked Hough, and despite his protestations to the contrary, he obviously enjoyed the attention Hough's articles generated. "An unexpected crowd of business" delayed Hough, though, and he did not leave Chicago until Thursday, November 21, 1895. [4] Coincidentally, when he changed trains in Memphis the next day, Hough met Tom Divine in the station returning from Coahoma County. Divine, it seems, had been called back to Memphis by his own unexpected crowd of business.

Divine told Hough the party had already killed six bears and he gave the writer instructions for reaching Bobo's bear camp. Thus informed, Hough proceeded by rail to Shelby, Mississippi, where he hired a teamster to haul him and his baggage to the bear camp. Finding that his driver had no clue as to the way to the camp, Hough directed him according to the Divine instructions. At times they could not locate any trail and were reduced to following bayous. Even so, they found the ford across the Sunflower. As they crossed, Hough loosed a blast from his hunting horn. To his delight, what sounded like "a thousand dogs" roared their response. [5]

Hough and his driver rode into camp as night fell and found a scene similar to that at the logging camp Hough had visited the fall before. Hough declined to disclose the site of the camp—probably because of the unwanted hunters who flooded into the Bobo Bear Country following Hough's articles about his hunt of the previous year. From his description, however, it appears to have been the same logging camp at which Hough had stayed on his first Bobo hunt. [6]

Two "good-sized" cabins made of "upright boards" and joined by a common roof in the Southern dogtrot style served as bunkhouses for the more than a score of hunters in the party. The structure differed from most dogtrots by having a common rear wall connecting the two rooms. A "low fence and gate" intended to keep the hounds out of the area between the cabins bordered the wall-less side of the dogtrot. Within the enclosure blazed a "glorious big fire of oak and ash and hickory slabs." Despite the fence a number of dogs had managed to secure warm spots in which to curl up in the ashes at the fire's periphery, their proximity to the fire determined by more of the endless fights that were the daily life of the bear dog.

The one canine that rarely participated in the incessant battles was the fierce Old Rock who almost always "slept pretty close to the fire." Even if a human approached with a stick to "poke him in the ribs" to shoo him back among the other hounds, he would resist, "stand[ing] with lowered head and bared teeth awaiting the onslaught very calmly." While "the continuous conflict for precedence among the other dogs" raged around him, "this disturbed him not, for he had fought himself up to his bad eminence, and the rest of the pack knew he was entitled to the hottest ashes in the place."[7]

By the firelight Hough saw a dozen or so members of the party.[8] Some he knew; others, he did not. Bobo, of course was there, and he was "smiling." Jim, a cook from Memphis who had accompanied the Divine party to south Louisiana the year before was there, as well, much to Hough's delight. Jim's presence, the writer knew, meant that fine food would be coming from the kitchen shanty. Bears or no, all would be well in the dining shack.

Hough also recognized Noel Ernest Money,[9] one of the more interesting characters of the 1890s sporting world. Capt. Money, then 28,[10] made his living as an agent of the American branch of a British concern, the E. C. Powder Company.[11] In that capacity he traveled the U. S. and abroad participating in trap shooting competitions and socializing with wealthy sportsmen.

Money, in fact, just had arrived in Coahoma County from an appearance at the Atlanta Cotton States and International Exposition "in the interest of the E. C. Powder Company."[12] The young Canadian-born outdoorsman was already well-known as a crack shot and had hunted and killed bear on at least two continents by the time he arrived in Coahoma County. Money carried a hunting knife of unique design, forged from "fine steel [and] inlaid with gold." It had been given him by an eastern nobleman whose life he had saved during a scuffle with an Indian wild boar.

Noel was not the only prominent member of the Money family. His little brother, Harold, ten years his junior, became a celebrated shooter in his own right, as well as the subject of one of Memphis outdoor writer Nash Buckingham's most famous stories, "De Shootinest Gent'man."[13]

Hough explained the reason for his delay and then declared he had come for a bear and would stay until February if it took that long to get one. Pleased to hear it, Bobo recapped the preceding days' hunting for Hough. "You ought to have been with us," Bobo said. "You've missed a heap of fun by being late." The bears, Bobo explained, were "thick as rabbits" and "fat as hogs," gorging themselves in a good mast producing stretch of woods "about six miles away." Divine had been wrong about the bear count when he had said six bears in six days. It had been eight in six.

The Bobo pack, though, had suffered as much or more than the bears. Always interested in the dogs, Hough surveyed the canine mob and found it contained the same basic mix as the year before: a few purebred foxhounds ("or nearly so") to maintain some cold noses in the pack; some big terrier crosses with staghound or pointer; and a variety of dogs with bloodlines mixed beyond recognition. Hough saw a few of the dogs from his first Bobo hunt: there was New York, a smallish, short-haired, mongrel,[14] who would occasionally point a bear trail as a bird dog might point a covey of quail,[15] and a shaggy mutt called Texas. "Old Henry, the aristocrat of the pack," who refused "to eat unless served in a clean dish by himself," and who would not permit other dogs to touch him as he slept, was there, as well.

Most of the dogs Hough had hunted with the last season, though, had gone the way all "bear dogs go sooner or later, and usually sooner," the writer noted. Raphael, the cold-nosed strike dog whose voice always signaled a true trail, had been "killed by a bear on the field of honor," as had many other members of the pack. Two dogs had been killed within the previous 48 hours, in fact. This process of death and replacement of dogs, Hough observed, had gone on with the Bobo pack for decades. A look at the dogs in the current pack, Hough believed, "showed them willing to take all the risks of the field on which their ancestors had been slain. There was 'war' written over each rough face—a very goodly thing to see where one is afoot for war himself, and looking for allies," Hough said.

Injuries, too, had visited the pack, with many of the dogs "crippled up a good deal," Bobo told Hough. Eleven were convalescing, "bit up too bad to" hunt. A half dozen more were questionable.[16]

Bobo had come close to getting "bit up... bad himself." Earlier in the week—Wednesday—a bear had run past Bobo and Money. To wait to shoot around Bobo was to forfeit the game—Money knew that from experience. Bobo's "impulse to kill bear," Tom Divine would later say, "was irresistible. He would frequently invite people... to hunt, and would take a solemn promise not to kill a bear himself but to leave it for the visitor to dispatch." Though he meant well, Bobo usually could not honor his vow. "When the time came and the animal got within range of his gun, he could not resist the impulse to administer the quietus." Bobo, in fact, had done such a thing to Noel Money when Tom Divine had first brought Money to Coahoma County. During one exciting bear drive Bobo "found himself between Mr. Money and the bear." Bobo "couldn't resist."[17] That "cold blue shooting eye," having fixed on the quarry, took on a death-dealing life of its own beyond the will of the hunter to control.[18] "He raised his gun and fired, and there was nothing for the guest to do but watch...." Bobo was remorseful: "That was a mean trick on my part. Money would have killed that bear sure. But I just couldn't keep from killing" it.[19]

Having experienced Bobo's propensities in that regard previously, the Canadian had fired first this time, and a bit prematurely. Although the game went down, "it was a very big bear and would not quit easily." Almost immediately it rose and ran, only to be shot again by Bobo and a third hunter. The shots seemed to have had little effect other than to slow the bear enough for the dogs to catch up. The fight was furious. The bear had to be stopped before it seriously injured or killed any dogs, but shooting was out of the question because of the danger shots would pose to the pack. Bobo and Money drew their knives and were running toward the ruckus when "Bobo tripped and fell almost in the bear's mouth." Money quickly stabbed the bear with his ornamented East Indian blade, not killing it, but distracting the beast for the split second Bobo needed to finish the job "with his huge bear knife."[20] Money, for the second time, had saved a potentate from a savage beast. This time, though, the autocrat protected was of the Mississippi Delta, rather than the Indian, variety.

22 Bobo Sings

Bobo was none the worse for the experience and the prospects for the already successful hunt were looking up. The number of hunters in the Bobo entourage the week before had been so large that at times it was difficult to tell whose shot had killed the bear. Too, despite "Bobo's best efforts to get away from" interlopers, there were no fewer than five big groups of out-of-state "still-hunters" congregated within a four mile square area. Still-hunting, a method of hunting without dogs, either by taking a stand and waiting for game to come by, or by slipping stealthily through the woods in hopes of encountering game, was the most difficult method for hunting bear, even for locals familiar with the country and its wildlife. As an Arkansas hunter told writer Horace Kephart, "there are two impediments" to still-hunting for bear in the canebrakes—"the cane and the bear," meaning it was almost impossible to approach a bear in the cane thickets without it hearing you coming.[1]

The out-of-state hunters served as a case to prove that point. True to Bobo's predictions about nonresident hunters, none of the still-hunters had killed a bear. One group of ten very disappointed hunters "from Illinois had been there four weeks, and [had] killed only four deer in that time." Most of those non-residents were leaving, returning to their homes with little to show for their trip to the Delta other than perhaps a touch of malaria, something newcomers to the swamp country frequently contracted except during the dead of winter.

Several members of the Bobo party were returning home that weekend, as well. The hunters would be fewer, and Bobo was sending for more dogs. Hough was ready for the chase to begin.[2]

Others were not. As is the case in many present day hunting camps, a certain contingent of those present preferred lounging around the cabin to hunting. Chief among them was one R. W. Foster, "a leading cotton factor"[3] from New Orleans. Hough noted that when he had first arrived, a "pleasant" Mr. Foster had "just awakened from a profound slumber."[4] A little while afterwards Mr. Foster had "put [back] in practice his theory of a vacation, and had peacefully dropped off to sleep, with his boots on." Around midnight, the men roused him and suggested he would sleep better without his boots. He surprised them by getting up and telling "stories to the rest of us until daybreak. You could never tell what Mr. Foster's means of taking rest might mean." Later, Hough observed that Foster could "sleep as well as ever, and that is saying a great deal. He averaged about twenty hours a day...."

Capt. Napoleon "Boney" Leavell and Col. Dick Payne, who had not known each other prior to the hunt, had become fast friends. Most of the time when the others were hunting they stayed in camp talking and playing cards, pretending a single white poker chip was worth an entire plantation. They particularly enjoyed discussing the late war and re-fought it "from the first Manassas up to Shiloh." In the process, the friends would draw battle diagrams and "war maps" in the dust with sticks, only to have a hound occasionally lie down on their makeshift chart or sweep his tail across it. C'est la guerre.

The pair's preference for the camp over the canebrake worked to Hough's advantage: he was permitted to use Boney Leavell's wise and experienced mare, the great bear horse, Gladys, as his mount in following Bobo.

The majority of the party, though, had come to hunt. They set out on Friday morning, November 22, 1895, with an air of confidence pervading the party of around a dozen men. "We had only about half the pack," Hough later recalled, "the rest being crippled or lost." The sun already had traveled well above the horizon, but the late start dampened no spirits. Neither did the absence of so many of the regulars from the pack concern anyone. The hounds they had were as good as any bear dogs in the Bobo kennel. The hunters figured that Bobo had the bears figured: the bruins were fattening on acorns, pecans, and persimmons on the blue cane ridges about eight miles from the camp. During the previous week the hunting parties had started bears within a half hour's ride from the camp. There was no reason for this day's hunt to turn out differently. Everyone was expecting to kill a bear quickly and to be back in camp well before nightfall. The group, though, had not included the Hough luck, or lack thereof, in its bear hunting calculus. That morning, Hough reported, fortune "took its first turn against the party and we met with only disappointment."

The dogs were "cast on a heavy ridge...." Some of the younger ones opened up almost immediately, but it was the kind of vocalizing experienced bear hunters knew signified something other than bear scent. Soon there were three or four bunches of dogs running their own false trails here and yon through the cane. For more than an hour the hunters strained to listen without hearing any "token of serious business" from any of the more trustworthy members of the pack.

Suddenly, the reliable Rounce hit what sounded like a bear trail, but he was running alone, the other segments of the pack being too far away to join in. Until well after noon the hunters crisscrossed the cane, listening for dogs, hoping for the pack to unite on a single track. Late in the day, as the party traversed the edge of a long cypress swamp, a few of the dogs opened up on hot bear scent. Within moments, half the pack, including some of the stalwarts, was in full cry. From across the swamp came the baying of the other hounds as they rushed to join the chase.

Next, the humans split into groups, each rushing to what it believed would be the most strategic route for encountering the bear. Hough once more fell in with Felix Payne, and the two marked a course beside a long slough paralleling the path of the pack.

Capt. Money and his horse soon appeared out of the cane and joined them. The men rode along, doing their best to track the barely discernible sounds of the dogs. Payne abruptly shouted: "They are going to the Hurricane, sure!"[5]

Among the old timers a "hurricane" was a windfall—an area where a storm had blown down trees. The Hurricane, to which Payne referred, however, was not just any windfall. In her wonderful memoir, *Trials of the Earth*, Delta backwoods pioneer and logging camp cook and manager, Mary Hamilton, described this same Delta feature, which she called "the Cyclone."

According to Hamilton, a mammoth tornado had ripped through Sunflower and Coahoma counties many years before the time Hough and Bobo hunted there. The storm had skipped along the Delta landscape like a pebble thrown across the surface of a stream, cutting a swath eighteen miles long and up to four miles wide from the Sunflower River to the present site of Parchman, Mississippi. "In all that stretch," Hamilton said, "not a tree was left" in place. "Maybe there would be half a mile where every tree had been uprooted and left lying," Hamilton remembered. "[T]hen it would look like the wind had lifted gradually and cut the timber off like hay by a mowing machine; then down the wind had dropped to the ground again, lifting trees by the roots." [6]

Within the path the tornado had taken, Hough wrote, "giant trees—many of them five, six, and eight feet in diameter, [lay] heaped and crossed in a gigantic windfall whose like few men have seen." [7] Wild fires had raged through the area since the tornado, stimulating the growth of cane, blackberry, greenbrier, and poison oak. [8] The resulting profusion of thorn and vine, "all growing to enormous size out of that rich Delta ground," and inter-woven with the downed and dead trees, formed an impassible barrier. "No horseman on earth" could penetrate such a natural fortress, wrote Hough, "not even Bobo."

This interlacing of vine and bush and cane had a most peculiar acoustic effect: it naturally baffled sound. Hunters and hounds within this densest of thickets could scarcely be heard by those outside in the more open woods. It was, said Hough, a "frightful" and "weird strip of solitude." Once, Hough was told, a bear pursued by the hounds took refuge in the Hurricane and was killed about 200 yards from its edge. Those outside the thicket thought the pack to be at least a mile away. When the hunters with the dogs blew their horns to call the others to the kill they could scarcely be heard just 300 yards away.

Except when denned up in the winter, even the bears avoided the Hurricane, resorting to it only when necessary to elude hunters and hounds. On the other hand, Hough learned, the Hurricane was "the home of many wolves, panthers, and wildcats" [9] and, accordingly, a potential graveyard for bear dogs. The Hurricane, it seemed, bore some kind of curse. Only days before, old Fly, one of Bobo's better hounds, had followed a trail into the Hurricane and had not been seen again.

About two years after Hough's hunt along the Hurricane with Bob Bobo, one Leo Minkus, [10] an agent for a European stave company, almost met a similar fate. According to Mary Hamilton, who worked with the man, it was June and time for Minkus to settle up with two camps of laborers for their winter and spring logging work. The primary camp was on one side

of the Hurricane; the other lay on the opposite side on the banks of Black
Bayou. Minkus paid the workers in the first camp on Saturday and planned
to pay those in the second camp the following day.

Five miles of road hacked out of the Delta wilderness led, in a round-
about way, from the first camp to the second.[11] Although an Austrian
immigrant,[12] Minkus was acknowledged as an expert Delta woodsman.
He determined he could cut three miles off the trip by going straight
across the Hurricane. Minkus set out for the Black Bayou camp on Sunday
morning with a cane knife, a compass, and $472 in payroll money. When
Minkus failed to show up at Black Bayou by Wednesday, the foreman in
charge of that site rode to the main camp in hopes of learning the reason
for the delay.

By the time the foreman informed Minkus's co-workers at the main
camp of his failure to appear, it was too late in the day to organize a search.
Trackers left camp the first thing Thursday morning, though, to hunt for
the missing man. Bits of cloth torn from Minkus's clothing adorned briars
and branches along the circular path he had forged through the Hurricane.
The search party found Minkus's compass, shoes, cane knife, and hat, but
not the man himself. It was indeed a Hurricane mystery.

Elsewhere in the same vicinity that early morning a crew of railroad
workers was riding a fresh cut right of way along the edge of the Hurricane.
As they were dropping rail ties out of a wagon to be used in laying track for
a new piece of road, they spied a strange, naked figure emerging hurriedly
from the brush. "Minkus?" called one of them who had heard of the man's
disappearance, but there was no response. Instead, the man, apparently
frightened, turned back into the thicket from whence he had appeared.
Some of the workers quickly mounted their mules and chased down the
wild man, who turned out to be, of course, Leo Minkus. After wandering
for days the bewildered Minkus had come out on the same side of the
Hurricane from which he had entered!

Half-crazed from thirst after having been lost four days and nights in
the Delta wilderness, his clothes ripped from him by the briars, brush, and
brambles of the Hurricane, the man fought and struggled with his rescuers
until he was subdued. When he settled down enough to ask for water it
was in a voice so weak it was hardly a whisper. When given the drink he
could scarcely get a drop down, so swollen were his tongue and throat from

dehydration. Always a good steward of his company's assets, however, he still held the $472 tightly in his hand.[13]

Minkus recovered and by 1904 was identified in a national trade publication as "a well-known stave exporting agent"[14] of Memphis, Tennessee. Just a month later, however, another stave trade journal announced that Leo Minkus had been "found dead a short time ago with two bullet holes in his head and a pistol in his hand containing two empty shells. The opinion of the police is that he committed suicide, while his family maintains that he had difficulty with another man" and was "murdered."[15] Little wonder some thought the Hurricane to be "haunted by something or other."[16]

Whatever the reason—malevolent spirits or otherwise—"if ever the [bear] chase got into this mysterious, demonish stretch of ghostland," Hough said, the hunt would be over for the day. Not surprisingly, the men rode hell-for-leather to head the bear[17] and the pack before game and hounds could enter the Hurricane.

A few minutes of riding brought the hunters to the edge of an uncrossable cypress slough that "served as a moat to the fastness" of the Hurricane. "Far on ahead we heard the faint and phantom-like baying, as of the pack of the Wild Huntsman,"[18] the headless ghostly hunter of Norse mythology, "baying in the clouds."

"They've headed us and gone on in" the Hurricane, said Payne, who believed the dogs were running not a bear, but a wolf. While Hough thought Payne's wolf theory unlikely, it was a fact that they could not hear any of the more reliable hounds that would have verified a bear trail.

Payne determined it was pointless to continue the hunt. The only thing left to do was to blow the horns to try to call the dogs off the trail. That is what they did. Not much later, however, the men met an exasperated Bobo. He confirmed that the dogs had indeed been running a bear; he had seen it earlier and had been riding to turn the chase away from the Hurricane when he heard Payne's horn blowing. He took the notes as the signal for a kill and rode toward the sounds. As it turned out, the horn-blowing had simply interrupted a chase that could have ended in a kill. Hough, Money, and Payne tried to salvage the situation by riding the edge of the Hurricane with Bobo in search of the pack and bear, but to no avail.

The day was indeed a disappointment to most in the party. To add to the bad luck, Capt. Money caught a stick of cane in the eye as he was galloping after the dogs. Hough could tell by Money's instability in the saddle that he was in immense pain, and he rode to the Canadian to render aid. Money, almost certain that the eyeball was ruptured, was trying to survey the damage with his hand. Hough pushed the lid of the injured eye back and discovered a "deep red, bloodshot spot... where the cane had struck...." Much to Money's relief, however, "the eyeball was not ruined...." Hough suspected the injury would sideline Money from the hunt, but it did not. The powder company representative was soon back on the trail.

By that time the day was well spent. Dark was falling, and most of the hunters already had returned to camp. Finally, Bobo, Payne, Money, and Hough called it quits and rode back to the logging camp with no bear and 17 of their 23 dogs unaccounted for.

Hough had no complaints at all about the day. He was not accustomed to easy hunting. "For my part," he would later write, "I think they get bears entirely too easy down there."

Bobo, though, plainly hated that he had once more failed to produce a shot for the writer from Chicago. As they rode through the dark woods, Bobo "sang very loud and continuously," a behavior that Hough had learned "was a sure sign that [Bobo] was in a deuce of a temper...."[19] In his novel, *The Law of the Land*, Hough's character, Col. Calvin Blount, supposed to have been based on Bobo, likewise burst into song when in a poor humor. In Blount's case, the old sacred harp standard, "On Jordan's Stormy Banks," was the tune indicative of his foulest mood.[20] It likely served as a similar barometer for Bobo and might well have been what he sang as he and Hough rode back to camp:

> On Jordan's stormy banks I stand
>   And cast a wistful eye
> To Canaan's fair and happy land
>   Where my possessions lie.
> I am bound for the Promised, Promised Land,
>   I am bound for the Promised Land.
> Oh, who will come and go with me
>   I am bound for the Promised Land.

23 Rainbound

Upon arriving in camp the hunters discovered nine of the missing dogs already there. Some wandered back later that night, but the next morning several were still absent. Among the unaccounted for was Scott, Bobo's favorite. While most of the hunters rested on Saturday, Bobo and his older son, Fincher, rode far to the east of the camp searching for the truant hounds. By noon, all but two had come back into camp. Scott remained missing, however, and is to this day.

Rain set in Saturday night and did not let up until Tuesday, forcing a temporary halt to the hunting. Hough used the down time to watch and listen. As usual, he paid special attention to the dogs, which, he observed, "are more uncomfortable and fight each other" more readily in wet weather. Breaking up dog fights, he noted, at least gave the rainbound hunters something to do. Most of the hounds were "much disabled by continuous fighting (with bears and among themselves)." A number "lay around" in what Hough called "different stages of discomfort." The most miserable, though, were too crippled even to do that. They were the ones that had been "bitten through the back by the bears."[1]

Such was the bear's specialized way of dealing with dogs. "With his immense paws," hunter James Gordon once wrote, the bear "strikes down at the nearest dog,... and woe to the dog that is caught in those giant arms...." The bear does not "hug them to death," Gordon explained. "[T]hat is a hunter's fable....." Rather, "he holds them until he can get his teeth on them...." Even if the bear fails in that, "his long claws leave lasting impressions."

"[W]hen [a bear] gets his favorite hold, the small of the back," Col. Gordon said, "one bite is sufficient."[2] The back-bitten dogs Hough saw were the lucky ones. They had escaped what is usually certain death for a hound seized in that way by a bruin.

No doubt the poor hounds did not feel lucky. Hough learned that a dog so wounded in the "small of the back is unable to lie down, or to get up if he does lie down." Some of the dogs thus injured were so tired they were falling asleep standing up. "They would waver and stagger as the drowsy influence came over them; then there would be a swaying of the body and a sharp cry of pain as the wrenched back felt the sore muscles used...." The dog would wake a bit, walk a few feet, and then go through the same thing again. The back-bitten dogs were "almost dead from lack of sleep." Almost all of the members of the pack "were thin and sorry looking from their wounds...."[3]

One particularly sad canine case named Alcorn had caught a bullet meant for a bear with the result that his jaw was "shot off," or so it appeared.[4] The unfortunate hound had poor prospects—how long could a dog unable to bite or chew survive amidst the free-for-all of the Bobo bear pack?

One of the healthier dogs, a hungry black foxhound, slipped into the bunkhouse and raided the "refreshment table" maintained for the hunters by Jim the cook. The dog got away with an entire "cheese and the biggest part of a cake." To the hunters' amusement, despite being run out, the dog returned repeatedly. "[N]o one could tell what he was after," Hough joked, "unless it was a glass of whiskey, which was all he had left on the table."[5]

Hough also heard more of the hunting adventures of his comrades. Bobo, he learned, had on more than one occasion captured bears alive, lassoing them and leading them home behind his wagon—always reluctantly (the bears, not Bobo). Bobo told Hough that he had once caught a panther.

It happened around Christmas many years before. Bobo and his stepbrother, Curt Clark, with half a dozen of the plantation hands had gone into the woods "on a kind of lark." The dogs brought to tree a sizable panther. "Let's catch him alive and tie him," Bobo suggested. Bobo had one of the hands cut and strip the limbs from a stout sapling. Once a heavy pole had been fashioned from the young tree, he directed another man to shoot the panther in the tip of the tail with a shotgun. Stung by the shot, the panther leaped from the tree and was covered with dogs immediately upon hitting the ground. Bobo and one of the stronger hands, holding opposite ends of the pole, used it to pin the cat's neck to the ground "while the others tied his legs together." It was surprisingly easy to keep the cat immobile, Bobo said. The pinning down part, though, was easier than the tying. "Curt Clark had his hands badly clawed in the operation," Bobo recalled.

The men placed a noose around the panther's neck and tied the free end to a tree. The cat became sullen. Despite the men's best efforts to elicit a response, the cat refused to growl or make any other aggressive displays, much to the men's disappointment. When prodded with a stick, the panther would simply turn its head away.[6]

When they failed to realize the entertainment from the cat for which they had hoped, they decided to carry their prize back to the plantation house some two miles away. The hunters passed the pole between the cat's hog-tied legs, two of the hired men each took an end, and the group proceeded back to the main house with the panther.

Almost immediately the rear man experienced "some anxiety… when the front man raised his end too high,"[7] causing the cat to slide back toward the rear. Soon thereafter the entire project took a southward turn when the cat worked one of his legs free. The men holding the pole were taken by such surprise they dropped the suspended feline, at which point they were treated to far more action than they had bargained for. The beast became so enraged that the men reflexively killed it.[8]

The fireside talk shifted from men carrying panthers to how panthers transported their prey. The big cats, which hunted deer, primarily, hauled their kills by dragging them by the neck, Hough learned. The hunters told Hough that sometimes two of the felines would cooperate in such an enterprise, each seizing one side of the dead deer's neck. "They will go through the thickest cane at a great pace that way,"[9] Hough learned.

Bill volunteered that bears, which have a fondness for pork, occasionally preferred not to go to the effort of killing and then carrying their prey. Rather, he said, a bear would sometimes straddle a hog, and with the swine between his forelegs, walk the hog to where he intended to eat it and dine there.

That story may or may not be of the same suspect cloth as another old Mississippi tale about a bear that captured hogs, penned them in the woods, and fed them corn to fatten them up before eating them.[10] Bill added that bears would sometimes take a bite out of hog and leave it alive, a tale somewhat easier to believe than his first story.

The talk inevitably returned to bear hunting. The hunters' consensus was that the black bear, though potentially dangerous in tight quarters, generally was not an aggressive animal. Accordingly, Hough did "not think the rifle the proper weapon" for hunting bear. Rather, he concluded that the knife was a far more sporting weapon. Money recalled hunting bear with the knife during his time in India. That country's custom, he said, made use of large, heavy, catch dogs that would take jaw holds on the bruins. Once the bear was thus immobilized, the hunters would slay it with the knife. Money believed large dogs could be put to the same use with Mississippi bears.

As it was, however, the smaller dogs common in Coahoma County could not stretch out a large bear, India style, and hold it for a knife wielding hunter. Consequently, firearms typically were used, if possible, before the fight between the bear and the dogs became too close in order to keep the mayhem among the pack to a minimum.

The knifing talk prompted a tale by Boney Leavell and his family's long-time and esteemed retainer, the hoary-haired Uncle Joe. As a younger man back before the War Between the States, Uncle Joe had been the favorite servant of and hunting companion to Boney's father. What must have been Joe's most interesting hunt took place with the younger Leavell, though, after the War.

Somehow, Boney and Uncle Joe found themselves on a bear hunt with no gun. The pair's only weapons were a "stout club" and a knife highly prized by Uncle Joe. Somehow, too, they came face to face with a bear. Despite the fact that they "were not very well equipped for a bear fight," as Hough put it, they went after the beast with the weapons at hand.

It was a grueling labor. Leavell clubbed the bear in an effort to knock it down; then Uncle Joe attempted to kill it with his knife. The bear, though, was too quick and escaped with hardly a scratch—but with Joe's knife lodged in its thick hide and fur.

"Hit him. Hit him," Uncle Joe screamed frantically at Boney. "He's got my knife." The situation struck Leavell as funny. He stood there, immobilized by laughter, unable to bring the club to bear. Boney would not have been much help anyway. Besides being gunless, Leavell had only a wooden prosthesis where his foot and ankle, lost in the War, had been. He walked with a cane and "could not... get about very well" on foot in the woods.

Uncle Joe, though, was not giving up. He ran after the bear, catching it by the long hair along its back. Hanging on, he was able to slow the bruin down enough to retrieve his knife and strike a death-dealing blow.[11]

The old bear hunting stories and the rain notwithstanding, young men like Hough and Money could not sit by the fire for long. The next day (Sunday) they braved the downpour and took a hike through the cane thickets along the Sunflower River. Less than a mile from the camp they found the fresh track of a big bear and mentally filed the sighting away for future reference.[12]

The rain continued on Monday, and Felix Payne and Boney Leavell, along with a Mr. Dunn, left camp to return to their normal pursuits. They took with them, no doubt to Hough's dismay, Jim the cook. The rain broke Tuesday, and those still in camp organized another hunt, except for Mr. Foster and Col. Dick Payne, who were scheduled to leave that day.

The entire party, or at least what was left of it, rode to the Sunflower ford where Payne and Foster took their leaves. Like departing lovers, the newfound friends, Foster and Col. Payne, bid their adieus to one another from opposite sides of the river before going their separate ways: Foster to Bobo station to catch the train for New Orleans, and Payne to follow the stream southward toward his home in Yazoo County.

Leavell had ridden away on his bear horse, Gladys, leaving Hough without a mount. Foster, though, left a replacement: "a little rat-tailed roan swamp pony," whose owner, Foster supposed, would show up at some point claiming rentals due on the animal. Hough preferred that arrangement. He had not been comfortable using Leavell's horse and putting the man on foot.[13] The new arrangement would not be an entirely comfortable one, either, Hough would learn.

Bobo, to Hough's relief, moved the party in the direction of the river bank scouted by Money and Hough two days before rather than going back to the accursed Hurricane. About a half mile beyond the spot they had seen the big bear print, the dogs began to work a trail. At first the hounds were half-hearted; the hunters assumed the pack was scenting the deer whose tracks dotted the soft earth of the brake. Then, Bobo, leaning in his saddle, pointed to "a series of deep holes in the leafy mold" along the deer trail. "Here's your bear," he said, "and you can bet he's a big one, too. Turn in the dogs!"[14]

24 The Bull of the Woods

Right on cue the entire pack hit the trail in full cry. "It was," to Hough's ears, "a glorious chorus, enough to set every drop of blood tingling in one's veins." The hunters lined out, deserting the marked path, each looking for the best route for following the pack. As always, Hough's chief aim in coursing through the canebrakes was to keep within sight of Bob Bobo so as not to become lost. That had been hard enough before with a horse seasoned to the bear hunt. Unlike the well-trained Gladys, however, the "rat-tailed roan swamp pony" was neither accustomed to the chase nor inclined to learn its ways. She was, in fact, entirely uncooperative. Rather than keeping to the brake and following Bobo, the little horse broke for the open woods where she would not be beaten constantly by whipping cane. When Hough urged her back toward his chosen route she retaliated by running him against a tree, painfully bruising his leg, causing him to fall off, and resulting in the saddle sliding around her girth.

When the pain in his leg finally subsided, Hough tried to reset the saddle in its proper position. No matter how hard he pulled at the cinches, he could not achieve the needed snug fit. The pony was just too small for the saddle. Hough did the best he could, remounted, and rode off again, his knee still hurting from its collision with the tree. In the meantime, Bobo had disappeared from sight.

Miraculously, Hough caught up with Bobo. Fincher Bobo, the planter's son, meanwhile, had struck out to Hough's right, following a hack through the cane. A man named King, unknown to Hough, had joined the party. Horseless, King was walking a line parallel to and to the right of Fincher. Meanwhile, Bill and Capt. Money, about half mile away, raced back and forth along a narrow slough where they expected the quarry to break from the thickets at any time. In their racing, Money, too, had faced mount problems, breaking his saddle girth. Bill hospitably swapped saddles with Money, leaving Bill with a very loose saddle—a situation much the same as Hough's. In one of their passes through the slough a large buck leaped from its bed right in front of Bill's mount, startling the old mule almost into apoplexy. The mule then executed a series of what Hough termed "mulesquian pyrotechnics" that ended with Bill flying through the air and hitting the ground in a seated position, a painful turn of events for Bill. Fortunately, Money carried a bottle that contained the remedy for such upsets. Though Bill's "innards" were seriously jarred, a generous and steady internal application of Money's elixir apparently resolved the situation favorably. Bill was so comforted by Money's solution that he offered to carry the container. When Bill returned the bottle some while later, Money was not too surprised that the liquid all had "leaked out," or such was the theory Bill offered for its disappearance.

While Bill and Money struggled with the mule, the bear and hounds were making through an old "burning" (a strip in the woods subjected to fire in the recent past) that began not 100 yards away. The undergrowth having been stimulated by the fire, the burn was now something like the Hurricane in miniature: "dead cane and the briers made such a mat of cover that a man could not get into it." Money occasionally could hear the ruckus and at one point suspected the melee was fewer than 20 yards away. Yet, the cane and briar thicket was so dense that he saw neither bear nor hounds.

Unbeknownst to Money, the bear and the dogs were in a moderately open stretch just beyond the relatively narrow band of dense cane. An old hack, the opening to which Money and Bill had passed with each trip along the slough, would have taken them right through the cane to a somewhat more open area through which the bear and hounds were running. The man King, without a horse, was keeping abreast of the chase on foot in a thin strip of cane on the far side of the bear from Money.

Bobo and Hough simultaneously rode along a bayou, hearing nothing. They followed a "cross-hack" through the cane leading away from the watercourse. As the hunters moved down the trail they began to hear "the chase plainly." Fincher, on orders from his father, left in search of a hack to take them directly to where the elder Bobo supposed the bear to be. Hough and Bobo continued to follow as best they could the "flood of savage music [that] came swelling down… from the heart of the wilderness of cane."

"It's a running fight," Bobo said. "[T]hey'll surely cross in here some-where. He's our bear, sure, and you'll never have a better chance to kill one. Just tie your horse when they get a little closer, and run [into the cane] on foot."

The dogs were fewer than 300 yards away in the cane and moving closer. Such a din came from the pack that Hough could not understand how Bobo could have heard anything but the maniacal voices of the hounds. Bobo, though, believed he heard a gunshot. Then, the baying lessened, and the movement through the cane ceased. Curious, Bobo and Hough spurred their mounts and quick-timed along the hack to the opening near the large bayou at the trail's end.

In the clearing was the pedestrian hunter, King. At his feet "summoned as if by magic out of the depths of the wilderness, lay a vast black object," as Hough later described it, "inert save in such motion as twenty fighting dogs gave it in their still unappeased rage."

Bobo surveyed the beast. "He's the bull of the woods. I knew by his track he was a big one." The hunters estimated the bear's weight at 500 to 600 pounds. Hough believed a novice would have guessed the animal weighed two or three hundred more. The beast measured seven feet from nose to tail, and eight and a half feet from paw tip to paw tip when its front legs were extended.

King, the only man on foot, had made the kill. From the thin strip of cane between the burning and the big bayou, he had followed along as the bear fight moved back and forth through the burning. When he had heard the pack turn in his direction, he had taken a stand atop a fallen tree in a clearing and waited.

The bear had burst from the burning ahead of the hounds, King said, and paused, not twenty yards from the hunter, "half standing up and looking back at the dogs, his tongue hanging out and himself blowing like a bellows." He had never suspected King's presence.

The first dog out of the burning was a "little one-eyed cur called 'Bad-eye.'" Just as the feisty little dog made a leap for the bear's neck, King fired the first of three shots from his model 1886 Winchester .38-56. He shot for the bear's ear. His aim was low, but deadly. All three shots, any one of them fatal, struck the bear in the neck. Hough suspected that Bad-eye's bravery—or foolhardiness—the distinction being a fine one among bear dogs and bear hunters—would lead the little dog "to an untimely end one of these days."

The hunters blew their horns to announce the kill. Money and Bill rode up in response along with a Mr. Beard, known to Bobo but not to the others. Beard had been on his way to the Bobo camp when he heard the horns and joined the party.

The bear was much too heavy a load for any one horse or mule. They butchered the kill and divided it among the mounts for the ride back to the camp. The bear skin, Hough estimated, was larger than his rat-tailed pony's hide would have been had the horse been skinned, something Hough might well have been tempted to do an hour or so earlier. The hunters made a present of the hide to Hough. He put it to a very practical use, wrapping it about his mount to make the saddle fit. A year later, tanned and cured, the bear skin would adorn Hough's office in the Chicago headquarters of *Forest and Stream*.

The hunt, though, was not yet over.[1]

Two men from a nearby still-hunters camp visited the Bobo logging camp Tuesday evening and reported seeing new tracks of a sow and cub near their site earlier in the day. Hough recognized the location as near the blue cane ridges where the party had enjoyed so much success the previous week. Bobo determined the morrow's hunt would move in that direction.

Fincher returned to other plans Wednesday morning, leaving the party at its smallest numbers since Hough had arrived. Besides the Chicago writer, there were left but the senior Bobo, Mr. Beard, Mr. Money, and the hands, Big Sam, Bill, and Pete.

The hunters began by casting about the vicinity where the still-hunters had seen the tracks. Making no strikes there, they next tried a nearby waterhole where bear sign had been noted a couple of days before. The dogs struck no bear scent, but some of the pups raised a deer, which led a sizable contingent of the pack on a fruitless chase. The disgusted hunters required more than an hour to round up all the "delinquent hounds." As the dogs were caught, Hough said, the hunt degenerated "into a general dog-whipping bee." Once apprehended, each offending hound was taken by a hunter to the nearest sapling. One hunter would hold the dog by the forelegs, one on either side of the tree, which prevented the dog from biting or escape, while another man tore into the hound's hindquarters with a stout branch. The dogs, said Hough, began to wail even before the punishment began, and doubled the volume once the whipping actually got underway. "[T]he serious business of educating the bear pack," Hough lamented, thus produced "more music than we cared for."

The poor canines must have wondered heartily as to the nature of their offense. The hounds that started the deer had just been added to the pack and previously were in fact used for deer hunting. They had been conscripted into the Bobo ranks because the "ravages of the chase" necessitated additional troops and the pool of volunteers had been low at the time. Such was the hard life of the bear dog—even one pressed into service without its complete and informed consent.

Little wonder the hunters "had nothing but trouble with the pack" or that "the dogs acted in a most puzzling manner...." Perhaps fearing a thrashing if they bayed the wrong game, they were entirely unreadable, "opening repeatedly" and "running for hours" for no obvious reason.

At one point a goodly number of the dogs, including some stalwarts, made a run looping back toward the blue cane ridges near where the morning's hunt had begun. Bobo, Money, and Hough "rode hard for two miles" and headed the pack in the open woods. A score of dogs, tightly bunched, bore down on them in full cry, all appearing quite confident as to their game. Bobo was unconvinced and directed Hough and Money to help him whip the hounds off the trail.

The rest of the day was spent in such "false starts." Bobo could not figure "what had got into the dogs." Addicted to the breakneck pace of the hunt in the bruin-rich Delta, he became depressed if a trail failed to yield immediate results. Hough, accustomed to places where a man might hunt "all day for a rabbit and [be] elated to find a track," could not help but wonder what Bobo would do were he forced to hunt in ordinary country. When dark came, the hunters returned to the camp with Bobo "singing very loud, apparently very happy and therefore really very much discontented." Bobo believed that luck had turned on the party. "It looks like [you will] have to stay till February, sure enough," he told Hough. "I don't reckon we ever will kill another bear now."

Hough really would not have cared but for his friends back in Chicago. He did not want to return without having fired a shot, "one's friends not always knowing the value of plain luck in a bear hunt." Otherwise he would have been perfectly happy with the hunt's progress.

Hough saw a good omen, though, in the return to the hunt of Capt. Boney Leavell and, especially, in the appearance of Leavell's constant companion, the venerable Uncle Joe. Once in camp, Uncle Joe "took a half a tumbler full of straight whiskey" for his "rheumatism," and the hunters retired for the night.[2]

25 Moonlight Bear

Thursday dawned another sunny day. Bobo appeared when the hunters assembled, mounted, not on his customary battle charger, which had gone lame the day before from a cane stab to the soft of its foot, but on a more plebeian mount: a plantation mule that, like its rider, was called Bob. The hunters struck out toward the woods along the river where the horseless hunter King had killed the big bear two days earlier. Bad fortune followed, though, or so it seemed. A quick start by the hounds fizzled to nothing and "Capt. Bobo anathematized his pack as having degenerated into a lot of deer dogs," apparently forgetting that deer dogs in fact were what many of the dogs actually had been before being drafted for the bear chase. Instead of hunting, the party worked the better part of the morning in an effort to round up the errant hounds.

A Mr. Kimmerer, owner of a neighboring timber operation, appeared at midday with a half-dozen mounted hunters, almost doubling the size of the hunting party. As the group rode along, single file, Hough counted fifteen rifle-carrying men and realized his chances at a bear had dropped to one in 15, not particularly encouraging odds. He had no choice, he decided, but to rely upon what he dubbed the *Forest and Stream* luck, which of course, had left him bearless on a trip the year before and thus far on his second Bobo hunt.

The dogs finally rounded up, the hunters decided that the local bear population, being hard pressed for the last week, must have resorted to the dreaded Hurricane. Accordingly, they moved the hunt in that direction. Their approach to that forbidding covert followed a succession of blue cane ridges interspersed by long, slender sloughs, all leading to the cypress swamp that bordered the Hurricane. Bobo, concerned that excessive noise from such a large party would interfere with the listening so crucial to the bear hunt, divided his forces, sending the greater portion of his troops "down one of the sloughs." Hough remained with the smaller party consisting of

Bobo and the other most seasoned hunters: Bill, Pete, Sam, and Uncle Joe. Bobo's contingent scouted the heavy cane ridges and "along the persimmon sloughs." With the exception of a momentary glimpse of Leavell and Beard, it was the last Hough would see of the main party until ten that night.

Bobo's group struck fresh bear sign in some low, boggy terrain. The dogs confirmed the visual indicators by immediately opening and dashing off as a body. The horsemen followed the hounds over a ridge of cane and down through a slough. As they rode up onto the next rise the trailing tongue of the hounds exploded into a full, savage cry that bellowed an unmistakable message: the dogs had raised a bear, had him in sight, and were closing in.

The bear was moving toward the thickets across a slough lying perpendicular to the hunters. Bobo issued his battle orders. "Ride on down the slough, hard as you can," he told Hough. "You'll head him as he crosses if you hurry." The writer, accompanied by Sam, charged off immediately as instructed.

Based on the location from which the sounds of the pack were coming, Hough picked the spot where he thought the bear would break from the cane and kept his eyes glued to it. That, he would learn, was a mistake. The sound of the pack only indicated where the dogs were and where the bear had been. There was no guarantee that the bear would cross the slough directly in front of the pack, and it did not.

Even before the horses came to a complete halt Hough noticed in his peripheral vision Sam struggling to raise his rifle, which had become ensnared in vines. "There he goes," Sam hollered.

A disgusted Hough turned to see a sizable bruin darting across a sliver of open cover some 60 yards beyond the expected point of emergence. The bear reentered the cane on the slough's opposite bank as quickly as it had exited the first brake. The hunters never had a chance at a shot.

Hough and Sam conferred with Bobo, Bill, Pete, and Uncle Joe. Those who had seen the bear concluded it was indeed a large one, as big as "a mule," said Sam—an exaggeration, perhaps, but one surely appreciated by the other hunters. Bobo and Bill decided to ride back toward the cane ridges. Uncle Joe, Sam, and Pete elected to head down the slough. Hough had been around the Bobo outfit long enough to know his best chance for a shot lay with Uncle Joe and he directed his pony accordingly. Almost simultaneously the sounds of the pack disappeared as if they had entered another dimension.

Even with the dogs out of earshot the hunters moved confidently through the woods, Uncle Joe in the lead, the younger Sam and Pete—although themselves bear hunters of great experience—deferring to their elder's woodcraft. Hough immediately knew he had thrown in with the right men. There was none of the fevered racing through the cane to which Hough was accustomed from his hunts with Bobo. Bobo's style, Uncle Joe's mannerisms suggested, was just that: a style, and a not a necessity, and a style more ordinary men, like Hough, found difficult. Uncle Joe paced his mount no faster than a walk.

Despite his years Uncle Joe had the sharpest ears of all the hunters. The men paused in the open slough, removed their hats, and listened, slowly turning their heads, scanning the woods for any distant popping of cane or muffled yelp of hound. One of the marks of a good bear horse, Hough learned, was the ability to "stand motionless when his rider is listening for the dogs," even if it means not having so much as a "bite of cane leaf all day…." Any horse that dared "stir a leaf or munch a bit cane" at such a time met quick chastisement.

Uncle Joe, his bald head slightly tilted and his face maintaining a sphinx-like countenance, extended the arm and hand holding his hat like a dowsing rod to indicate the direction from which he heard the sounds of the pack. Sam and Pete murmured a disagreement that really only reflected their disbelief that the old man could pinpoint the location of sounds they were not even sure they heard. Hough, on the other hand, was certain he heard nothing.

As the ancient Joe sat motionless on his horse, pointing into the woods like some equestrian statue, the others began to register, first surprise, then agreement, as they gradually heard the distinct sounds of the dogs coming from the direction Joe pointed.

From the noise of the dogs, the race was taking a great turn, "crossing the [cane] ridges higher up" from the location of the hunters. The bear, it appeared, was not making for the Hurricane after all. Pete, Sam, Bill, and Hough galloped off for the slough where the dogs first took the trail. Uncle Joe, unperturbed, maintained his standard pace behind them. The "voice of the pack," lost for some minutes, suddenly returned. "The chase was coming right for us," Hough later wrote.

All was excitement as Hough and his companions "broke cane for a quarter of a mile," riding in ahead of the dogs until they found themselves in an offshoot of the dreaded Hurricane that reached out from the main body of that labyrinth like an ensnaring tentacle. Somehow they picked their way through that tangle of vine, briar, and logs, searching for the pack they expected to see burst through at any moment.

Then, without warning, and as on previous hunts, the pack split, the greater portion turning in a direction away from Hough's group. "One big-voiced dog" Hough took to be the hound called Jolly continued "baying in one place…." Part of the pack was with him, leading Hough to believe some of the dogs had treed. The other hunters, unconvinced, urged their mounts back toward the cane ridges. Hough followed as best he could, all the time falling further behind. After some half-dozen circuits back and forth across the same series of brakes he suddenly found himself "alone in the middle of the Mississippi Delta, a bear hunter on [his] own hook."

Hough rode through the woods solo, looking and listening, but heard no sound of the pack. Finally he gave up any hope of finding a bear and rode back in what he hoped was the direction of the ridges where he had last seen Bill and Pete and Sam. He came upon a large dry bayou channel and, in the grip of the panic that sometimes seizes those lost in the woods, ran his horse along it at full speed for a mile or more.

Hough, without a clue as to his location, must have been close to despair. Then he "saw a quiet, white-headed figure jogging calmly along ahead" like some apparition. While the other hunters had been spurring their mounts through the woods and brakes like mad men, neither Uncle Joe nor his mule had broken a sweat. Hough should not have been surprised, but was, when Uncle Joe also turned out to be closest to the pack. "I hear 'em sir, right over there," he told Hough. "They're coming across above here a little way. I reckon if you ride up there right fast you'll get to kill the bear."

Following the old gentleman's directions, Hough rode a half a mile, watching for the pack all along the way. For once Uncle Joe had miscalculated. The dogs took a turn back into the same square mile of woods "they had been working at full cry for over two hours." A crackle of cane took Hough's attention. Someone called out from the thicket, and Hough answered. In a moment Bobo and Bill emerged from the brakes onto the bank of the dry bayou.

Bobo was fit to be tied. Never, he insisted, had he seen bear dogs act so irrationally. "I don't know what they're after," he declared with obvious disgust. His best dogs, he observed, would "be trailing along right out in the open woods on a cold trail, apparently, and then all at once they [would] jump in together," baying furiously, "just as if they [had seen] the bear right in front of them" even though there was nothing there. "It's been that way all the afternoon," he complained. "I can't tell a thing about what they mean or what they are doing and I feel like killing the whole pack. Listen at them! There they go, three different packs and not one running a bear, I'll bet a dollar! I never saw anything like it!"

Bobo was so outraged, in fact, that Hough feared he might break into song. "I didn't want him to do that," Hough later wrote, "so I tried to divert his mind with pleasant speculations."

They reversed their course and rode a while more. It was late, around 5:00 p.m., and the sun's light was quickly fading. There was no quitting yet, though. The men rode further along the perimeter of the area the dogs were working. Pete and Sam met up with them on that path.

Then, not unexpectedly, Uncle Joe came ambling along on his steady old mule, "very tranquil and unconcerned." Hough's little group that had separated from the main body of hunters so many hours and miles before was entirely reassembled in the near dark and "about six miles from camp, in the middle of the wildest and roughest of that wild country."

Bobo remained on the verge of song. "It's no bear, that's one thing for sure. The bear don't live that my dogs wouldn't have run to a standstill before this. I don't know what's the trouble, but it's no use fooling. Call in the dogs."

Everyone blew their horns to bring in the hounds. Sam and Pete, insistent that the dogs were on a bear, did so reluctantly. A few of the inexperienced pack members responded. The backbone of the pack, though, the old soldier dogs, remained on the trail. Bobo told Sam to fire his Winchester. Still convinced that his boss was wrong, Sam obeyed under protest. The loud reports of the rifle, which almost always brought the dogs running en masse, failed to raise the cream of the Bobo pack.

Bobo, unused to being ignored by man or beast, stood speechless. Night had fallen in earnest, and with it, a pervading, dewy chill. Out of the evening cold and damp came the faintest hint of something to warm a hunter's heart: a barely audible chorus of stationary canine voices emanating from deep within the dark wood. Above all could be heard the distinctive voices of Bobo's finest dogs.

Pete and Sam, their opinions bolstered by the cries of the pack, became more assertive: "That's him," one said. "That's ol' Rock in there, Cap'n. Ol' Rock, he ain't never opened on nothing but bear. That's bear, sure as you're born, sir!" Uncle Joe took off his hat and extended it with his bear dowsing arm in the direction of the music. "I reckon [they have] treed," he declared.

The angry expression Bobo had shown for the last hour dissolved and, as Hough put it, "his face shortened about one foot." Out of fear of disappointment, perhaps, he could not yet bring himself to acknowledge what the others insisted was true. No, he said, the dogs must be on a coon.

Sam, emboldened by the ever-swelling volume of the hounds, emphatically disagreed: "Don't you never believe it! That ain't no coon. That's bear!"

Whatever it was, Bobo would find out. "Come on, Hough!" he shouted, and spurred the mule Bob into what appeared to Hough as "a jet-black wall of braided wire fences," which, of course, was the canebrake at night.

In that instant, said Hough, was where "the Bobo of the [bear hunt] came in,… [for] no man on earth [could] ride cane with Bobo, the bear hunter." Even Bobo, of course, had to have a mount fit for the job. The mule Bob was more than up to the task. The thicket before them presented a formidable obstacle, even in the daylight. It was the densest of brakes. Reliable Bob "lowered his head and plunged in…." The cane parted before him like saloon swinging doors. All Hough had to do was to keep his rat-tailed pony close enough to Bob the mule's hindquarters to make it through the doors before they closed.

For a quarter hour they rode, the briars and branches and cane snatching and slashing at them like the enchanted trees of a fairy tale forest. In that time they probably progressed no more than four or five hundred yards. All the while the sound of the pack continue to emanate from the same place and grow ever louder.

When the raging battle noise told the hunters they were only 100 or so yards from the fray, Bobo stopped, dismounted, and silently signaled the others to do the same.

Without a word, Bobo led the final approach. Hough, Pete, Bill, and Sam followed, creeping through the black density of the brake. Even before Hough could see the dogs, Bobo stopped, pulled Hough toward him, and pointed to the top of a massive oak some 50 yards distant. High in the tree, at least 25 yards up, Hough saw a large black mass, about the size of a pumpkin, but pointed on one side, and appearing to be attached to the oak's trunk. On closer inspection he made out a shadowy form, curved and blacker than the other shadows. The "pumpkin," he realized, was the head of a substantial bear. On a limb protruding from the far side of the tree the beast stood, "looking calmly and happily at the dogs, each of which was trying to jump 75 ft. high."

The moon was rising on the opposite side of the tree from the hunters as Bobo and Hough made the final stalk to the base of the oak. Though it would have been better had the moon been to their rear, it still brightened the sky enough that Hough could make out some detail. The cane around the oak in which the bear perched was well over 20 feet tall, providing plenty of screening for Hough and Bobo. As the men neared the bottom of the tree, the bear swung its head about "uneasily." Hough, no longer able to see the bear's body, again wondered if the moving, pumpkin-sized object might actually be the entirety of the creature up the tree. "Coon?" he whispered to Bobo. "Bear!" came the quiet but forceful response. The outline of the animal once more came into focus for Hough. He levered a round into his big Winchester, raised the rifle, and, unable to see through the sights in the dark, lined up his shot along the breech and barrel of the piece as best he could.[1]

26 Insubordination

Don't shoot," Bobo told Hough. "Wait till the boys get here," referring to the young hands, Sam, Bill, and Pete. In giving that instruc-
tion Bobo exhibited a standard reluctance of the practiced bear hunter. As
George Alexander explained in his treatise on black bears, "[d]ogs are more
apt to be killed by wounded than unwounded bears. Hence, old bear-hunt-
ers are always fearful of letting a novice get the first shot at a bear at bay."[1]
That, no doubt, is one reason Bobo often shot so quickly—before any guest
could pull a trigger.

Decades before, Dr. Henry Peck had warned of the dangers of sloppy
shooting:

> [e]ndeavor to shoot him above the bridge of the ribs, tolera-
> bly low down, and you will be apt to shoot him through the
> heart; on the contrary, if you shoot in a hurry you will prob-
> ably make a bad shot, which will render the bear furious
> and he will probably kill and cripple many of your dogs, for
> bear dogs rush into close quarters upon the firing of a gun.

Most to be avoided was the frontal head shot. For one thing, the bear's
head was almost constantly in motion, presenting obvious problems for
the shooter. Secondly, at least according to the conventional wisdom of
the nineteenth century bear hunting fraternity, the shape, thickness, and
hardness of the bear's skull made penetration difficult. "A bullet striking
the front of the head of [a] bear will, if not driven by a heavy charge of
powder, almost invariably glance off, causing only a momentary stunning,
from which it rises with increased ferocity; and unless the hunter is close
enough to use his bowie or cane knife, he may be either fearfully lacerated
or killed."[2]

That appears to be what happened in the case of Dr. Hamberlin, some
half century before, whose tragic history is described previously herein.[3]

Accordingly, unless he was confident enough "to be sure of killing [a bear] stone dead," Bobo said, he would "never try to make a head shot."

Neither would Bobo ordinarily attempt "a shoulder shot. In running bear with dogs, you do not want to cripple a bear or stop him when you shoot him." Just as Dr. Peck had said years before, Bobo believed the ideal shot would be "well back through the hollow of the body—pretty low down is best [i. e., the heart, lung area]—and then let him run." A bear so hit would start to run but quickly drop dead without killing or crippling any dogs. On the other hand, a shot that broke a bone without mortally wounding the bear would simply stop or slow him down "before the fight [was] out of him." Such a crippled bear would be "sure to ruin the pack for you."[4] Recall the canine devastation that resulted when A. B. Wingfield shoulder shot a bear thinking such a hit would protect Zack Jones's dogs.

It was the dogs, Bobo knew, that had the most to lose from a poorly placed shot. Bobo gave Hough an example: "My dogs," he had learned, "will pile in on a bear as quick as they hear a shot, thinking he is killed." On one occasion, a fellow hunter shot but only grazed the bear's head. The dogs charged "and [the bear] killed eight of them before I could get up" and kill it. Given that experience, Bobo "never like[d] to take any chances" where his dogs were concerned and was very particular as to the shot placement he counseled.[5]

Hough considered such advice to be "ex cathedra,[6] for," at least in Hough's view, "Bobo's equal in bear hunting does not live to-day, if, indeed, he ever lived."[7]

As to the bear up the tree before them, Bobo no doubt feared Hough would miss or superficially wound it. The result in such a case would be that the beast would bolt and be lost entirely or, worse yet, wreak destruction amidst his dogs or even the hunters. For that reason he wanted the intrepid Sam, Bill, and Pete present as back-up in case Hough made a mess of things. Hough, though, had learned that given the slightest chance the three hired men would beat the rest of the hunters to the shot. What is more, the Chicago writer, though new to Delta bear hunting, was no tenderfoot. Quite to the contrary, he was a veteran outdoorsman who knew how to shoot to kill and had the skill to do it. It was "the only time," Hough later wrote, "I deliberately disobeyed orders" from Bobo.

A column of fire and brimstone belched from the muzzle of Hough's Winchester as the rifle's report rattled the moonlit stillness of the canebrake.

"You broke his back," shouted Bobo, apparently forgetting Hough's insubordination in the excitement of the moment. Hough stepped to the side of the cloud of blackpowder smoke for a clearer view. The bear slumped onto the limb, obviously mortally hit. Hough levered and fired a second round to make certain the job was finished. As the bear tumbled from the limb, Bobo fired as well. Simultaneously, a fusillade erupted from the three men still approaching from the cane.

The bear was dead before it landed on the woodland floor, hitting the ground like "400,000 four-bushel sacks of beans," as Hough described it. Bobo erupted in what Hough called "his regulation war whoop" he loosed at the conclusion of every successful hunt: "Good Lord A'might, dog-gone! We killed a bear!" Each time Bobo let out that yell, Hough noted, it was always with "joy and surprise, as if he had never seen [a bear] killed before." The planter "was happy," said Hough, "in the only way he ever gets really good and happy." His usual pleasure at bringing a bear to bag was magnified by finally being able to put his writer friend in position to make the kill.

"So you've got your bear," said Bobo, "and I'm mighty glad of it. I wouldn't have missed this for $100. I knew you'd get your bear before long. We've had a long, hard day of it, and I'm glad we didn't go home beat."

Sam couldn't restrain himself. "I told you, ol' Rock...." Bobo cut him off, but with a laugh. "Oh! You go on away about old Rock! You go on and cut up the bear, and let's get out of here if we can."

Bobo and the others, by the light of a dry cane fire, conducted a postmortem. The bear was an old she, milking, indicating she had a least one cub, which, given the time of year, should have been around eight months old and big enough to take care of itself. Hough was glad of that. No one else was quite so sentimental. The old she's cub, no doubt, was the reason the hound Jolly, who had just arrived on the scene after the gunshot, had been baying at another tree about 100 yards away.[8]

Hough had used a Winchester .45-70-405, a heavier firearm and load than the .44 and .38 caliber carbines favored by his companions. The gun was a full-sized rifle and, as such, too long for convenient carrying through cane. It was death on bears, though, as Hough discovered. It was not the gun, so much, as the ammunition it used. Based on a military round that had found popular use among buffalo hunters in the late 1870s and '80s, the .45-70-405 cartridge fired from Hough's gun was manufactured by the U.M.C. Co.[9] The load included a bullet "made expansive by means of [a] copper cylinder in the center of the lead projectile," a design that produced a devastating mushrooming effect upon the ball's striking the game.

Hough had not broken the bear's back as Bobo had thought. Both of his first two shots had been clean-killing lung shots, either of which would have been almost instantly fatal to the 300 pound bear. Hough's third shot apparently had been a miss.[10]

Despite the demonstrated power of Hough's heavy rifle and ammunition, Bobo did not adopt the larger format firearm. His chief measure of a good bear gun remained overall practicality. He liked a gun that would sustain "hard knocks" and required as little cleaning as possible.[11] Bobo maintained his preference for shorter, lighter carbines. The firearms he eventually passed on to his descendants were the lever action 1892 model Winchester .44-40 used on his hunts with Hough and a similar carbine in the .30-30 caliber he acquired some while later. The .44-40 was barely 33 inches long from muzzle to butt.

Col. James Gordon once said that when it comes to quail hunting, the next best thing to being a good shot is "being a good claimer of doubtful birds...."[12] The hired man, Bill, it appeared, was from a similar school of thought regarding big game hunts. "I expect I done killed this bear," he declared to the others. "I done shot him right square in the head. You'll find my bullet right in his head, sure." The bear's head, unfortunately for Bill, was unscathed. They did find "someone's bullet in the [bear's] opposite extremity, it having struck the ham" of the falling bruin after Hough's killing shots.

Hough took no great pride in shooting the bear. "[P]otting a bear out of a tree—even in the dark—was not so exciting" to his way of thinking "as killing a quail on the wing. ...I can't see elements of much sporting glory in that sort of situation. Your friends insisted you must kill a bear; and so you must, or pass for a duffer. You do kill him, and then you feel as if you really were a duffer."

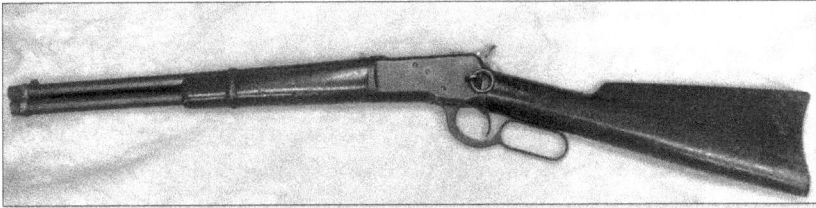

Bob Bobo's .44-40 Winchester carbine. *Photo by author.*

The shooting of the bear, Hough insisted, was not where the sportsmanship of the chase lay. Rather, the thrill and the challenge were in the riding; the staying with the pack; and the testing of one's own luck and the ability of the hounds "against the speed, strength and cunning of one of the largest of animals pursued as game." In the end, Hough knew, he was in his hunting success but the simple "beneficiary of Uncle Joe's ears and Capt. Bobo's courtesy." He claimed no glory in the conquest of the bear.

After the hunters "skinned and divided" the kill their thoughts turned homeward. Should they spend the night in the woods even though they had no water with them? Or should they try to find their way back to the camp through the dark Delta swamps and brakes by moonlight. Bobo, as usual, constituted a majority. "If we can get back to that slough where we stopped to listen before we came in here," he said, "we can ride down that slough till we come to the big bayou and then we can ride up the bayou that will take us to camp. Will your mule take us back the way we came in, Bill?"

Bill was confident that his mount, known for its woods savvy, could "pilot [the hunters] out of the wilderness" and back to their base camp. He gave the mule its head and the beast "sought for the winding trail… [the party] had made coming in." The hunters followed through the sea of cane, which closed up behind them, leaving no wake.

Bobo, Hough, Pete, Bill, Sam, and the ever tranquil Uncle Joe, in the competent custody of Bill's mule, arrived safely and found the other members of the party, whom they had not seen since the morning, already comfortably ensconced in camp.

Hough had his bear and it was time to return to Chicago. The next morning, a Friday, Hough and Capt. Money caught a train north. "I disliked to say good-by [*sic*] to my Southern friends," Hough wrote, "for the only unpleasant thing about your visit to the South is the time when you have to say good-by."

On the pages of *Forest and Stream* Hough thanked Bobo profusely "for his courtesy" and wished that he would "live to see plenty of sport yet in his beloved Delta country...." It was a country, Hough said, "whose richness is its own worst enemy, since eventually it must attract the covetousness of men perhaps not so fit to occupy it as those who now claim it as their homes and as their hunting grounds."[13]

27 A Year Goes By

Forest and Stream serialized Hough's account of his autumn 1895 hunt over four issues in February and March of 1896.[1] Hough and the Bear Hunter remained fast friends, and Bobo never left Hough's thoughts for long.[2] By August 22, 1896, Bobo was back in Hough's regular column, if only for a cameo appearance in a short discussion of wild hog hunting in Tennessee and Iowa.[3] Autumn was approaching, but a third annual fall bear hunting trip to Mississippi was not to be a part of Hough's calendar. The *Forest and Stream* readership, however, would not be deprived of a report on the fall bear hunting escapades of Bob Bobo.

The first report came in the form of a letter to Hough from Tom Divine, which Hough reprinted without first asking Divine's permission. A gentleman, Hough admitted, would not do such a thing. "Some years since however," Hough said, tongue well in cheek, "I gave up the business of being a gentleman, because I found there was nothing in it...." Besides, he added, "in the *Forest and Stream* family there are not secrets."[4] Furthermore, Hough insisted, "in Memphis the boys all read each other's telegrams and letters and often get on to good things that way."[5]

Divine's letter began with a few reminiscences of the Bobo place as it was when he had first visited it with the railroad engineering party hardly more than a decade earlier. In the brief ten years since, Divine said, those hundreds of acres of dense bottomland forest and canebrake had metamorphosed into "the most magnificent [fields of] corn, cotton, potatoes, barley, rye and wheat that one ever saw." Where muscadine vines once had hung in profusion from virgin timber there stood a new plantation house, "the garden overgrown with beautiful roses" and "the ground covered with soft grass...."

Some things had changed little, however. Upon his arrival at the Bobo place, from whence he was writing to Hough, Divine had given "one blast of the horn" and had been "greeted [by] about 100 tried and true bear dogs."[6]

Bobo, absent when Divine arrived, returned that night. "[W]e talked over the various things of our lives," Divine wrote to Hough, "the many changes that had taken place, and… particularly of you and [Noel] Money.

Among the news reported by Divine was the addition of new blood to the Bobo dog stock. Knowing Bobo's fondness for the "cold foxhound nose,"[7] Money, following the previous fall's bear hunt, had sent Bobo "several fine English hounds," including "some young puppies…." Bobo named the little ones for some of his favorite hunting partners: Hough, Money, Divine, and Foster, the latter being the namesake of the bear camp's champion sleeper. The pups called Hough and Foster, Divine jokingly wrote, "may be fine hounds, but they are the sorriest looking ones I ever saw…." What was more, the one called Foster, Divine had discovered, "seems to be willing to do a great deal of sleeping." The one named Divine might well have been as homely as the rest, but it died, a fact in which Tom Divine claimed to take some solace. "Money will be glad to know," he added, again, in classic Divine jest, "that the one… named for him went mad and had to be killed."

The supposed mad dog was not the only thing killed at the Bobo place. Shortly before Divine's arrival, Bobo's hunters had slain a 400 pound bear. Divine reported, no doubt to Hough's surprise, that one of the dogs that acquitted himself especially well in that hunt was Alcorn, "the dog that had his jaw shot off" during Hough's Delta hunt the previous year.

Alcorn, it seems, was almost indestructible. In addition to recovering from a bullet to the jaw, the dog had survived an ordeal that should have killed him or at least taken off a leg or two. While hot on the trail of a bear, Alcorn had stepped squarely into a huge steel-jawed bear trap. Fortunately, "a little block of wood kept the jaws apart just enough so it didn't hurt his leg very bad."[8]

Bobo, who was present when the trap snapped shut on Alcorn, held the little dog tightly so that he would not break any bones from struggling. Meanwhile, two men from the hunting party "opened the trap." The instant Alcorn was freed, "off he went with the rest of the pack, [in] full cry."[9]

In those times bear traps must have presented an ever present danger in the lower Mississippi valley to horses and men as well as to dogs like Alcorn. The Delta was touted in the sporting press as a trapper's paradise. Fur hunters from as far away as Pennsylvania and Wisconsin journeyed to the bottomland swamps of Mississippi and Arkansas to set their steel-jawed traps for all manner of furbearers, from mink and muskrat to black bear.[10] One can only imagine the injury a trap designed to hold a 400 pound bear could do to the leg of a man or a horse.

Mississippi hunter, surveyor, and engineer, Augustine Lee Dabney, the son of Thomas Gregory "Coahoma" Dabney, almost learned that first hand while on a "reconnaissance survey" in Phillips County, Arkansas, just across the Mississippi from Coahoma County. Writing under the pseudonym "Tripod," the 25 year old told the readers of *Forest and Stream* of his own close call with a bear trap. Following his crossing of "Yellowbanks Bayou on a fallen tree trunk," he jumped from the log to the stream's bank and "was startled by a sharp 'click.'" The surveyor thus "discovered that [he] had struck [his] foot on a 20 lb. bear trap with teeth of tenacious length...." To his great relief his foot had landed "near enough to the place where the teeth are, to spring the trap, but fortunately without getting caught." The owner of the trap, wrote Tripod, had failed to post the legally required warnings to humans with near disastrous results.[11]

Besides the good news about Alcorn, Hough learned that the pugnacious "little one-eyed cur called Bad-eye," who had flung himself so recklessly at the great bear Bobo had dubbed the "bull of the woods,"[12] had exceeded expectations and also survived another year—no small feat for a Bobo bear dog.

Divine concluded his dispatch with a demand that Hough join him at Bobo's in December to "kill a bear." It is "[e]asy, nice work," he wrote, "and the music of the hounds will make you a boy again."

To Hough's great surprise and satisfaction, even as he was lifting paragraphs from Divine's letter for his upcoming "Chicago and the West" column, Tom Divine himself strolled into the *Forest and Stream* office. "It snowed yesterday in Chicago," Hough wrote, "but immediately on Tom Divine's arrival the snow began to melt in front of his beaming smile, and at the time is entirely gone in the vicinity of the city." Divine, who was in Chicago on business, reported that Bobo had ridden off for a two week bear hunt "further down in Mississippi." Divine was in Chicago but for two days, at the conclusion of which he planned to travel to Canton, in central Mississippi, for an extended quail shoot. Before leaving he promised to send up "large quantities of venison, wild turkey and quail for the Thanksgiving dinners of his Chicago friends," or so Hough wrote.[13]

About a month after Divine told of a Bobo party killing a 400 pound black bear, Hough reported a very different Coahoma County scenario. "I am told," he wrote, "that the Delta Country of Mississippi, where the black bears were so numerous last year, has this year almost no mast at all." There were, consequently, "no bears to be found in all that country," the bruins apparently having voted with their feet and departed for more fruitful precincts. "Capt. Bobo," Hough lamented, "is practically without an occupation, and expresses doubt whether he will ever see the good old bear days which he has known so long in the past." Hough "supposed that the bears have gone to Arkansas or the hereafter."[14]

The "no mast" report began a series of comments by Hough decrying the disappearance of bears from the Delta and the demise of the sport of bear hunting in "the Bobo Bear Country." Certainly bear hunting was not what it once was in Coahoma County. Indeed, it is hard to imagine that the natural reproduction of the species could have kept pace with the rate at which Bobo and other hunters were killing them. More likely, though, Hough's deprecation of the state of bear hunting in the "Bobo Bear Country" was an effort at counter public relations in hopes of undoing some of the damage his previous articles had wrought. Some negative reporting, Hough must have decided, could, perhaps, discourage and send elsewhere the mobs of out-of-state hunters who had invaded the Delta since he first began publicizing Bobo.

The following spring, though, came an event that had serious and undeniably negative effects on the Delta, its human population, and its wildlife. "For many days," Hough wrote in his April 17, 1897, column, "the press dispatches have been filled with the accounts of devastating floods which have been raging across the Delta country of the South, from Tennessee to the mouth of the Mississippi River."

The loss of life and property was so great that Hough was reluctant even to speak of the effect on game and probably would not have except that such was his job. The bear, deer, and turkey, Hough supposed, would have been forced onto the few ridges of dry ground they could find, making them easy prey for hunters. Most of the country he had hunted with Bobo, he assumed, was inundated. The Bobo homestead, however, and much of the attached farm land, was situated upon some of the highest ground in Coahoma County and would have escaped the worst of the flooding, he guessed.[15]

Bobo's name again surfaced briefly in a discussion on camp and hunting knives in an article Hough wrote in June 1897 about a hunt he had taken the past winter in the Rocky Mountains. The Hudson's Bay Company knife carried by one of his hunting companions (Billy Jackson) on that trip reminded Hough of "a Bobo bear knife." Like the Delta hunter's knife, he said, it "weighs about 4 lbs, and has a blade about 3 in. wide, so it can be used as an axe, as a meat axe, as a knife, a hammer, or several other tools."[16]

In October Hough received a visit from his and Bobo's old friend, levee engineer Maj. Thomas Gregory "Coahoma" Dabney, who was on his way home from a "Waterways convention" in Davenport, Iowa.[17] Despite the unpromising reports Hough previously had published concerning the Delta bear situation, Dabney found, in Hough's words, "that the redoubtable bear hunter, Capt. Bobo, still gets his bear every now and then, and remains as hearty as ever and as full of hunt."[18]

The Bear Hunter may have been "as full of hunt" as ever, but, regardless of his appearance to others, he was not "as hearty as ever...." Bobo had begun to experience problems with "some sort" of "malignant growth assail[ing]" his cold blue shooting eye.[19] While he continued life as usual, Bobo had a problem, and it would worsen.

In *Forest and Stream*'s Christmas issue that same year Hough made yet another fleeting reference to Bobo, this time in connection with an update for the readership on Noel Money's latest adventure: "trying the temper of the bears of Russia in company with, and under the guidance of, his host, Baron Hirsch." Money, Hough noted, had "given chase to bears in the Mississippi bottoms" under the "tutorship of Bobo."[20]

What Hough did not mention in that column was that he was about to take a bride. On the day that article appeared, December 25, 1897, Hough, 40, married Miss Charlotte "Lottie" Amelia Cheesebro, 34, of Chicago.[21]

28 Bobo's House in the Hills

Bear hunting continued "in the Mississippi bottoms" whether or not it was up to Bobo's standards, and Bobo continued to appear in accounts of such hunts, even when he had not been involved in them. In February 1898, for example, New Orleans resident Walter Ganong wrote of something of an accidental bear hunt he had made the preceding fall in the wilds of the Mississippi Delta. This was the same Ganong who, as a teenager, had shot the panther off the lamp post in downtown Memphis. Ganong, 32, had left New Orleans for his family home in the little plantation village of Jonestown in Coahoma County to visit his parents. Four days later he read in the newspaper that the first case of yellow fever of the summer had been confirmed in the Crescent City. Because he had a "fifteen-year life insurance policy to outlive," as well as "a few suits of old clothes [that] had not [been] worn threadbare," Ganong elected to remain in northern Mississippi until the fever abated in New Orleans. That proved to be a longer wait than he expected. To Ganong's delight he was still in Jonestown in November, the month of the "annual bear hunt" of a group of residents of that vicinity.

Ganong and thirteen of the Jonestown villagers set out by horse at 11:00 p.m. on November 15 for "Talla-Quit," a wilderness hunting camp named for its location on the border of Tallahatchie and Quitman counties about 45 miles southeast of Jonestown, Mississippi. The trip, an overnight ride, required eleven hours to complete, six of which were in a drenching autumn rain.

The hunters, wet and cold, lost no time in pitching six tents "in cane such as [Ganong] had not seen before." This hunting party included a dimension apparently absent from the Bobo hunts: four of the group were women. Ganong was pleased that "the ladies had everything shipshape in short order, and camp life didn't seem so bad after all."

The ladies, Ganong hastened to add, were not there merely in auxiliary roles. "[O]n the contrary," he said, "they handle the rifle equally as well as

---

168

they manipulate a venison steak, and are thorough woodswomen," something Ganong knew from personal experience. "When I and my chum were hopelessly lost," he confessed, one of the women "piloted us safely to camp after" the two men had "wander[ed] several hours," lost in heavy cane.[1]

On the opening day of the hunt a local man with the party killed a large bear, the only one that would be taken by the group. After losing several others over the next two days, the hunters turned their attention to deer with much success. While deer hunting, Ganong on two different occasions saw panthers. He shot at one of them, but missed, perhaps because the cat was in the canebrakes instead of on a lamp post in downtown Memphis.

Ganong wrote that their group had encountered a number of other hunting parties, including a Mr. Oliver Clay and a Capt. Ben McKee who, as "bear hunters... are without a peer, unless it be the great and only Bob Bobo, whose reputation is so well known that comment is unnecessary." Bear hunting apparently continued to be a viable sport in the Mississippi Delta, Bobo's and Hough's protestations to the contrary notwithstanding.[2]

Forest and Stream was quiet on the subject of Bobo for the rest of the year. Bob Bobo's son, Robert Eager Bobo, Jr., in fact, had married a Miss M. A. Anderson from nearby Panola County, Mississippi, in September 1898 without mention by Hough in his columns.

Bobo's name resurfaced at last in the January 21, 1899, edition of "Chicago and the West," once again in the context of a discussion on hunting knives. One of Hough's hunting companions had made a Christmas gift to him of one of the Hudson's Bay Company knives he admired so much, this one a custom crafted duplicate of the one carried by his friend, Billy Jackson, during their winter Rocky Mountain hunt some two years before. "It was something like a foot and a half long, and three inches across the blade, with a backbone like a beam and a total weight of a couple of pounds or so." Hough had never been happier with a knife. "From this time on," Hough wrote, "Capt. Bobo of Mississippi, has got none the best of me in a bear fight, when it comes to a show down of knives."

In the same column Hough published a letter from one Ernest A. Bigelow, of Sutton, Quebec, who asked for "the address of Capt. Bobo, or of anyone else you know of who keeps dogs for bear hunting" because he "wish[ed] to buy a pair."[3]

"I presume Capt. Bobo can still be reached by addressing him—Capt. R. E. Bobo, Bobo, Miss.," Hough responded. "Whether he would part with any of his bear dogs is another question."

Hough well knew that Bobo was loath to give up a good bear dog. Poindexter Dunn, a United States congressman from St. Francis County, Arkansas, had once offered Bobo 640 acres for a pack of 14 seasoned bear hounds. Bobo had declined, telling the congressman "they could not be bought." Still, Hough did not discourage Bigelow from asking. "Capt. Bobo is the soul of generosity, and it may do no harm to try him anyhow."[4]

Bear dogs were not on Hough's immediate agenda, however. Tom Divine had promised Hough some stellar quail shooting if he would just come down to Memphis. Hough obliged, and after several days afield in west Tennessee with dog and comrades reported only a single bird falling to his shotgun—the Hough luck at work again. From there Hough took the train to "dear old New Orleans, quaintest and most lovable of all American cities," to spend a few days in some "plain sight-seeing, most of our time being spent in the pawnshops and graveyards, which, as is well known, are among the main attractions of that city."

Most likely Hough was in Louisiana vacationing with his still fairly new bride, for he did no hunting while in the Crescent City area. Moreover, he noted that his fishing was limited to sampling the seafood of the "old French Market" and "in the many excellent restaurants we discovered." Hough reported that the "pompano of New Orleans is a dream, the red snapper is a reverie,... the tenderloin of trout is pure and delicate imagination," and the "oysters are beyond description." Before leaving New Orleans Hough made a visit to the Old Absinthe House in the French Quarter as well as a tour "through the great sugar plantations" of the outlying areas.

Hough did meet up with one of his companions from his Coahoma County hunts while in New Orleans. "It was very good of our friend of earlier bear hunts, Mr. R. W. Foster, to show us to the depot, as we left [for Memphis and then for Chicago], though he was at the time ill...."

While Bobo did not join Hough in Louisiana, a meeting with the Bear Hunter at his Mississippi Delta plantation was on Hough's itinerary.[5] Hough had written "to Bobo at his place, and said we would call," he told his readers, "but... we did not hear from him."

Hough stayed over for a few days in Memphis. As Hough sat in a Memphis café on his last day in the Bluff City, in one of those coincidences that is not especially rare where Delta folk are involved, "who should come into the [place] and sit down at arm's length... but Bobo himself, looking just the same and talking just the same as ever." Bobo, Hough wrote appreciatively, "ought never to forgive me" for ruining him "in the bear hunting business, ... [but he] does."[6]

Bobo explained that he had not replied to Hough because he recently had moved to his newly purchased home and acreage among the rolling hills and ridges of DeSoto County, Mississippi, just southeast of Memphis. Bobo's new place, which he called his "hill farm," was located near the village of Byhalia, right across the road from his friend and sometime *Forest and Stream* contributor, W. I. Spears.[7] Bobo had only that day received Hough's letter at his Byhalia home. It had been forwarded to him from his Coahoma County plantation some 80 or 90 miles to the southwest. Bobo told Hough that, while the hunting was far from what it once was on his old hunting grounds, he "might could squeeze out one little, measly, small, poor bear if [Hough] should be out of meat." The Delta man also told Hough he would visit him in Chicago in the spring. "All these Southern folk," lamented Hough, "promise to come to see you, but they don't come, ... which is the one thing that can be urged against them." Bobo, though, would visit Chicago, but not in the coming spring.

Hough took his account of his conversation with Bobo as an opportunity to shame their mutual friend, Noel Money, who had been incommunicado for some time, into making contact with his old bear hunting comrades. Capt. Bobo, he wrote, in what amounted to an open letter to Mr. Money, "has got at his house... the big set of bear tusks" Money had said he "want[ed] to put in the head of a walking stick." Bobo also had for Money, Hough added, "the curiosity of the claw of a bear, which is white instead of black, it being rarely that the black bear has a white claw." Bobo would give those things to Money, Hough wrote, if only Money would "write as a decent fellow should, and tell us where to send them."[8]

In July 1899 Hough once more invoked Bobo's name in a discussion of a knife. A Mr. H. A. Jackson, of Greene, New York, traveling on business to Wisconsin, stopped by the *Forest and Stream* Chicago office and made a gift to Hough of a custom hunting knife. "This knife would delight the heart of my friend Bobo," said Hough, according the gift the highest praise he could, "for with it he could both kill and cut up a bear."[9]

Two weeks later Hough mentioned Bobo once more, this time on the occasion of Noel Money visiting Hough in Chicago. Hough recounted Money's success hunting red deer and brown bear in Russia with hollow point bullets fired from a .303 Holland and Holland double rifle. "Whether he will get to meet Captain Bobo again on a bear hunt is a question," wrote Hough, "but if so the worthy Captain had better do something to protect his bears."[10]

In November 1899 Hough reported news that suggested a very real possibility that neither Money nor anyone else would again hunt bear with Bobo, whom he called "out of all America... best entitled to wear the name of Big Bear Chief." Hough wished, he wrote, that "I might give only the best reports of Capt. Bobo's health and happiness, but I am told today that he is having very bad trouble with his" left eye.[11] The problem, reported Hough, was that the eye had "become involved with inflammation from a little tumor. It is sad to think of Bobo not hunting bear, but I think he is not hunting this fall." Hough reiterated the awe in which he held the Mississippi hunter: "There never was a bigger-hearted man than this same Bobo, and his like in the canebrake never crossed a saddle."[12]

Bobo was not to undergo his trials without friends at his side. As the twentieth century dawned, two fellow sportsmen from the Memphis area, W. A. Powel,[13] and a Maj. La Rue, joined Bobo in Byhalia. As Hough humorously put it, "Mr. Powel has moved all his family, including La Rue, down there, ...and the whole outfit has taken charge of the house of Mr. W. I. Spears, where they seem to be living in a state of great contentment."

Spears had put together a collection of leases totaling some 25,000 acres to form the Ivanhoe Club, which must have been one of the earliest privately leased hunting clubs of Mississippi.[14] Hough was thoroughly impressed with Spears's project, which had arisen primarily from Spears's desire to stop the market hunting of quail. Market hunting apparently was not as prevalent in the South as in the North, and Spears wanted to keep things that way. The South, Hough believed, "always instinctively rebelled at this market shooting idea, and it has stopped it far more generally than was ever done in the North." That was one of many things about the South that made it, in Hough's estimation, "a great country...."[15]

Hunting at the Ivanhoe Club was a small game proposition with fox, raccoon, rabbits, and quail being the primary objects of the chase. The hunting for those species was outstanding. "I think it would be easy to put up fifty coveys of birds a day here," Powel wrote to Hough. Besides the native bobwhite quail, Spears had stocked pheasant on the place, as well. Moreover, Powel declared that there were "at least 200 rabbits within a quarter mile of the House."

A stay at the Ivanhoe Club was not just a matter of shooting. The "cooks here are artists," Powel reported with obvious glee. "Every meal we have a big turkey at one end of the table and a ham at the other, with quail, rabbit, pigs' feet, sausage, spare-ribs, pork and greens, and most everything you can think of in between." Regularly seated at such a straining board during the course of his visit, said Powel, he felt as though he "would never be hungry again."[16]

The Ivanhoe Club lay in upland farming country some 40 miles from the northeast edge of the Delta swamps, with not a bear trail in the vicinity. That was probably just as well for Bob Bobo. His "doctor [had] told him he would have to quit bear hunting, or it would kill him," Hough told his readers, "so he has quit...." Hough could not lie to his readers, so he added, "or is tapering off...."[17]

Veteran Delta bear hunter James Gordon would have agreed with Bobo's doctors as to the high toll exacted of a man by the rigors of bear hunting. The sport subjects the hunter, he wrote to a British audience in 1885, to "strain on the system from exposure to wet and cold, intense excitement, over heating and cooling suddenly, plunging into bayous, straining every muscle and fibre of the body until exhausted.... [You undergo] every hardship and exposure, until the constitution is shattered, then [you] fall victim to the first little illness that strikes you...." That, concluded Gordon, "is why bear hunters and bear dogs die young."

"I found," Gordon wrote in another article, "that bear hunting was killing my friends and undermining my own constitution." He said he "felt the warning in nervous twinges and sciatic pains, and sought for sport in less arduous fields."[18]

Bobo did something similar. While ordered by his doctors to quit the bear chase, he had not been prohibited from hunting small game[19] and would join in a fox race "once in while to keep his horn in tune."[20]

The old Bear Hunter "did not at all distain such tame sport; except for rabbit hunting, in which he refused to participate." Bobo, jested Hough, was "degenerating into a fox hunter." In W. I. Spears's estimation, Hough admitted, the change marked an improvement in Bobo's social standing, not a decline.[21] Fox hunting, after all, was considered "the chief end of man in that precinct,"[22] the *Westminster Shorter Catechism* notwithstanding.[23] Bobo, being a Methodist, no doubt concerned himself little with Calvinist theological propositions anyway.

29 Bobo's Trials

Within a few days of the report from Powel Hough was "down in Mississippi" once more. Hough, in fact, had traveled all the way to New Orleans again for reasons not disclosed in his "Chicago and the West" column. It being February, perhaps he was using the Crescent City as his headquarters for a Gulf and marsh fishing trip. More likely, New Orleans had become a favorite get away spot for Hough and his recently acquired wife. Whatever his purpose, rain had set in, and Hough was confined to his hotel. Growing weary with "hotel life," Hough decided to head back north. In anticipation of the trip home, he wrote Bobo a letter asking the hunter to watch for him and his wife at the platform at Bobo Station.

When Hough arrived in Coahoma County, Bobo was not to be found. Unable to secure any reliable information as to the Bear Hunter's whereabouts, the Houghs proceeded to Bobo's "hill farm" in DeSoto County. When no Bobo was found in residence at the hill place, Hough again telegraphed Bobo, this time joking that he "was running [Bobo's hill] farm, and liked it pretty well, and he need not come home unless he felt like it, as we were very comfortable."

Despairing of finding Bobo, Hough and his bride departed DeSoto County for Memphis, and there, "face to face at Gaston's* (every Southern man knows where Gaston's is at Memphis), we met Bobo, and Bobo was mad."

"Where've you been?" demanded a clearly irate Bobo. "I've been wiring after you all over the South. I wired you at New Orleans to come on ahead to the Delta, and then I got word that you were over at my other place a-running it. I gave up trying to catch you, and concluded to come here to Memphis and lay for you when you started back North. Do you know what you have done?"

---

* An exclusive restaurant on Court Square in the Memphis of the late 19ᵗʰ century.

The only thing Hough could think of that he had done was to have eaten "up everything there was at [Bobo's hill] farm."

Bobo quickly set him straight. "We postponed the wedding for you."

Bobo explained that he had received Hough's letter on Saturday, February 10, and immediately had responded by telegram, inviting Mr. and Mrs. Hough to the marriage[1] of his son, Fincher, 27, to 18 year old Elizabeth "Bessie" Brock.[2] Fincher and Bessie were to have been married on Tuesday, February 13, 1900, in Bobo, Mississippi. When Hough failed to appear, Bob Bobo told his son his marriage plans would have to be continued until the following day. When Hough was not there on Wednesday, February 14, St. Valentine's Day, the couple proceeded with the wedding. The cause of all this exasperation, Hough determined, was "the most grossly stupid of all hotel clerks" who had failed to see that Hough received Bobo's telegram.

Although he did not hunt with Bobo on that trip, he did manage a brief conversation with the man. Bobo, "the king of all bear hunters," wrote Hough, was distraught over the destruction of the Delta bottomland forests by timber companies clearcutting the Delta woodlands. "There is but little of the old Delta wilderness left," Bobo reported. Still, Bobo believed "he might get a bear, if he had to."[3] Despite the berating he took for missing Fincher's wedding, Hough obviously enjoyed thoroughly his short time with the Delta hunter.

The following day Bobo was back at the Ivanhoe Club participating in a 20 mile run after a red fox. The next day he assisted in the bagging "of three coons and five possums on an all-night raid in Pigeon Roost Bottoms."[4]

By June of that same year, what William Faulkner would later call the "deswamp[ing] and denud[ing] and deriver[ing]"[5] of the Delta was proceeding at double time. That very month Geo. T. Houston & Co., a Chicago lumber firm, acquired from the Illinois Central Railroad for a price in excess of $1,000,000, "a tract of land seventy miles long and from eight to twenty miles wide, situated in Sharkey and Washington, counties, and on the Sunflower and Yazoo rivers," wrote Hough under the heading, "The Bobo Bear Country Gone." With "[t]wo branches of the Yazoo & Mississippi Valley Railroad... being extended into the property... the saw mills will soon begin their work," Hough predicted, adding that the same thing was happening to the remaining "hunting grounds" throughout the country. "This ends the Bobo Bear Country, which within a decade will be a thing of the past."[6]

Hough reported in September that Bobo had "been down in bed with fever for quite a while," but was at last up and around. Whether the fever was related to his ongoing eye problem or the result of some other malady such as the recurring malarial agues that afflicted many Mississippi Delta natives in those days, Hough did not say. Hough's report left no doubt, however, as to the general optimism that was a hallmark of the Bobo character. Despite doctor's orders to refrain from bear hunting and in total disregard of Hough's obituary for the "Bobo Bear Country," the old hunter's first act upon arising from his sick bed was to "buy twelve brand new hound pups" in anticipation of the beginning of the Bobo bear season the upcoming November. What would Bobo do, Hough wondered, "if he had to live in a city where he couldn't have forty or fifty hounds around the place?"[7]

Two months later Bobo was in Chicago for surgery necessitated by the "malignant growth" on his eye[8] first mentioned by Hough to his readers almost exactly a year before. Hough, for the first time, indicated the seriousness of Bobo's condition, at last admitting that the tumor had gotten "no better and [had] occasioned both Bob and his friends much uneasiness."

Though the problem obviously was taking its toll on the man, Bobo had ignored it for three years. In early November 1900, as he "was on the point of starting for a bear hunt in the bottoms," Bobo's "friends got about him and urged that he go to Chicago instead of the Delta cane brakes." The intervention worked. Bobo agreed and left for the north immediately for medical treatment, arriving in Chicago on Tuesday, November 6, 1900. He submitted to anesthesia and surgery for the removal of the tumor that very afternoon.

Hough visited Bobo in the hospital the next day. After what must have been a physically traumatic operation, Bobo already was sitting up and talking, declaring "he had never felt any pain at all." Though confined in his room by doctor's orders for a week, Bobo was up and dressed the second day and did not get back in bed again, except for his regular night's sleep. The surgeon told Hough he had never seen "a patient like Bobo...." Bobo would be on his way home immediately upon release from the hospital, Hough wrote, "unless [he] frets himself to death from being caged up...."

The depth of the friendship between Hough and Bobo is apparent from the fact that the Chicago editor of *Forest and Stream*, who, no doubt, had plenty to do to see to his part in the production of a national weekly sporting paper, spent four days talking with Bobo in his hospital room. In one of their conversations Bobo attributed his rapid recovery from his surgery to the fact that "[t]hings never did seem to hurt me much...." As an example, Bobo recalled a time he "was out in the woods, where a man was chopping wood." The ax slipped out of the woodsman's hand in mid swing. The bit of the ax, Bobo said, "struck me right square in the thigh" with the "handle sticking up in my face." How his leg was not ruined, Bobo could not figure. He knew the blade had buried itself in his femur, for when he pulled the ax out of his leg, he heard the same "cluck" an ax makes when it is pulled out of a tough chunk of wood. Despite the terrible wound, Bobo mounted his horse and rode for home, which was "a good ways" away. When he reached his house, he could not dismount without help. His "boot was full of blood," he told Hough, "and I fainted... and near bled to death." Bobo, Hough concluded, was "a pretty hardy sort of citizen" and a survivor.[9]

Hough, no doubt, understood the dire state of his friend's health and realized Bobo's time in the Chicago hospital could be the journalist's last chance to learn of the ways of the bruin from the master. Hough wisely used his time with Bobo to continue his "investigations in bear lore at the fountain head" by pursuing with the hunter a number of questions concerning the habits of bears.

Among other things, Hough and Bobo revisited a subject considered by the campfire during Hough's second visit to Mississippi in the fall of 1895: how a black bear eats a hog. While a wolf or a panther will kill a hog, Bobo told Hough, "a bear never troubles about that. He just begins to eat him, always beginning at the back of the neck." The bear, Bobo explained, "just lies right down on the hog's back" and goes "to work on him...." The Bear Hunter had seen many a hog "come home mutilated in this way," for "[w]hen a bear has eaten enough of a hog, he turns him loose." Bobo added that one of his neighbors "had a fine sow which came home with pretty near her whole back eaten off." From then on, Bobo told Hough, that sow's pigs were all "born with a sag or a hole along the back bone."[10]

Whether he expected Hough to believe that story, who can know?

Despite their conversations about Delta bear lore, Bobo's prospects for recovery must have been the real, if unspoken, topic foremost in the minds of both Hough and the Bear Hunter all the while they talked. Certainly there was never a sidelined outdoorsman who exceeded Bobo in zeal for the hunt and determination to get back behind a gun. Because the surgery had been on his left eye, the left handed hunter[11] naturally feared that he could lose all sight in that eye and thus his ability to shoot. During one of his visits Hough caught the Delta man "sitting up on the bed… trying to see if he could shoot from his left shoulder and use his right eye." Hough told Bobo that "a good many men are able to do this by means of cast-off gun stocks," a bit of information that "seemed to relieve his mind." Hough held out hope, however, that Bobo's "left eye has not yet lost its cunning, and that it will continue to look through the rifle sights for many a year yet to come."[12]

Within a matter of weeks, however, it became obvious to Bobo that he would not recover the use of the damaged eye. Not only was the eye "inefficient" and "more or less motionless in the socket," it was generally "a source of considerable annoyance" to the hunter. By April 1901 Bobo had made the decision to have what Hough had once described as his "cold blue shooting eye"[13] removed. In his April 20 column Hough reported that Bobo was again in the hospital in Chicago, this time recovering from the removal of the bad eye and "declaring that he is better in his mind again, can see much better out of his good eye, and that all he needs is a little exercise."

Again, Hough lauded Bobo's recuperative powers. The doctors, he told his readers, were of the opinion that Bobo was "a wonderful man physically, and confidently express[ed] the belief that his head could be cut off and that it would grow out again in the course of a couple of weeks." While it pained Hough to see "the old bear hunter… lose his shooting eye," he found it "a matter of very great congratulation that he [was] recovering so nicely from so serious a trial."

Meanwhile, Bobo was learning a new skill—the tying of the mule packer's "diamond hitch"—from Hough's friend, Billy Hofer, who had stopped by the hospital for a visit. Hofer had explained to Bobo the use of the diamond hitch by Western hunters to secure supplies and equipment to a pack saddle cinched to a mule's back, something all new—and very exciting—to Bobo. Bobo resolved to buy some pack saddles when he returned to Mississippi and to commence trail camping for bear in the style of Rocky Mountain hunters. With such an outfit and using the diamond hitch, Bobo determined, he could "put a little tent and a couple of weeks grub on the back of a mule and take one or two men and just go flying anywhere [he] want[ed] to... ." There would be no "need [to] bother about where we are going to stop," Bobo told Hough. "If we run out of corn or grub, I can send a man and a mule back with the pack saddle." Bobo, who just months before was concerned about the disappearance of the Delta bear country, now resolved, with the help of his newly developed pack saddle plan, "to kill all the bears in Mississippi" the following spring. Hough doubted not that Bobo would "wreak a horrible revenge on the bear family" once he was "turned lose again in good shape."

Bobo left the hospital on April 20, 1901, "as well as one could be," Hough wrote, "after so sad a misfortune as his."[14] Despite his health problems, Bobo seems to have continued bear hunting. Once source reported that he killed 43 bruins that year.[15]

In November 1901 Bob Bobo's sons, R. E. Bobo, Jr., and Fincher Bobo, joined the Ozark Lake Hunting and Fishing Club on its annual hunting trip. Named for an oxbow lake situated on the border of Bolivar County, Mississippi, and Arkansas County, Arkansas, the club was comprised primarily of prominent lawyers, businessmen, educators, and politicians, including Tennessee governor Benton McMillin.[16] The club members assembled in Memphis and traveled by the steamer *Kate Adams* to Sunflower Landing in Coahoma County. There the Bobo brothers boarded the vessel with saddle horses and their father's dogs for the short trip downriver to Ozark Lake. The elder Bobo, however, was not among the hunting party.[17]

It is not surprising that both Bobo brothers were together on the Ozark Club trip. The importance of family to the Bobos is obvious from the historical record. Almost every documented hunt and significant event involving any Bobo typically happened in the company of relatives or in-laws.

In January 1902, two months after his hunting trip with the Ozark Lake Club, Robert E. Bobo, Jr., was visiting in the home of his first cousin, Katherine Harris Hopson, daughter of Sheriff Nels Harris, brother-in-law and close friend to Bob, Sr. Whether the younger Bobo was ill when he arrived at the Hopson home, or whether he fell sick at some point thereafter, is not clear. On January 24, 1902, however, the *Clarksdale Challenge* reported that the preceding Tuesday, January 21, Robert E. Bobo, Jr, had died at the Hopson's home "[a]fter a week's illness of pneumonia...."[18]

Oddly, Hough appears to have made no mention on the pages of *Forest and Stream* of his friend's loss of his son. Indeed, Hough had been quiet on the subject of Bobo since the spring of 1901. That silence was about to be broken.

30 Bobo and the President

During the time the Bear Hunter was suffering the death of his son and experiencing health problems, the nation was undergoing traumas of its own. Much had transpired in the maturing republic since Hough's second bear hunting trip in 1895. There had been a presidential election—the new president, William McKinley, took office in 1897—followed by a war with Spain in 1898. Theodore Roosevelt, the man who some say was responsible for starting that war, was one of its heroes that same year. Elected vice-president when McKinley was reelected in 1900, Roosevelt became president upon McKinley's assassination in 1901, the same year Bobo endured the personal anguish of having his eye removed. The new President Roosevelt was about to shine the national spotlight on the Mississippi Delta bear woods and put Bobo back in the newspapers.

Roosevelt was a serious outdoorsman and the author of books on hunting and the outdoors long before he rose to national political prominence. He was on an outing in the Adirondacks, in fact, when he learned that McKinley's death had raised him to the highest office in the land.

Roosevelt was also a ground-breaking politician, especially regarding racial issues. New York schools had been desegregated during his tenure as governor of that state, and upon his accession to the presidency, he had sought the advice of Black educator Booker T. Washington and entertained him at the White House. While those may seem inconsequential things by today's standards, by the political mores of Roosevelt's time they indicated a coming fundamental change in societal and governmental attitudes.

Roosevelt would also leave in place one of the last vestiges of Reconstruction in Mississippi: a Black female postmistress in the Delta town of Indianola. In the Deep South, where vivid memories remained of the indignities suffered by many ex-Confederates during the not so long before ended Republican Reconstruction regimes, the Republican Roosevelt and his progressive racial policies were not very popular.

Roosevelt, though, was not without affection for the South. He had grown up hearing Southern hunting stories from his Georgia-reared mother and had read with his own unique enthusiasm "Wade Hampton's chronicles of Mississippi black bear chasing."[1] What better way for the president to cultivate some alliances and sympathies in Dixie than to go bear hunting in Mississippi? Mixing politics with bear hunting, after all, had been a hallowed tradition in the Magnolia State since at least 1841 when Seargent Prentiss, a then prominent Whig orator in Mississippi, made his famous Indian Mound Speech during a hunt in Sunflower County.[2]

Acquiring an invitation for a presidential hunting trip would prove to be no great problem. Roosevelt had many friends in the South, including John McIlhenny, of Avery Island, Louisiana, whose family created and marketed Tabasco® Sauce. McIhenny had served in Roosevelt's Rough Rider regiment during the Spanish American War. Perhaps more importantly, Roosevelt had appointed as U. S. Marshal for the Southern District of Mississippi one Edgar Wilson, the brother-in-law of then Mississippi Governor Andrew Longino. Wilson also had been designated by Roosevelt as the chief operative for reorganizing the Republican Party in the South.[3]

On June 1, 1902, the New York *Sun* announced that President Roosevelt had been invited to the Magnolia State. To political observers it probably came as little surprise to learn that Mississippi governor Longino had issued the invitation. Roosevelt, the article said, would "visit the state and take part in a grand bear hunt in the Yazoo canebrake, covering a large part of Sunflower, Coahoma, and Tallahatchie Counties," a "district… famous for bears and… said to be the best bear hunting region of the country."Bob Bobo, the press reported, would be in charge of the hunt.[4]

The following fall, John Parker, then a prominent New Orleans businessman who would later become governor of Louisiana, wrote a letter to Bob Bobo. Parker's correspondence, Bobo later told his friend Tom Divine, "referr[ed] to [an upcoming] hunt and ask[ed] about the dogs." Parker, at least in Bobo's recollection of the letter, did not mention the president's name and Parker's name was unknown to Bobo. It is not surprising that Roosevelt's name was not mentioned. The President wanted the details of his trip "kept as secret as possible" lest an onslaught of reporters force him to cancel the hunt.[5] Assuming the man was just another "someone who wanted to come down and hunt, as they often did," Bobo tossed the letter aside and thought no more of it.[6] Bobo had no further communications from Mr. Parker.

The presidential entourage was to roll into Smedes Plantation in Sharkey County in the lower Mississippi Delta on Thursday, November 13, 1902. The Sunday before, while Tom Divine had been visiting at the Bobo plantation, Bobo had mentioned in passing the letter from the Parker man from Louisiana. Divine, who recognized the name and knew of Parker's role in the Presidential hunt, explained to Bobo "the identity of Mr. Parker" and on whose behalf Parker had inquired about the Bobo bear pack. Bobo "was extremely sorry, and said he would have been glad to have gone with the [President's] party or to have done anything to make the Presidential hunt a success" had he realized the inquiry involved Mr. Roosevelt.

Bobo also told Divine that he had a prior commitment to friends from Illinois coming to Coahoma County for a bear hunt. Bobo entered the woods with his guests shortly after his visit with Divine. Five days later Bobo returned from his hunt just as the president's band of hunters was arriving. With the Roosevelt party was Illinois Central Railroad president Stuyvesant Fish who also invited Bobo to hunt with the President. Bobo declined.

Why, the press wondered, did Bob Bobo refuse a command performance for the President of the United States? One newspaper announced that Bobo, as a loyal son of the Confederacy, "had refused to allow his pack of hounds to associate with the President's because [Roosevelt] had invited Booker T. Washington to dine with him at the White House."

Bobo was incensed. While he was indeed a loyal son of the South, for precisely that reason he would never have been inhospitable to the president of the United States. Interviewed at the Gaston Hotel in Memphis, Bobo told the *St. Louis Post-Dispatch*: "I cannot imagine how any man could have circulated such a false story so monstrous in its exaggeration and revolting in detail. I lay claim to being both a patriot and a gentleman," continued the outraged Bobo, "and I cannot persuade myself to believe that my friends placed any confidence in the awkward and uncouth attack made against the President at my expense."[7]

In defense of his friend Tom Divine would later assure the press that Bobo "never entertained any other than a sincere desire for the success of the Washington hunting party."[8]

Bobo's good friend and one man public relations firm, Emerson Hough, heard of the alleged Bobo slight to the President up in Chicago and immediately began preparing a defense of the Mississippian to appear in the next issue of *Forest and Stream*. First, though, Hough's column gave Bobo's analysis on an entirely unrelated matter: the periodic phenomenon of gray squirrel migrations. Only then did he turn to the matter of the Roosevelt bear hunt.

"It is late now," he wrote, "to speak of President Roosevelt's bear hunt in Mississippi, but in view of certain inaccurate statements which have appeared in different parts of the country, Bobo wishes to be set right before the sportsmen, and is anxious that the *Forest and Stream* shall have what will perhaps be the only accurate statement of the matter published."

The confusion over Bobo's role, or lack thereof, in the presidential bear hunt, believed Hough, had at least part of its root in politics. Without explaining further, Hough said that as to that aspect of the hunt, "we need not concern ourselves." It was a Memphis paper, however, Hough said, that "printed the somewhat astonishing announcement that Col. Bobo had declined to enter the hunt at Smedes, and assigned an unworthy reason for this action."

Bobo had been outraged by the story. In hopes of disabusing the public of the notion that he was anything other than respectful of President Roosevelt, he had taken "out a card"[9] in several papers denying the allegation, a "card," in those days being the term for a paid space in a newspaper containing a response to a libelous charge.[10]

Bobo's card read as follows:

> Mr. Stuyvesant Fish wired Capt. A. A. Sharp to ask me to join the President's party. When I got the message I had been five days in the woods, hunting with personal friends from Champaign, Ill. I regretted more than words can express that I could not see any honorable way to comply with Mr. Fish's request, and I so wrote him. I should have been delighted to join the President's friends and to aid in extending him every courtesy, which would be due not only the man but his exalted office. The President of the United States is never slighted by any true American, and anything published to the contrary as coming from me, no matter

by whom related, is so related under total misapprehension
and in error.

(Signed) R. E. Bobo.

Having published his friend's card in his own column, Hough added
some praise of Bobo and his dogs. "The Bobo bear pack," Hough said, "is
by comparison the only one in the State of Mississippi. It is a pleasure to
see it when it moveth itself aright on its accustomed grounds; and when
Bobo goes out after bear, he gets bear." Hough also offered this advice to
those planning any future chief executive bear hunts in the Delta: "the next
time the President wants a bear hunt, it is to be hoped he will go to Bobo
direct." [11]

31 The Curtain Falls

As anyone who had been reading *Forest and Stream* over the previous year must have realized, Hough knew that there would be no next time. Although Hough had given Bobo's public reason for failing to join President Roosevelt's party—the hunter and his pack were spent from five days in the woods with a group of Midwestern hunters—there also was a private, personal reason for Bobo's declining to participate in the chief executive's bear hunt that would soon be apparent to all.

Even when the press first announced Gov. Longino's invitation to President Roosevelt, Hough had understood the end was near for the Bear Hunter. He had written at that time: "There are bears yet to be had in the canebrakes of Mississippi, and there are good bear packs to be had, but it is doubtful if, even plucky a man as he is, our dear friend Rob Bobo would be able to join in even this notable bear hunt."[1]

Perhaps it is indicative of the continued development of the friendship between the two men that for the first time—in print, at least—Hough referred to Bobo as "Rob," the name by which Bobo was called by his family.[2] Bobo's decision to have his surgeries in Chicago must have said as much about his affection for Hough as it did about the skills of the physicians in that city.

Bobo, Hough told his readers, once more had been under medical treatment concerning the tumor that had taken his left eye the year before. He had undergone a course of radiation therapy in Chicago[3] and had spent a considerable amount of time in clinics and hospitals in Memphis, Tennessee, and in Champaign, Illinois. Months before the presidential hunt Hough had written that "Bobo has been, and no doubt now is, in a critical condition."

Besides "destroy[ing] one eye for the old bear hunter, [the cancer] had taken away nearly all of one side of his face." Despite Bobo's "splendid courage and iron nerve," which Hough had witnessed "both in the field and under the surgeon's knife, it would be little short of a miracle," Hough wrote, "if he were able now to pike the saddle for even a day or so of his beloved sport of bear hunting."

For all Bobo's excuses for his failure to hunt with the Roosevelt entourage, the fact is the great Bear Hunter was physically unable to join the presidential party. Even as Roosevelt was still in Mississippi, Bobo was leaving Coahoma County for emergency treatment in Chicago.[4] He died there on December 17, 1902, three days before Hough's defense of the hunter appeared in *Forest and Stream*.

Bobo's death was greeted with shock and sadness from Coahoma County to Chicago and in many quarters around the country. In Memphis the press reported that "strong men" unrelated to Bobo by blood or marriage openly wept upon hearing of the death of their friend and hunting companion.[5] Surely Tom Divine was among those mourners. The extent of Bobo's influence and friendships is evident from the fact that his death was a news item, not only in Hough's column in *Forest and Stream*, but in the Memphis *Evening Scimitar*,[6] the St. Louis *Post-Dispatch*,[7] and many other papers.

Two days after Christmas, 1902, Hough announced Bobo's death to the *Forest and Stream* readership. "Last week," he wrote,

> there was printed in these columns some mention of that veteran bear hunter and prominent citizen of Mississippi, Col. R. E. Bobo. It is sad reading to offer in this time of cheer, yet I am obliged to chronicle the death of this friend, who was also the friend of thousands of other sportsmen in America. Col. Bobo died in this city at eight o'clock on Wednesday morning last, and his remains, in charge of his son and a friend, left this city yesterday morning for their final resting place in the soil of Mississippi. The immediate cause of death was an acute complication which resulted in something like severe jaundice, the liver being badly involved. Bobo was accustomed all his life to hunt in the malarial swamps of the cane brake country. Perhaps the swamps finally had their revenge on the man who had done so much toward conquering their secrets, and so much toward changing that country from a wilderness into a land of civilization.

"It was my sad office," continued Hough, "to help Col. Bobo's friends to assemble his effects." Hough found Bobo's pockets contained "telegrams and letters bearing upon the recent presidential bear hunt in Mississippi," evidence of how deeply the false reports concerning his failure to hunt with the president had affected the dying hunter. Hough could not resist once more defending his friend.

Hough did not think it any exaggeration to call Bobo "without question, the most expert hunter of the black bear which this country ever knew. … There was no master of bear hounds in all the country," he was confident, "like this same energetic Mississippian, as I am sure earlier mention in these columns must have shown fully." Moreover, added Hough, it was Bobo's "delight to take his friends out upon these hunts." That was Hough's chief reason for believing the charge against Bobo in the matter of President Roosevelt was so absurd. "No one who knew Bobo," he wrote, "doubts that he was the soul of courtesy and hospitality." The Bobo home was open practically to all in "the old time Southern fashion."

By way of example Hough pointed to an incident "a few months" before Bobo's death. There had been a railroad mishap near Bobo station stranding some 155 passengers and train crewmen in the Delta backcountry without breakfast. Every one of them "tramped over to Bobo's house and there they were fed, each and all of them." Although they offered to compensate Bobo for the food, the planter refused. He had "never charged a man for a meal in all his life," he told them, "and was too old to begin it then."

That Bobo graciousness was apparent to all and it won admirers for him wherever he went. "I may say also," Hough added, "that, during his stay [in Chicago], he made a wide circle of friends who not only respected but loved him, even" after knowing him only for those few days at the end of his life.

Bobo not only had been rich in friends, he had accumulated considerable financial wealth, as well. "He died possessed of a fortune of $200,000 or $300,000 (a tremendous amount of capital in those days)," wrote Hough, "all of which he had amassed by his own energy and foresight. He was at one time offered $100 an acre for land for which he paid less than $2 an acre." The soaring value of that Delta cropland, however, was not without its costs: "Col. Bobo lived to see fertile plantations stretching over much of his old bear hunting grounds.…"

"'There will be no one to take the place of Bobo, the bear hunter," wrote Hough. He added this observation: "The Delta is changing very rapidly."

That was an understatement, indeed. Between the railroads, which Hough described as "going through [the Delta] at distances of every few miles,"[8] and the ever-improving levee system being constructed under the supervision of Bobo's friend, T. G. Dabney, the Delta was becoming a much easier place in which to live. By the late 1800s, settlers, attracted by the fertile and relatively inexpensive land cleared by logging concerns, already had begun to pour into the Delta in previously unheard of numbers. From 1880 to 1900 the Delta population had increased by well over 100,000 persons.[9]

Bear hunting could not last much longer in the Delta, Hough knew. "The Bobo bear pack will perhaps be scattered," he supposed, but predicted that

> [t]he memory of its owner will not readily die, certainly not in the minds of those of us who have ridden with him, slept with him in camp, and known that friendship which arises only between men who know each other for what they are in the outdoor air, wide of all the artificialities and conventions of city life. I knew Bobo and loved him, and am only one of very many of whom the same might be said. I feel sure it is my privilege to speak for them in expressing this sense of loss. R. E. Bobo was no ordinary man. He was a big man and was rapidly forging ahead into still bigger stages of life. We cannot have too many American citizens of his type, men of courage, fearlessness and a fine and delicate sense of personal honor.[10]

EPILOGUE

Bob Bobo was gone, but Emerson Hough, as he would confess a couple of years after the great bear hunter's passing, could "never get done thinking" of his "old friend, Col. Bobo."[1] It is difficult to overstate the gaping hole Bobo's death left in the North American sport hunting fraternity. A bear hunt with Bobo had been an adventure coveted by notables from across the United States. Not three weeks after Bobo's death Hough recorded in his "Chicago and the West" column that a former Chicago alderman, one William Kent, and a Mr. Fred M. Stephenson, who recently had killed deer in Wisconsin and Michigan and hunted grizzlies and mountain lion in the Sierra Madre of Mexico, were "intending to have a hunt with the Bobo pack of bear dogs in Mississippi this winter...." Their plans were derailed, of course, by "the sudden and wholly unexpected news of Col. Bobo's death...."[2]

California manufacturing executive and hunting and fishing writer, Charles Cristadoro, sang Bobo's praises on the pages of *Forest and Stream*, as well, though he confessed that he only had "met him once in Mr. Hough's office in Chicago." Nonetheless, he named Bobo among the ranks of "Daniel Boone, Davy Crockett and the scores of other mighty hunters who have crossed the silent river."[3]

Bobo would continue to influence the *Forest and Stream* readership long after his death. When sportsmen gather in person or in print arguments often arise concerning the existence (or not) of some unusual creature or natural phenomenon some have claimed to have observed but that others, usually in the scientific community, doubt. Recall the horn snake discussion in which Hough found himself embroiled in Tennessee the year he first journeyed southward to hunt with Bobo. Even in death Bobo was at the center of such a controversy.

Shortly before he died, Bobo visited Hough in his Chicago office. During the course of their conversation that day Bobo told Hough of his observing on four occasions great migrations of gray squirrels. These spontaneous movements covered large areas of the countryside with the squirrels letting no obstacles block their movements. Bobo said they even swam substantial streams, including the Mississippi River. Not only had Bobo witnessed such squirrel migrations, Hough reported, he had "seen parties... in boats... picking up the squirrels by the tails and throwing them into baskets or bags in the boat"[4] to supply meat for their own tables or, perhaps, to be sold in a local market. After all, as late as 1895 writer Horace Kephart reported that squirrels were bringing 60 cents a dozen in the Memphis game markets, which, according to Kephart, made the squirrel, pound for pound, and effort for effort, a more profitable quarry than bear.[5]

Forest and Stream correspondent, naturalist, and celebrated painter, Martin Johnson Head, of St. Augustine, Florida, would have none of it. Writing under the appropriate pseudonym of Didymus, the biblical Greek name for Thomas, the doubting apostle,[7] Head declared: "Col. Bobo was a great bear hunter," and if he "had stated that he had seen bears in countless thousands swimming the Mississippi and rowed among them..., picking them up by the tail and throwing them in a basket, I wouldn't have dared to doubt it." The fact that Bobo did not say the hunters killed the squirrels before throwing them "in the bags and baskets," though, caused Head to reject that entire idea of migrating squirrels.[8]

Readers from Wisconsin to Quebec[9] and from New York[10] to Georgia[11] immediately came to Bobo's defense, all attesting to the reality of the squirrel migration phenomenon. Lest their voices go unheeded for their failure to marshal evidence from "naturalists," as happened to the proponents of the existence of the "horn snake," contributors quoted from such observers as John James Audubon and John Bachman and even from the Ohio Geological Survey[12] as proof of the occurrence of squirrel migrations.[13]

Confronted with such overwhelming opposition, Didymus conceded defeat and offered "a hatful of apologies...." As far as Hough was concerned, however, the question of squirrel migrations was "settled when Col. R. E. Bobo described what he had seen."[14] Thus, Bobo won a final victory. One cannot fail to note in Hough's articles following Bobo's death his posthumous promotion of the Bear Hunter from captain to colonel.

By the publication of *Forest and Stream*'s July 4, 1903, issue, the squirrel migration argument had been replaced by another burning question: "whether or not a horse can swim and carry a man on its back" simultaneously.[15] While Bob Bobo himself was not the direct instigator in this controversy, he bore responsibility indirectly, for the question had arisen while DeSoto County, Mississippi, resident and friend of Hough, W. A. Powel, was visiting at the Bobo plantation, which was administered by Fincher Bobo since his brother's and father's deaths. Another guest at the Bobo place insisted a horse could not carry a rider and swim at the same time. "[H]e had seen it tried on a wager at Meridian, Mississippi," Powel said, with "fourteen different horses from livery stables being tried, and not one of them being able to keep his head above the water" with a rider on his back. Powel pursued the question, though, and came to the conclusion that a horse could indeed swim with a rider. Hough added that many a rider had discovered that if he sat "low and well back the horse [could] get along." Such, however, was not the optimum way to swim a horse, Hough noted. "[I]t is much better to slip off of the horse, take the down stream side of him and hold on to the saddle horn or to his mane."[16] There scarcely could be a definitive answer (by Hough's way of thinking), however, for Bob Bobo was no longer around to settle the question.

In January 1904 a J. B. Morrow of Massachusetts wrote to *Forest and Stream* to ask where he might find a "good bear dog." Hough, of course, immediately thought of the Bear Hunter. "The lamented death of my friend Col. R. E. Bobo," Hough wrote, "makes it impossible to put this question before the greatest authority on bear dogs we ever had...." Hough did note that the "Colonel's" son, "F. G. Bobo," or Bob Bobo's friend in Byhalia, Mississippi, Mr. W. I. Spears, might know of some good bear dog stock.[17]

That same year another sign of the passing of an era in the Bobo Bear Country became manifest: the first automobile was spotted on the streets of Clarksdale, the seat of government for Coahoma County.[18]

Hough and *Forest and Stream* had little more to say about Robert Eager Bobo. No doubt Fincher continued to hunt bears at least occasionally, but there is scant evidence of it. The bear population being already in drastic decline in Coahoma County at the time of his father's death, Fincher, most likely, found seriously diminishing returns in the bear hunting enterprise and discontinued the famous Bobo hunts. As Hough had expected would happen, the famous Bobo bear pack was sold.[19]

Sometime between 1906 and 1910 an unexpected call came for Fincher from New Orleans. His mother, Anna Prince Bobo,[20] who had run away with the railroad man Norton some two decades before, was on the line. Mr. Norton had died, she told Fincher, and she had terminal cancer. She wanted to come home to die.

Betty Bobo Pearson, Fincher's granddaughter, tells it this way: "Fincher was understandably furious that his mother had left him, and at first said, 'no,' but my grandmother [Bessie], who was a saint, said 'She is your mother, and of course we are going to welcome her.'"

When the dying Anna arrived she had with her the big trunk she had left with years before, a small boy whose relationship to her was never explained, and a pet monkey. Upon Anna's death a short time later, her relatives came to Coahoma County for her funeral. When they left, they took the little boy and the monkey with them. Anna's grandson Bob, who told the story of Anna's return many times, always would end it by saying, "I sure did hate to lose that monkey."[21]

There remained pockets of bears scattered about the Delta—in the Carrier Woods in nearby Panola County, for instance. The highly publicized Roosevelt hunt only had added to the glamour and romance of the Delta as a sporting destination, and the out-of-state hunters continued to come—especially the wealthy from Memphis and even the Northeast—seeking out the last strongholds of the Delta's rapidly disappearing bear population. The late University of Mississippi history professor, James Silver, wrote accounts of the outings of two such wealthy hunters in 1957 for the *Journal of Mississippi History*.

The first of those hunts occurred in October 1905, almost three years after Bobo's death, when multi-millionaire Herman B. Duryea hosted what must have been among the more extravagant bear hunts ever undertaken in the Mississippi Delta or elsewhere. Besides his home among the society elites in Newport, Rhode Island, Duryea owned an expansive hunting preserve in Hickory Valley, Tennessee, in prime fox and quail hunting country about 70 miles east of Memphis. Duryea, who had made a fortune breeding and racing thoroughbreds and who would later become the only person known to history to have hired a train for a dog's funeral, knew how to be extravagant. After securing permission to hunt in the Carrier woods, Duryea had his employees begin preparation for his Delta bear affair.

First to arrive at the bear camp were some 25 trunks of silverware, linens, clothing, and jewelry, including Mrs. (Nelly) Duryea's $60,000 necklace. Next came butlers, cooks, and Nelly Duryea's personal lady-in-waiting. Also in the Duryea entourage was James (Jim) Monroe Avent, co-founder of the nationally known bird dog field trials held annually at Grand Junction, Tennessee, and perhaps the foremost dog trainer of his day. Avent, who was Duryea's neighbor in Hickory Valley as well as his dog handler for field trials,[22] drove some 30 saddle horses down from Tennessee to be used as mounts by the guests. Meanwhile, 100 bear dogs were arriving by train. Even a pet bear named Susan was brought in for use in educating the young dogs.

"[T]he hunt went smoothly for a few days and the [bear] skins began to pile up," wrote Silver.[23] The press reported, in fact, that Nelly, with a single rifle shot, killed her first bear—a 300 plus pounder—"after twenty-four hours' continuous chase."[24]

"Then it began to rain." The rain came, in fact, in a deluge reminiscent of the great flood of Noah—fourteen inches in 36 hours. The sluggish Delta bayous quickly rose from their typically low fall levels and overflowed into the surrounding woods as torrents of water rushing down from the hills to the east added their volumes to the more than a foot of rain that had already fallen in the bottoms.[25]

As the water levels rose to between four and six feet, the hunters, leaving a camp watch of servants, made for the Yazoo-Delta Railroad station some miles to the west as quickly as possible to see Nelly, her jewels, and her maid off to Hickory Valley by way of Memphis. Once Nelly and company were safely en route to Hickory Valley the men of the party caught a southbound train from Memphis to Sardis, one of the two seats of Panola County, to begin rescue and recovery operations for persons and property still in the bear camp.

A hundred loggers temporarily out of work due to the rains and flooding were recruited for the effort. Any boat that could be found was pressed into service, as well, to be carried by train to Bobo Lake,[24] a body of water named for the Bear Hunter's kin, and paddled from there. When the rescue party arrived they found the camp guard detail had eaten most of the good food, drunk all the liquor, and gone absent without leave. The horses brought down by Jim Avent were close to drowning. The dogs, able to perch on flotsam drifting among the trees, fared somewhat better. About the only piece of equipment that had remained dry was a single wagon that had been left on relatively high ground. In it, defending her position against all challengers, was Susan the bear. Amazingly, all the dogs and horses had survived.

Three weeks passed before the rain and high water abated enough to permit extraction of the animals and equipment. In the meantime the workers kept the horses, dogs, and bear out of the water with makeshift platforms and rafts and fed them with provisions brought in by rowboat.[25]

As prodigal as Duryea's 1905 hunt had been, Robert M. Carrier, the lumberman for whom the Panola bear woods were named, would organize an even more extravagant bear outing in 1919. According to Professor Silver's account, Carrier's bear camp, which included numerous tents, was pitched about three miles to the east of Lake Carrier, formerly known as Bobo Lake, between the Tallahatchie and the Little Tallahatchie Rivers in western Panola County.[26] The temporary city boasted sizable kitchen, quartermaster, and dining tents. There was even a lounge tent for use by the hunters. All the tents were furnished with tables and chairs built on the spot and were well provisioned with "half the visible supply of groceries in Memphis" purchased by Carrier for his guests. A line was strung to the telephone company in nearby Sardis in case guests required contact with the outside world. For those who felt no urgent need to use the phone, there were other distractions in camp, including 185 quarts of bonded whiskey shipped by river boat all the way from Caruthersville, Missouri. James Silver likened the whole thing unto "a Hollywood medieval tournament set...."

The guests were described by a lumber trade journal of the time as an "assorted bevy of lumbermen, politicians, businessmen and others." A first hand observer attested that he "counted a hundred millionaires" among the campers. Professor Silver doubted that figure. There were, he said, actually only "about 75 hunters" in the camp. Moreover, probably only a paltry dozen or so qualified as true millionaires, Silver supposed. Among those notables were the oil rich governor of Oklahoma and Col. Tom James of Tallahatchie County, Mississippi, a champion hog farmer and cattleman. West Virginia vaudeville comedian and raconteur, Riley Wilson, was hired for a princely $1000 to provide the humor, and he apparently earned his wages.

Millionaire bear and lion hunter,
Paul J. Rainey. *Photo from author's collection.*

Also in the company was adventurer Paul Rainey, recently returned from extensive safaris in Africa.[27] An Ohio born playboy and heir to his family's coal and coke fortune, Rainey had first come South for the bird dog field trials at Grand Junction, Tennessee. Impressed by the quail hunting he experienced in northeast Mississippi's hill country during that trip, Rainey had acquired 13,000 acres in that region's Tippah and Union counties where he operated a farm and hunting preserve. When not cavorting with the socialites of New York City and Newport, Rhode Island, Rainey frequently was with his horse and hounds hunting bear in Panola County.[28] It was Rainey, in fact, who had purchased the last of the Bobo bear dogs from Fincher Bobo, which hounds and their descendants became part of the pack Rainey used in his many mounted African lion hunts that were inspired by the style of the old Delta bear hunters.[29]

Despite the presence in the Carrier bear hunting camp of all manner of diversions, Silver notes in his account that "a few bear skins were actually brought out of the woods...." Silver leaves no doubt, however, that camp shenanigans, especially gambling, were the focus of most of those in attendance. The "tireless hunters never wearied," says Silver, quoting the facetious words of a reporter on the scene, "and the shooting was fast and furious, sometimes continuing far into the night," referring, in all probability, to shooting craps.[30]

Gambling certainly appears to have been a chief activity of the Carrier hunting party. In one all night poker session, Silver said, "Riley Wilson dropped his thousand dollar fee in a matter of minutes." The Mountain State comedian could afford the loss. The young banker from St. Louis who lost two years' salary could not. When the game finally ended "in the glare of the morning sun," however, the generous winners made a gift of their respective takes to the young man who, no doubt, returned up river both richer and wiser, having learned a merciful and memorable lesson about gambling with millionaires.[31]

Back in Coahoma County Fincher Bobo continued his father's farming operations, but the bear hunting side of Delta life was almost a thing of the past. An article that appeared in the Sunday edition of the Memphis *Commercial Appeal* on November 17, 1918, illustrates well the changes wrought in the Bobo Bear Country since the death of the Bear Hunter. Whereas the press once carried stories of oversized bears or panthers killed by Bob Bobo, Fincher, his sole heir, was now famous for gigantic specimens of another species.

The Memphis paper, it seems, had been amazing its readers over a number of days with successive stories about exceptionally large sweet potatoes. First, the paper reported a ten pound potato, then a twelve pounder, and then an 18 pound one. "But if you were surprised by the size of the potatoes we have" reported previously, the article read, "prepare now to be knocked down. We have in our office a sweet potato weighing 30 pounds grown on P. B. Abby's plantation" near the Delta town of Webb, Mississippi.

News of an even more titanic tuber would be forthcoming from the *Commercial Appeal:*

> [T]he day following [the newspaper office] received a potato grown upon the plantation of F. G. Bobo, of Bobo, Miss. . . . sent to us by Guy Clark, editor of the Clarksdale (Miss.) Register. The potato weighs 32 pounds—32 pounds.

We have the potato in our office. We are printing a picture
of these two potatoes. Notice the foot rule between them.
We have these potatoes in The Commercial-Appeal office,
second floor, Second and Court.[32]

Sic transit gloria mundi.[33]

Emerson Hough, meanwhile, continued his very successful writing
career. Shortly after the United States entered World War I the then 60
year old Hough joined the U. S. intelligence service with the rank of
captain. Thus, Capt. Hough became one of the few of all his old Delta bear
hunting comrades to hold a title actually derived from a military officer's
commission. He died on April 30, 1923, about two months shy of his 66th
birthday and a week after attending the Chicago premier of the film version
of his book, *The Covered Wagon*.[34] His life was not an especially long one,
but, as he once said of the bear dog's allotted time, it was "full of action, as
that of the warrior should be…."[35]

That same year the Bear Hunter's sole surviving child, Fincher, called
"Captain Jack" in his later years, suffered a stroke. Fincher's son, Bob, thought
a visit to relatives on the Mississippi Gulf Coast would be beneficial to his
ailing father. While Bob remained in Coahoma County, Fincher and his wife,
Elizabeth "Bessie" Brock Bobo, Bob's wife, Lenora Corley Bobo, and their 18
month old baby girl, Betty, spent a few days on the Gulf Coast with their kin.

On Halloween night the Bobos were returning home. Lenora was driving. Fincher sat in the front passenger seat. Bessie held her granddaughter
Betty in her lap in the back seat. In Glendora, Mississippi, about 30 miles
south of Clarksdale, Lenora stopped at a railroad crossing—the same railroad that had been built across the Bear Hunter's land some 35 years before
—to await the passing of a northbound train. As the last cars rolled by the
brakeman leaned out from the caboose and waved to Lenora to proceed
across the tracks. Unbeknownst to the brakeman, another train was fast
approaching the crossing. As Lenora drove onto the tracks the second train
struck the Bobo family Buick broadside.

Fincher "was killed instantly." Bessie's pelvis was broken. Lenora, at
the time expecting a baby (who would be the fourth Robert Eager Bobo),
miraculously was unscathed. Baby Betty was thrown from the car onto the
cowcatcher of the locomotive.

When the engineer finally brought the train to a halt the toddler rolled off onto the side of the tracks. A little boy found her, picked her up, and carried her back to her mother. Baby Betty appeared unhurt.

The same train that stuck the Bobos took Fincher's body and the survivors back to Clarksdale. Subsequent x-rays indicated that baby Betty had suffered a broken left arm and right shoulder blade. Betty Bobo Pearson, like her great-grandfather, apparently was little inhibited by bodily injury. She recovered fully and, as of this writing, is 93 years old.[36]

Fincher G. "Captain Jack" Bobo (r.) (1872–1923) and son, Robert Eager Bobo (1901–1979). *Photo by Mary Brock Bobo, from original, courtesy of Fincher Gist (Jack) Bobo.*

The old plantation house burned in 1928. If the "old home had left a diary," Fincher's widow, Bessie Bobo, told WPA interviewer Florence Montroy in 1936, "it would have been full of rich hunting lore,"[37] it having seen so many fascinating hunts and hunters. Unfortunately, neither the house nor its original owner left any records of the hunts and hunters they hosted.

The clearing of the last large tracts of timber continued in the 1930s and 1940s as increasing mechanization made farming large acreages easier and cheaper. Descendants of the Bobos who pioneered the Delta, not surprisingly, were at the fore of that modernization of farming. Beginning in the 1930s International Harvester began testing its prototype mechanical cotton pickers at Hopson Plantation. The owners of the Hopson place, Howell Hopson, Jr., and Richard Hopson, were the grandsons of the Bear Hunter's sister, Katherine "Kate" Rivers Bobo Harris, and her husband, Sheriff Nels Harris. In 1944 the Hopson Plantation became the first farming operation to plant and harvest a cotton crop entirely by mechanical methods.[38]

Three years later, in 1947, Fincher's granddaughter, Betty Bobo—the same one who had been thrown from the touring car in the accident that killed Fincher—married William Wallace Pearson. "Bill and I... went to Chicago on our honeymoon," Mrs. Pearson wrote in recent correspondence. "Dad"—the third Bob Bobo—"was in touch with [Emerson Hough's] son, who invited us to his apartment and took us to the Stockyard Inn for a steak dinner!"[39]

The descendants of Robert Eager Bobo have thrived and prospered. Bobo the Bear Hunter is well represented by his progeny today in Clarksdale, the county seat of Coahoma County, in the state capital of Jackson, and elsewhere.

The bears have not fared as well. Although there continued to be a legal hunting season on bruins in Mississippi until 1932, by that year only a few remnant populations, probably no more than a couple dozen animals, total, remained in the State. The bears were never entirely extirpated from Mississippi, however, and sightings, though not frequent, continued to occur over the next fifty years.

Since the 1970s confirmed bear sightings have become increasingly common, including some in Coahoma County. The bruin's numbers are rapidly increasing.

There is still no bear hunting season in Mississippi, but the black bear, like the family Bobo, is a survivor. At the rate the population of this iconic Delta game animal is expanding it is entirely reasonable to expect that there once more will be Mississippi Delta bear hunts in the not too distant future.

The bear is back; the Bobos never left. Given those two facts, the Bobo story cannot be said to end here. There are chapters to the chronicles of Bobo, the Bear Hunter, no doubt, yet to be written.

APPENDIX I
Location of the
Bobo Bear Country

Bobo left no record of exactly where he hunted, but some of those who wrote about him left helpful clues from which I have drawn conclusions about the location of the Bobo hunting grounds. I emphasize that what I have written in this appendix is merely my opinion and that only. I cannot certify to the accuracy of my ideas about where Bobo hunted, but I do believe they are reasonable based upon the evidence.

Bobo's earliest hunting as an adult, which took place during the years following the War Between the States, appears to have been done on the western side of Coahoma County and in northwestern Bolivar County. The first of his hunting trips of which we have record occurred on Anise Ridge immediately following the Bear Hunter's return from the War. Based on the location of what is now called "Annis Ridge" on some maps, the Anise Ridge of Bob Bobo's time appears to have been approximately two miles northwest of the present site of Bobo, Mississippi. The county road that connects the hamlets of Bobo and Sherard runs over much of Annis Ridge.

We also know from James Chism's 1876 letter to the Memphis *Daily Appeal* that Bobo hunted in the Friar's point vicinity in northwestern Coahoma County during the postwar years.

When T. G. Dabney first attempted to interview Bob Bobo in 1886, the Bear Hunter was not at home, but hunting along the Hushpuckena River, which rises in southwestern Coahoma County, flows southward into Bolivar County, and from thence into northwestern Sunflower County where it joins the Sunflower River.

Apparently, prior to his first hunt with Emerson Hough in 1895, Bobo hunted almost exclusively west of the Sunflower in Coahoma and northern

Bolivar counties—at least Hough reported that Bobo was unfamiliar with
the country east of the Sunflower at that time.

THE FIRST HOUGH HUNT

Bobo was a quick study, though, when it came to bears and their
habitat. On his first hunt with Hough the party left Bobo station and rode
about 20 miles to a logging camp operated by Bobo's son Fincher on the
east side of the Sunflower River. That 20 miles, of course, was an estimate,
and probably was not 20 miles as the crow flies but a wandering 20 miles
along wriggling bayous and around sloughs and brakes. On the other hand,
the settlers back then surely reckoned distances as well or better than we
do today. In any event, we know the camp was on the east side of the
Sunflower because Hough reported fording the stream about two hours
before reaching the place.

Hough says that on the following day the party hunted along "the
breast of Surveyor's Lake." I find no record anywhere of a Surveyor's Lake in
Coahoma or Sunflower counties or anywhere else in the Mississippi Delta,
for that matter. I do find on the Coahoma County highway map (and on
nineteenth and early twentieth century maps) a "Sevier Lake." I am confident
that either the northern writer misunderstood the southern accents of his
hosts and wrote "Surveyor's" for "Sevier's," or else the typesetter could not
read Hough's handwriting and spelled out the more familiar "Surveyor"
rather than the somewhat unusual surname, Sevier. Sevier Lake (also called
Sevier's Lake) is located on the west side of the Sunflower, about four miles
east and slightly north of Bobo.

I also suspect that Hough confused his lakes or days. While it is quite
likely the party hunted around Sevier Lake on the way to the Bobo camp—
they would have gone by it on their way—it is unlikely they hunted there
the first morning in camp. Bobo and Hough were east of the Sunflower that
second day, many miles from Sevier Lake, and Hough makes no mention of
going back across the Sunflower. Probably, they either hunted around Sevier
Lake the first day, or they hunted around one of the lakes on the east side
of the river, like Plummer Lake or Roundaway Lake, and Hough confused
the names.

In any event the hunting camp in which they stayed on that first trip was an active logging camp. Hough described the accommodations as "three shacks, or cabins, made of upright shakes, two used for sleeping rooms and one for a kitchen."

THE SECOND HOUGH HUNT

Hough revealed less about the location of his second hunt after his articles on the first hunt caused a flood of nonresident hunters into the area, much to Bobo's consternation. Hough does not tell us the route he took to the hunting camp, although we know from a Memphis *Commercial Appeal* article of that time that the hunters traveled to camp from the railroad station at Shelby in Bolivar County.

Hough's description of his ride by hired wagon to the camp suggests he traveled from Shelby to the Sunflower River following an easterly route roughly paralleling the Hushpuckena River and coinciding with the present Blue Cane Road and/or Mississippi Highway 32. The Hushpuckena enters the Sunflower from the west about a mile and a half upstream from the Sunflower's confluence with Black Bayou. From Hough's description of the route he followed from Shelby to Bobo's bear camp in 1895, it is my guess that the camp was on the east side of the Sunflower between the confluences of the Sunflower with the Hushpuckena and the Sunflower with Black Bayou. Hough also reported that, after he killed his bear, the hunting party followed "the big bayou" back to camp. No doubt he refrained from using the real name—Black Bayou—in order to maintain as much secrecy as possible concerning the location of the camp in hopes of preventing the onslaught of out-of-state hunters that occurred after he reported his first hunt with Bobo.

I also suspect that the camp for the second hunt was the same as the camp for the first hunt. Hough did not take a camera on the first hunt—it was shipped to New Orleans with some other of his baggage before he left Bobo Station for the bear camp. There exists, however, a photo of two buildings that meet the description of the sleeping quarters of the first and second bear camp(s). It shows two cabins made of "upright shakes" as he described in his account of his first hunt. The buildings are connected by a common wall with the space between fenced in, as he described on the second hunt. In the yard in front of the buildings are odd scraps of wood, such as one would expect to find around a logging camp. Five men, a saddled horse, and at least 15 dogs are visible in and around the buildings, suggesting the picture was taken at the bear camp or at the Bobo plantation as the hunters prepared to begin their hunt. I am not sure which.

No doubt the "upright shakes" were characteristic of a typical construction style. It may be that those buildings were outbuildings at the Bobo plantation house. They do meet the description of the sleeping quarters at the Bear Camp, though. Also, Hough describes the second camp as being an inactive logging camp. Either the camp was no longer used by Bobo for logging or it was a different camp from the first. Some serious work in the land records of the Coahoma and Sunflower county courthouses, no doubt, would shed some additional light on these questions, but that is beyond the scope of this book—at least of this edition.

By the time of Hough's second hunt with Bobo in the fall of 1895 Bobo's chief hunting ground seems to have been further down in the Black Bayou drainage. Black Bayou begins in southeastern Coahoma County and from there inscribes a great backwards S shape some 20 miles or more long moving southward into northern Sunflower County. It then turns back northward before curving toward the west and, then, southward again to its confluence with the Sunflower River. On the inside of the lower part of the S tributary bayous branch out like many boney fingers. The headwaters of another bayou form several other stream branches inside the upper part of the S. Other streams join Black Bayou just before its confluence with the Sunflower. Between these many small tributaries were ridges of slightly higher ground, the type of drier terrain conducive to cane growth. These ridges are still visible on modern topographic maps—see, for example, the U. S. Geological Survey's Baltzer quadrangle map. Hough describes riding through ravines and dry bayou beds interspersed with cane in the area of Black Bayou. He also describes the great windfall called the Hurricane, which we know from Mary Hamilton's writings ran for about 18 miles from the Sunflower River to Camp No. 1 of the Mississippi State Penitentiary at Parchman, located at the main gate of the prison on U. S. Highway 49, between the present-day towns of Rome and Drew in northern Sunflower County.

When Hough finally killed his bear, which he shot in the cane between the dry bayous near the thicket called the Hurricane, he was about six miles from camp. A six mile ride to the southeast from the spot where I place the Bobo bear camp for the first hunt would put a hunter right in the midst of the bayous feeding into Black Bayou and the ridges between them.

From these clues it appears that Hough was hunting with Bobo in 1895—the second hunt—all through the Black Bayou drainage and almost entirely in northern Sunflower County on what is now the grounds of the state penitentiary at Parchman.

Later, Bobo must have hunted far down into Sunflower County and maybe even into Quitman, Tallahatchie, Leflore, and Washington Counties, for Hough seems to have considered the entire Sunflower drainage to be included in what he called the "Bobo Bear Country."

·

APPENDIX II
The Bobo Photographs

To the best of my knowledge, there are but three photos extant of Robert Eager Bobo (1847–1902), the Bear Hunter: the Studio Portrait; the Pet Bear Photo; and the Horse and Hounds Photo. I first saw those three pictures in the office of the fourth Robert Eager Bobo (1924–2013) in 1987. There is also a studio portrait of the Bear Hunter's son, Fincher Bobo (1872–1923), with his son, Robert Eager Bobo (1901–1979) (the third Bob Bobo).

THE STUDIO PORTRAIT OF THE BEAR HUNTER

A copy of the studio portrait of the Bear Hunter to which I refer is among the illustrations in this book. The original is in the possession of the Bobo family. It appears beyond dispute that the photo was taken at Bingham and Hilliard photographic studio in Memphis, Tennessee, in 1895. I draw that conclusion from the humorous article that appeared in the November 17, 1895, edition of the Memphis *Commercial Appeal* entitled, "Extinction of Large Game." The article was accompanied by a line-cut illustration obviously made from that same portrait. The writer of the article said that the line-cut came from "a photograph made by Bingham last week." The author also indicated that Bobo sat for the portrait at the instance of his friend, Tom Divine. There may be other evidence on the photograph itself of its origins, but I have not had the opportunity to examine it that closely. From the similarity between the photo and the *Commercial Appeal* line-cut, however, I think it plain that the portrait is the one made by Bingham and Hilliard studios.

THE PET BEAR PHOTOGRAPH

The second Bobo photograph shows a man in the yard of what I am supposing is his home, the plantation house described by Emerson Hough. The yard looks bare and swept clean, as was the practice in those days. The man appears to be enticing a chained and collared pet bear to stand on its hind legs by offering it a bit of food. The man's arm obscures his face, but I think it is safe to assume the man is Bob Bobo. His descendants say it is he. The man is feeding the bear with his left hand, and Bobo was left handed. He also is wearing the same style slouch hat we see in the Bingham studio portrait. My guess is that this photo was taken by Hough when he first arrived at the Bobo plantation and that the bear is the yearling female named Alice that so fascinated the writer. We know that Hough had a camera with him at that point but that he sent the camera on with some of his baggage to New Orleans before he began his hunt with Bobo the next day.

Two men stand behind Bobo. The one to the left in the photo is bearded; the one to the right has a long mustache. A half dozen or so dogs stand at the feet of the mustached man, looking toward him as if awaiting food. Perhaps the men are Bobo's plantation manager, who probably often fed the dogs, and Bobo's friend and hunting partner, Felix Payne, who kept some of Bobo's dogs for him. My guess would be that the man closest to the dogs and without a visible necktie would be the plantation manager. These are just suppositions, however.

To the left and in the foreground is a long, narrow trough of the type often used in those times to feed large numbers of dogs. There is what appears to be a stake to the right of the trough. Since it appears to be the stake to which the bear's chain is fastened, my guess is that the trough was for feeding and/or watering the bear.

At the left in the rear is a young man leaning against a small, a-frame, structure that is probably a chicken shelter. Such shelters are still common today in rural areas. Two or three chickens can be seen in the yard. I suspect the young man is Bob Bobo, Jr. Hough's narrative suggests the younger Bob was around when Bob, Sr., was showing Alice to Hough.

THE HORSE AND HOUNDS PHOTOGRAPH

This photo depicts Bob Bobo standing in front of a wooden plank fence closing an opening between two sheds made of upright boards with gaps between them. The buildings share a common roof. On the plank fence sits what appears to be a McClellan saddle. Leaning on the fence, his elbow on the saddle, is a man with a neat mustache. Tom Divine, perhaps? There are also two men in the background and another in the foreground. Fifteen or so mixed breed dogs are bunched in front of the fence as if awaiting something. Some have obvious staghound and foxhound blood. The yard before the buildings appears grassy and is littered with sticks and wood chips

It is hard to know exactly where this photo was taken. When I first saw it in the office of the late Bob Bobo (1924–2013) in Clarksdale, Mississippi, in1987, I assumed that it was taken on the Bobo plantation, and that the connected buildings served as a stable or barn. I do not remember, but perhaps I got that idea from Mr. Bobo.

Many years later when I read the descriptions of Hough's hunts with Bobo and the buildings used for a hunting camp by the hunters on those outings, I decided that the buildings in the photo fit the description of those cabins. Hough, in his account of his first hunt with Bobo, describes buildings made of upright shakes as the quarters used by the bear hunters in their camp. In his account of the second hunt he describes the hunters' quarters as "two good-sized houses of one room each, built of upright boards and connected by a roof and back wall. The front side of the space between was left open, except for a low fence and gate...."

Those descriptions led me to believe that the Horse and Hounds Photo was a picture of the bear camp used on one or both hunts by Bobo and Hough. Since we know Hough did not have his press camera with him on the first hunt, I assumed that he took the Horse and Hounds Photo in camp on the second hunt. The wood litter in the yard suggests the place could be a logging camp, such as the logging camp(s) used by Bobo for his hunt headquarters on the trips with Hough.

On the other hand, the photo may have been taken near the plantation house about the same time the Pet Bear Photo was made. Bobo has a hunting horn around his neck—recall that he called in "a few dogs" with his horn on Hough's first day in Coahoma County—and there are some dogs in the photo. Also, since firewood was the chief fuel used in the Delta in those days, wood scraps would have been common anywhere wood was chopped or hauled. There are no guns to be seen in the photo, either, as one would expect in a hunting camp, although the guns could have been inside one of the sheds.

Hough, we know, had a camera with him on the first trip to the Bobo Plantation. There is no mention of a camera on the second trip. To my knowledge, he never published any photographs of either trip in *Forest and Stream*. So, it could well be that the photo was made when Bobo was giving Hough the plantation tour his first day at Bobo Station—if, in fact, the photo was made by Hough. All we can do is make educated guesses. We probably will never know for certain. I do believe it is almost certain, however, that Hough took that photograph.

FINCHER G. BOBO/ROBERT E. BOBO PORTRAIT.

Also included in the book is a portrait of Fincher Bobo (1872–1923), the Bear Hunter's son, and his son, Robert E. Bobo (1901–1979), grandson of the Bear Hunter. In the photograph, Bob appears to be teenager. Probably the picture was made around 1915 or 1916. Fincher, of course, was killed in a car and train accident in 1923 when the third Bob was 22 years old, eight years younger than Fincher was when the Bear Hunter died. I have known the Bobo family since I was a child and can vouch for the fact that the Bobos of the present generations still have amazingly strong family resemblances to the Bear Hunter, his son, and grandson.

APPENDIX III
Bobo Miscellany

Since publication of *The Bear Hunter: the Life and Times of Robert Eager Bobo in the Canebrakes of the Old South* in the first hardback edition in December 2015 I have come across additional information that I thought should be included in any subsequent edition of the book. Accordingly I am including that material in this appendix to this paperback edition of *The Bear Hunter*.

THE GUN ACCIDENT THAT KILLED PETE

Bobo once recounted a number of hunting and gun accidents with which he was well familiar, among them being one that killed a Black plantation hand named Pete.[1] In 1871 a Peter Bobo of Friars Point, then the seat of Coahoma County, Mississippi, was killed in a hunting accident. The newspaper account of his death reported that a Cary Strayhorn was using his cane knife to extricate his mule from a tangle of vines when his gun discharged striking Peter Bobo in the forehead and killing him instantly.[2] A Black farm laborer by the name of Peter Bobo lived in Friars Point in 1870.[3] Although the Bear Hunter said the gun that killed the Pete of whom he spoke was carried by one Sam it seems likely that both stories described the same incident. Both victims had essentially the same name and both were shot in the forehead. The variations in the details may have resulted from an attempt by Bob Bobo to protect the identity of the negligent hunter. More probably a faulty memory was to blame for the differences in Bobo's version – after all, the Bear Hunter told his story of the accident to Emerson Hough 29 years after the Peter Bobo of Friars Point was killed. It also is possible that Emerson Hough in writing the account conflated stories or otherwise misunderstood the facts. In any event it seems unlikely that two different Black men so named both would have been killed in such similar hunting accidents in the Coahoma County of Bobo's day.

BOBO SHOOTS IN SELF DEFENSE

The Bobos had a lady cooking for them and living in their home who apparently had fled to the Bobo place seeking refuge from her abusive outlaw husband, one Henry Simpson. One evening as Bob Bobo lay sick in bed and Mrs. Simpson was preparing supper, her husband, despite having been warned by Bobo not to come onto his property, strode into the house wielding a "very large knife" and declaring "that he had come to kill Bobo, then her and afterward burn the house." Bobo rose from his sick bed and moved toward the kitchen only to see Simpson advancing toward him with a knife in hand. Bobo pulled a pistol brought from his bedroom and fired just as Simpson struck at him with the knife, hitting Bobo's gun. Simpson fell dead "with the knife in one hand and a half-drawn pistol in the other." Bobo surrendered to the authorities but the matter was dismissed by a judge as "a clear case of justifiable homicide." The Bear Hunter expressed regret for the incident but asserted that Simpson had left him no choice in the matter.[4]

BOBO THE PANTHER HUNTER

Bobo once told Emerson Hough that he killed what appears to have been among the largest black bears every taken in Mississippi – or anywhere else, for that matter – a behemoth that weighed some 700 pounds field dressed.[5] I came across a story in an 1880 issue of the *Magnolia Gazette* reprinted from the *Vicksburg Commercial* in which Bobo claimed to have killed the state's record panther. "Mr. R. E. Bobo, the 'champion bear hunter' of Coahoma County," the paper reported, "recently killed a panther which measured nine feet ten inches from tip to tip, stood four feet high, and one of his feet which was measured covered eight inches from toe to toe." According to the paper, Bobo claimed the cat "the largest panther ever killed in Mississippi."[6] The measurements of that feline, no doubt, were exaggerated, most likely by someone other than Bobo. Ben Lilly, who probably killed more panthers than any other hunter of the lower Mississippi Valley, once wrote that the largest such cat he had ever seen measured from its nose to the tip of its tail 8 feet, 9 ½ inches, a full one foot shorter in length than the one attributed to Bobo.[7]

Exaggeration by newspapers on the subject of panthers was not usual in those days. Recall that another editor, four years before, had reported that Bobo had killed a panther that measured eleven feet, four inches, from "tip to tip,"[8] which, no doubt was a gross exaggeration based at best on stretching, in addition to the truth, the still wet skin freshly removed from the animal as far as it could be extended.

BOBO'S HOSPITALITY

On the occasion of the first through train leaving Memphis on the newly constructed Louisville, New Orleans and Texas Railroad, the September 18, 1884, issue of the Memphis *Daily Appeal* reviewed the stations along the line, reporting this about a stop at the Bear Hunter's plantation in Coahoma County:

> Bobo, the thirteenth, station, is eighty-four miles away and is the home of the great bear hunter and typical frontiersman, Bob Bobo, whose heart is as big as a house and whose house is always open, the abode of hospitality. Bobo Station is situated on the crown of Anise Ridge, the center of a tract of 2000 acres, which never overflows and which is covered with box elder, grapevines and pawpaws. It is as rich any of the alluvial bottom lands.[9]

Bobo's renowned skill at mixing mint juleps – recognized as far away as Washington, D. C. – augmented his native hospitality. "[T]he simple odor" of one such Bobo concoction, wrote one reporter, "would cause the corpse of an old time southern gentleman to turn over in its tomb."[10] Unfortunately Col. Bobo's mint julep recipe and technique have been lost to history.

ANNA PRINCE BOBO

Regarding the mysterious Anna Prince Bobo, wife of the Bear Hunter and mother of his children, who ran away with the railroad man, I have found but little more information. I wrote in the first edition of this book that Anna was "of Memphis." That was not entirely correct. The Princes, like the Bobos, originally came from South Carolina and were early settlers in Coahoma County where Anna was born in 1849. They moved to Memphis some years later, however, and were living there in 1868 when Anna and Bob were married.[11] After the wedding the young couple left Memphis "immediately for the home of the groom at Friar's Point, on the steamer Natoma."[12]

Anna Prince Bobo made her last appearance in the press in 1885 before disappearing with her railroad man. The March 20 issue of the *Friars Point Gazette* that year reported that "[p]rominent among the guests" at the ball "at the Grange Hall on Tuesday evening last [was] Col. R. E. Bobo . . . accompanied by his estimable lady . . . ."

Later that evening things got a bit out of hand as they sometimes could in the 19th century Delta. In Bobo's party that spring night at the Grange Hall was one Jack Kennedy, employed by a Capt. Hicks as a stave cutter. At some point during the festivities Mr. Kennedy repaired – for refreshment no doubt – to one Fogerty's Saloon where he was "approached by a long haired, wild-eyed[13] tramp" who accused him of plotting with Capt. Hicks to "beat [the tramp] out of his pay." Kennedy, offended by the allegation, launched a punch "straight from the shoulder" that decked his adversary. The tramp rose, found his opening, and "plunged his knife into Mr. Kennedy's left side." Fortunately for Kennedy the dull blade did not fully penetrate the heavy coat and vest he wore and the resulting wound was not serious. Unfortunately there was such a crowd in the saloon that night that the assailant made his escape before the arrival of the town marshal and his deputy.

Mr. Kennedy was assisted to one Dr. Coleman's office and shortly after treatment proved well enough to return to Fogerty's Saloon. The correspondent who reported the incident for the *Friars Point Gazette* noted that he and Col. Bob, as he called Mr. Bobo, became so "very solicitous concerning the welfare of the wounded man" that they insisted on leaving the Grange Hall to visit Mr. Kennedy at Fogerty's establishment "every quarter of an hour." So impressed was Mrs. Bobo with the pair's attention to their friend at the saloon, the gentleman wrote facetiously, that she remarked that they "would make splendid hospital nurses."[14]

BOBO THE MARKSMAN

I failed to emphasize the Bear Hunter's skill with the rifle in the first edition of this book. Apparently Bobo's mastery of that weapon was widely known in his lifetime. The author of the newspaper account of the Grange Ball at Friar's Point referred to Bobo not only as a bear hunter but as a celebrated "crack-shot."[15] Even after his death a Washington *Evening Star* reporter gave as an example of his shooting expertise "that he could put a bullet through the bung-hole of a barrel rolling down hill without chipping the edges."[15] Where a hill could be found in the Delta from which to roll a barrel the writer did not say.

MILITARY TITLES AMONG SOUTHERN PLANTERS

I noted earlier in this book that Bobo was posthumously promoted by Emerson Hough from Captain Bobo to Colonel Bobo. The Grange Ball article, however, written in 1885, also referred to the Bear Hunter as "Col. Bob," the earliest such reference to Bobo I have seen. Prolific outdoor writer and horticulturist D. B. Weir, of course, had called him Major Bobo as early as 1882.[16] I can recall no other references I have seen to Bobo prior to his death using a military title other than "captain."

The proliferation of military titles among southern planters who never held officers' commissions is a mystery to many. I gave one explanation for that in *The Bear Hunter*. A backwoods scribe who signed his work only as Tuckahoe offered another theory in a May 24, 1883, issue of *Forest and Stream*. Tuckahoe said the practice stemmed from antebellum days when military titles among southern planters were so common that had a "modern Napoleon" fired a few shells into plantation country "he would have bagged a 'little general' at every pop." Tuckahoe explained "for the benefit of the future historian" how the system worked. Such titles, he contended, "were bestowed in accordance with the number of cotton bales upon which the individual planter stenciled his brand." In those days "there were no captains . . . . The shipper of his five score bales never ranked lower than Major. When the packages of the fleecy staple readied to double that number he was promoted to Colonel, and when he rolled the comfortable figure of 500 out of his gin house, it was "Glad to meet you, General." If there were "brevets" for the intermediate numbers, the writer knew of none, unless, perhaps, it was "Judge."[17]

Col. George D. Alexander, a native of Virginia, whose title was bestowed on him by the Arkansas legislature when he was made founding commandant of that state's military institute in 1850[18] and who later served as a Confederate major during the Civil War,[19] wrote his observations on the subject in his journal in January 1848 after taking passage on a steamboat bound for Camden, Arkansas, via the Ouachita River.

> We were struck with a peculiarity which we had often heard of but never so strikingly experienced of every man being called by some pompous title. Not one passenger on board who was a resident but had a title and was formally introduced by the appellation General A., Col. B., and Major C., or Judge D. We remarked that none were ever less than majors, as one never goes amiss in giving the appellation above mentioned to any man to whom he is introduced. To call one by the plain title of mister would certainly be followed by the politest kind of an invitation to a breakfast of pistols and Bowie knifes [sic].[20]

Bobo, of course, did not become a planter until after the War Between the States when Captain apparently became an acceptable title for a planter, at least in Mississippi.

BOBO THE PUBLIC CITIZEN

Bobo's fame nationally is documented in the first edition of *The Bear Hunter*. That notoriety, though, well preceded Hough's visits. An 1890 article in the *Indianapolis News*, four years before Hough's first Mississippi hunt, in relating facts on the fine bear hunting opportunities in the Yazoo-

Mississippi Delta, noted that "Bobo's place is in this region," as if the readers would know who Bobo was. It was a country, the article continued "where Congressmen and public men have been so often invited on bear hunts."[21]

Even as his fame grew nationally Bobo took on leadership roles in the Coahoma County area. In 1887 Bobo's fellow citizens selected him to serve as one of three men to organize a local chapter of the newly formed Delta Farmers Association in his county supervisor's district.[22] That same year he also was elected as one of Coahoma County's delegates to his Congressional District's Democratic Party convention.[23] Bobo's son, R. E. Bobo, Jr., was appointed as a cadet to the United States Military Academy at West Point in 1893,[24] yet another indication of the Planter's increasing prominence. The Bear Hunter, always the progressive farmer, also was appointed to a task force charged with securing a state agricultural experiment station for Mississippi's Delta Region.[25] The Stoneville Agricultural Experiment Station, for many decades now a fixture in Washington County, Mississippi, two counties south of Coahoma, no doubt is the fruit of that group's efforts. Bobo also would serve as an officer in the local agricultural and stock breeders' association[26] and as chairman of the Coahoma County Democratic Party.[27]

1895 SPRING BEAR HUNT WITH BOBO

A not so public man, a Mr. M. M. Daily, of Duncan, Mississippi, known to Hough from the writer's visits South, wrote to *Forest and Stream* in early 1895, as follows.

> As you know, I managed Capt. Bobo's plantation last year. This year I am farming on my own account, planting some potatoes and cotton and raising some bear dogs. During the Christmas holidays we killed two large bears. Had forty-four dogs in the race, and they fought for about an hour before the bear was killed. I wished you were here, for they run over every man in the crowd, and finally Capt. Bobo had to kill him. The bear weighed 550 lbs. There are more deer here this winter than I have almost ever seen for ten years.[28]

In *Forest and Stream*'s May 4, 1895, issue Emerson Hough reported receiving on the morning of April 12 an express delivery from "our Mississippi friend, Mr. R. E. Bobo, of Bobo Station." The mysterious package – almost the size of a ham – proved to be the paw of a black bear – the largest Hough had ever seen, in fact – nearly three times the size of that of the largest bear" killed on Hough's Mississippi hunt the previous fall. "[I]f it had the projecting claws" of a grizzly, Hough wrote, "it would make a mighty respectable foot for" that species of bruin. The bear foot was "8 inches long, 5 1/4 inches wide, and 2 3/4 in. thick." Bobo sent Hough "a bear story" along with the foot. Hough published the account in the magazine's May 18, 1895, issue, with this introduction:

> Chicago, Ill., May 8.— A week or so ago I made mention of a very large bear paw which was sent me by our friend Mr. R. E. Bobo, the champion bear hunter of Mississippi and of the world, so far as I know. Mr. Bobo appends the story of the chase in which the big bear was killed, and from this it would seem that the bear chase had after all some revelations for him, even after so many years, experience at it. The weight of 600 lbs. is very large for the black bear, though Mr. Bobo told me he once killed one that weighed 700 lbs. after dressing. *Forest and Stream* must show this big foot, dried and shrunken as it must then be, in the exhibit at the sportsmen's exposition, and if anybody can tell any bigger true bear stories than these which have been coming from Mississippi, I reckon he will have to carry off the foot. But it will take more than 304 bears in one year to do it, and a black bear heavier than most grizzlies are thought to be will be necessary to beat the Mississippi record. Only the best of anything will get into the *Forest and Stream* exhibit, or get away with it.

BOBO'S BIG BEAR STORY

> A late hunt on the Sunflower recalls the pleasant times we had there last fall, when you were here. Our dogs being in full trim and the boys all anxious to go for a hunt, we arranged to leave Bobo station and round up at the Duncan place, that being as you know on the river at the east end of the tram road where we waited for the dogs,

when you and I were out there. In our party were Messrs.
J. R. Shield, Felix Payne, Mr. Heiler, Bob the Kid (my
son) and Tom Sims and Sam Russell, the colored boys [no
doubt the same Tom and Sam who would hunt with
Hough in November 1895]. We all started April 21, and
met successfully at the Duncan camp. Everybody told of
what sign he had seen and what we might look for on the
next day.

Early the following morning we left for the bit of
country known as Hell's Hundred Acres. When we got
near Mud Lake we heard Georgia Ann, Tom's favorite
dog, and everybody that knew the dogs said: "Yes, that's
all right." Then the whole pack went into cry, and away
we all went. The race went far to the north and then west
and south to the Pecan Bayou, then east to the river and
back west again. Crack! bang! bang! we could hear the
guns go along the tram road, then still for two hours and
a quarter a hard race went on, Tom and Sam and Mr.
Shield and everybody else getting a shot, but no meat.

At last the dogs caught and killed the bear, an 80 lb.
cub. We got back as fast as we could to the starting place,
knowing that the old she bear was not far away, and soon
Fly, Mr. Shield's favorite dog, gave mouth and off we went
again for a run of an hour and a half. We treed at last in
a big hollow tree, and the boys making a fire we soon
began throwing chunks at the hole, and after awhile Sam
put one in the hole and out came a 300 lb. bear, and was
on the ground before you could say what or how.

Well, you know the big knife I always carry, and this
came useful, for in a moment I had killed this bear with
the knife. The boys carved up the meat and we went back,
on the way discussing who should be called before the
Kangaroo court for doing all that shooting and missing —
the penalty of the court usually consisting of a shortening
of the guilty party's shirt tail by about 4 in. Our court
lasted till midnight, and I do not need say that some of
the boys had very short shirts on by that time.

The next morning we set out for some good grounds,
and very soon my favorite — the dog we could not find
when we were here — gave cry, and we knew a bear was
up. We gathered up, and came to the understanding that
we were to give this bear a chance for his life, and by fair
means take him without a gun being fired. The chase
went south a quarter of a mile and took a short turn to the

north of that tram road where I stationed you so often. We heard a gun go bang! bang! and then we heard a yell. "Now, boys," said I, "with forty-one dogs and no one to shoot the bear, I reckon we'll have some fun, and a little touch of high life in Mississippi bear hunting." We all tightened up for a hard run, but we got no run. It was all a disappointment. "What?" said I to Payne, as he came up, "you haven't killed it?"

"Yes," said Payne, with that honest look we all knew so well to carry the truth with it, "I did break the agreement. But that bear did look so black and fine that I shot and killed it before I thought — I did, honest!"

"Have you got your sack along to put the meat in?" I asked.

"Yes,"' said he, "I have. The bear only weighs 150 lbs."

"Well, keep that sack," said I, "for before our Kangaroo Court gets done with you, you are mighty apt to need it for a shirt."

Well, we got back to Pecan Bayou — you know where that is — and in a moment Ronco gave tongue again. We all closed in to see the size of the track, for it was in a sort of pond, a wet place. "Look! look!" cried Shield. "That track is as big as my horse's track."

It was indeed a monstrous track, and we laid plans to make no mistake in the run. I knew it might go south to the Hushpuckany River and cross and get clear away.

We rode to the front as best each could, two miles and a half to the river. At the bank I rode to the front and the bear turned back from the river and made for Hell's Hundred Acres, with me after him, and I reckon you know what that meant for followers. I rode hard a mile north and headed the pack all alone, the boys being far in the rear. Riding for the dogs, I came up with them, and at length saw a great black object going across a piece of burned cane, working hard to get to the cover a quarter of a mile away. I set spurs hard and heavy to my good horse Dan, and we closed with the bear. Holding my rifle like a pistol in my right hand and the reins in my left, I fired at the bear with the muzzle against its body, but the bear kept right on. Some of the dogs were within 5 ft. of him, and there were forty-one dogs strung out behind him. Fifty yards further I rode in and again placed the gun against the bear and fired, and down he came.

Off I piled on to him, and I tell you a 600 lb. bear and forty-one fighting dogs is something of a contract. A third time I placed the old rifle against the great animal and so I ended the hardest and most exciting bear race of my whole life, and my experience I think justifies me in saying this was one of the most pleasant hunts of the age.

I blew the call, and Shield and Payne, a quarter of a mile away, responded and came in. We had a general carving, for this bear was a monster indeed.

We had not had a dog scratched, and had killed four bears in two days, one of them this huge one. We thought this was the most pleasant hunt we had ever enjoyed. We all wished several times that you had been with us. When we pulled out for camp each man took all the meat he wanted and we had some of the finest hides we ever got. It is useless to say that when the court convened there were some short shirt tails, and Mr. Payne, who broke the rule by firing, had very little left of his shirt but the collar. We are making arrangements to have everything in good shape next fall, and you know you have a standing invitation to join us, something which you know too is not given to a great many. You have our best wishes.

R. E. Bobo.[29]

It is a shame Bob Bobo did not write down more of his hunting memories for he was indeed an entertaining story teller.

THE NEW YORK SPORTSMAN'S EXPOSITION

The first annual Sportsman's Exposition opened at Madison Square Garden in New York City on May 18. Over sixty dealers and manufacturers of sporting equipment from tennis raquets to rifles and shotguns to fishing tackle placed Exhibits in that celebrated venue. *Forest and Stream* sponsored an exhibit in the hall, as well. Visitors to that sporting journal's floor space saw a wide variety of persons and artifacts, including the female sharping shooting duo of Polly Cooke and May Clinton and impressive array of Native American hunting weapons. Also exhibited were the rifle given to Davy Crockett by the young Whigs of Philadelphia – lent to *Forest and*

Stream by the Alamo hero's grandson, Col. Bob Crockett, of Crockett's Bluff, Arkansas, and the big bear foot sent by Bobo to Emerson Hough.[30]

PRESIDENT CLEVELAND'S
HOPES FOR A HUNT WITH BOBO

According to news accounts of 1902, as recounted elsewhere in this book, Bobo was the intended guide for President Theodore Roosevelt's 1902 Mississippi Bear Hunt. The Bear Hunter's terminal illness, however, prevented him from serving in that capacity. Several years earlier, though, another president had expressed a desire to hunt the Sunflower River country with Bobo.

The Jackson, Mississippi, *Clarion-Ledger* reported in 1895 that President Grover Cleveland, having heard much of the great success of the famous bear hunter – no doubt from Emerson Hough's articles in *Forest and Stream* – spoke of visiting the Delta for a bear hunt. The Chicago Tribune confirmed that story. "The president," that paper said, "has long desired to go down into the Sunflower River country of Mississippi and try bear hunting. That region is the finest big game section of the South, and for some varieties the best in America. The pot hunter, the man who shoots game to sell, is utterly unknown there, and would be tolerated about 24 hours. The planters of Mississippi do not preserve their deer and other wild game for men from Chicago and other places to shoot and sell. With a judicious system of game protection the result has been that there is an abundance as would scarcely be credited. Col. John [sic] Bobo, a planter, about 100 miles below Memphis, killed in one year 200 bears, besides panthers, deer and other beasts. When [Mississippi] Senator [Edward C.] Walthall told the President this story and assured him he was not drawing the long-bow Mr. Cleveland said he must try to have a hunt in that region, and it is possible he may take the outing this winter. Col. Bobo is not only the greatest bear hunter in his State (Gen. Wade Hampton used to be), but a most agreeable host as well. He owns a fine estate and lives handsomely inplanter style. There is but one difficulty in attending a visit to him. It is almost impossible to get away."[31]

The Bear Hunter, Robert Eager Bobo, was a man of much energy and many abilities whose life came to an end far too soon. No doubt there are many other stories about the man out there in the historical record awaiting discovery. If you come across any not included in this book I hope you will share them with me.

If you enjoyed this book, be sure to have a look at ***Hunting Bear Bear and Panther in the Old South: The Writings of Dr. Henry J. Peck of Sicily Island, Louisiana***, with introduction and notes by James T. McCafferty and also published by Canebrake Publishing Company.

BIBLIOGRAPHY

Historic Delta Research Changed Cotton Farming. March 12, 2012. http://msucares.com/news/print/agnews/an08/080103.html (accessed April 14, 2014).

1880 Census about Fincher Gist Bobo. 1997–2013. http://search.ancestry.com/cgi-bin/sse.dll?rank=1&new=1&MSAV=1&msT (accessed November 8, 2013).

1900 United States Federal Census About W. A. Powell. 1997–2013. http://search.ancestry.com/cgi-bin/sse.dll?rank=1&new= 1&MSAV= 1&msT=1&gss=angs-g&gsfn=W.+A.+&gsfn_x=XO&gsln=Powel&gsln_x= XO&msydy=1900&msypn__ftp=Marshall+county%2c+ mississippi&cpxt= 0&catBucket=rstp&uidh=mm1&msydp=10&cp=0&pcat=ROOT_ CATEGORY&h=55179730&db=1 (accessed June 11, 2013).

1910 Census about Fincher Gist Bobo. 1997–2013. http://search.ancestry.com/cgi-bin/sse.dll?rank=1&new=1&MSAV=1&msT=1&gss=a ngs-g&gsfn=Fincher+gist&gsln=Bobo&msydy=1880&msypn__ ftp=Coahoma+County%2c+Mississippi%2c+USA&msypn=681&msypn_ PInfo=7-%7c0%7c1652393%7c0%7c2%7c (accessed November 8, 2013).

Evans, David, ed. "Afro-American Folk Music from Tate and Panola Counties, Mississippi." *Library of Congress.* http://www.loc.gov/folklife/LP/ AfroAmFolkMusicMissL67_opt.pdf (accessed November 9, 2013).

Alexander, George D. "A Sight Worth Seeing." *The American Field,* May 1883: 417, 418.

—. "Hunting Sketches—No. 4. The Death of the Big He Bear.– Fishing in the Hushpuckany." *The American Field,* November 25, 1882: 358–359.

—. "Hunting Sketches—No. 2. Booby's Encounter with a Ten-Year Old He Bear." *The American Field,* November 11, 1882: 328–323.

—. "My First Bear Hunt." *The American Field,* 1882: 291.

—. "The Big Mound Near the Hushpuckany." *The American Field,* August 25, 1883: 177–178.

Alexander, George D. "The Black Bear." In *The Big Game of North America,* edited by George O. Shields, 247–278. Chicago, Illinois: Rand, McNally & Company, 1890.

Alexandrov, Vladimir. *The Black Russian.* New York, New York: Atlantic Monthly Press, 2013.

Allen, Max. *Female Mountain Lion Screaming for Mates in Front of Trail Camera.* Edited by Yiwei Wang. October 10, 2012. http://www.youtube.com/ watch?v=hM2Sw8dsMDQ (accessed November 22, 2013).

American Kennel Club. *The Complete Dog Book.* 19th ed. New York, New York: Wiley Publishing, Inc., 1998.

Annis Brake Coahoma County. 2013. http://mississippi.hometownlocator.com/
    maps/feature-map,ftc,1,fid,666278,n,annis%20brake.cfm (accessed
    September 10, 2013).
Audubon, John James. "Hunting the Cougar, or American Lion; and Deer
    Hunting." *The Edinburgh New Philosophical Journal,* April–June 1831:
    103–15.
Auk, The. "Minor Ornithological Publications." October 1890: 389.
Backwoodsman. "The Ferocity of the Black Bear." *American Field,* December 18,
    1886: 383.
Barnes, S. D. "In Bruin's Stronghold." *Forest and Stream,* September 25, 1890:
    186.
Barram Bobo. 2011–2012. http://www.mytrees.com/newanc/South-Carolina/
    Born-1776/Bo/Bobo-family/Barram-Bobo-bo001087-2.html (accessed
    September 27, 2013).
Barrum Bobo. March 19, 2008. http://www.findagrave.com/cgi-bin/
    fg.cgi?page=gr&GRid=25374425 (accessed September 27, 2013).
Bartlett, John. *Familiar Quotations.* 12th ed. Edited by Christopher Morley.
    New York, New York: Little, Brown and Company, 1951.
Beers, Henry Putney. *The Confederacy: A Guide to the Archives of the Government
    of the Confederate States of America.* Washington, District of Columbia:
    National Archives and Records Administration, 1986.
Belant, Jerry. "Mississippi: A Home to Roam for Black Bears." *Mississippi Wildlife,*
    Summer 2013: 40–41.
Beldon, A. L., ed. "Bears." *Fur Trade Review,* June 1, 1894: 260.
Biographical and Historical Memoirs of Mississippi. Vol. 1. Two vols. Chicago,
    Illinois: The Goodspeed Publishing Company, 1891.
Birge, B. E. "Squirrel Migrations." *Forest and Stream,* March 28, 1903: 245.
Black Bear Color Phases. 2013. http://www.bear.org/website/bear-pages/
    black-bear/basic-bear-facts/16-black-bear-color-phases.html (accessed
    November 11, 2013).
Black Flies or Buffalo Gnats. Oklahoma State University Division of Agricultural
    Sciences and Natural Resources. http://entoplp.okstate.edu/ddd/insects/
    blackflies.htm (accessed March 18, 2014).
Blaine, Delabere Pritchett. *An Encyclopaedia of Rural Sports.* Third. London:
    Longmans, Green, Reader, and Dyer, 1870.
Blankenstein's Homepage. 1997–2013. http://www.blankensteingenealogy.net/
    generation_8_page_4.htm (accessed September 28, 2013).
Blankenstein's Homepage. July 4, 1997–2013.
    http://www.blankensteingenealogy.net/generation_6_page_1.htm (accessed
    September 28, 2013).
Block, W. T. *The Big Thicket Bear Hunters Club of Kountze.* Edited by William T.
    Block III. William T. Block III. 1998–2012. http://www.wtblock.com/
    wtblockjr/BearHunters.htm (accessed May 23, 2013).
Blue Flag. University of Florida. 2014. http://plants.ifas.ufl.edu/node/206
    (accessed April 20, 2014).
Bobo, Fincher Gist (Jack). "Letter to Author." Clarksdale, Mississippi, August 31,
    1987.

Bobo, Mrs. Fincher Gist, interview by Florence Montroy. "Robert Eager Bobo." *Historical Research Project of Coahoma County.* Clarksdale, Mississippi: United States Works Progress Administration for Mississippi, (November 20, 1936).

Bowden, Charles. "Return to the Arkansas Delta." *National Geographic,* November 2012.

Boyd, James Robert. *The Westminster Shorter Catechism.* Philadelphia, Pennsylvania: Presbyterian Board of Publication, 1859.

Browse Ancestry Archive By Surname—Barram Bobo. 2011–2012. http://www. mytrees.com/newanc/South-Carolina/Born-1776/Bo/Bobo-family/Barram-Bobo-bo001087-2.html (accessed September 27, 2013).

Buckingham, Nash. *De Shootinest Gent'man and Other Tales.* New York, New York: Rowman & Littlefield, 2000.

C., C. "On the Sunflower River." *Forest and Stream*, November 3, 1892: 379.

Cabinet Card Photos. http://historic-memphis.com/memphis/cabinet-cards/cabinet-cards.html (accessed April 14, 2014).

Cahalane, Victor H. "The American Cats." In *Wild Animals of North America*, edited by Merle Severy, 400, 212–213. Chicago, Illinois: National Geographic Society, 1960.

"Calendar." *University of Notre Dame Archives.* January 15, 2010. http://www. archives.nd.edu/cgi-bin/author.pl?c189207.xml+38 (accessed January 11, 2013).

Carter, Cathy. "The Black Bear In Mississippi." *Mississippi Outdoors*, December 1981.

Carter, Graye Harris. "Untitled Reminisences."

Cavalier. "Arkansas Game Grounds." *Forest and Stream*, May 27, 1886: 349.

Chesser, Barbara Russell. *Remembering Mattie.* Sunstone Press, 2008.

Chicago Tribune. "The Younger Boys." March 27, 1875: 7.

Chism, James G. "Editors Appeal (Letter to the Editor)." *The Memphis Daily Appeal*, November 15, 1876: 4.

Citizen, Old, interview by Mrs. J. L. McKeown. "Outlaw Days." *Historical Research Project of Coahoma County.* Clarksdale, Mississippi: United States Works Progress Administration for Mississippi, (1935–1942): Series 447, Box 10677, Outlaws File.

Clarion-Ledger. "Delta Lands." November 7, 1890.

Clarksdale Challenge. "Died." January 24, 1902: 3.

Clarksdale Daily Register. March 28, 1938.

Cobb, James C. *The Most Southern Place On Earth: the Mississippi Delta and the Roots of Regional Identity.* Oxford, Mississippi: Oxford University Press, 1994.

Cohen, Hennig. *Humor of the Old Southwest.* Athens, Georgia: University of Georgia Press, 1964.

Col. George Richardson Phelan. http://www.findagrave.com/cgi-bin/fg.cgi?page=gr&GRid= 101871360 (accessed May 10, 2014).

Col. George N. Saunders. September 28, 2006. http://www.findagrave.com/cgi-bin/fg.cgi?page=gr&GSln=SAU&GSpartial=1&GSbyrel=all&GSst=27&GScntry=4&GSsr=1361&GRid=15924942& (accessed September 27, 2013).

Commercial Appeal. "Extinction of Large Game." November 17, 1895, Sunday
    Morning ed.: 11.
Commercial Appeal. "One Potato Weighed 30 Pounds and Another Potato Weighs
    32 Pounds." November 17, 1918: 12.
Cristadoro, Charles Albert. "An Embarrassment of Literary Riches." *Forest and
    Stream*, January 20, 1903: 24.
Cross Keys House, Union County (S.C. Hwy. 49, Cross Keys). South Carolina
    Department of Archives and History. http://www.nationalregister.sc.gov/
    union/S10817744005/ (accessed September 27, 2013).
Cullen, John B. *Old Times in Faulkner Country.* Baton Rouge, Louisiana:
    Louisiana State University Press, 1976.
Cunliffe, Juliette. *The Encyclopedia of Dog Breeds.* Bath: Paragon Publishing, 2002.
Cuvier, Baron, Edward Griffith, Charles Hamilton Smith, and Edward Pidgeon.
    The Animal Kingdom. Vol. Two. London: George B. Whittaker, 1827.
Dabney, Augustine Lee. "In Bear-Trap Peril." *Forest and Stream*, February 1,
    1896: 94.
Dabney, Thomas G. "Bruin in the Canebrake." *Forest and Stream*, March 28,
    1887: 179.
—. "The Horn Snake." *Forest and Stream*, November 4, 1899: 365.
Dacus, Joseph A. *Illustrated Lives and Adventures of Frank and Jesse James and
    the Younger Brothers, the Noted Western Outlaws.* New Edition. New York
    and St. Louis, New York and Missouri: (New York and St. Louis: N. D.
    Thompson and Company, 1882.
Dalton, Daniel Webster 'Kit'. *Under the Black Flag.* Memphis, Tennessee:
    Lockard Publishing Company, 1914.
Dance, Donna E. "Supplement to Assignment XXX." *Historical Research Project
    of Coahoma County.* Clarksdale, Mississippi: Works Progress Administration
    for Mississippi, 1936.
DeAngelis, Jack. *Black Fly (Simuliidae) Bites.* 2004–2014. http://www.
    livingwithbugs.com/black_fly.html (accessed March 20, 2014).
Denison, Lindsay. "President Roosevelt's Mississippi Bear Hunt." *Outing*,
    February 1903: 603–610.
Dickson, Harris. "Bear Stories." *The Saturday Evening Post*, April 10, 1909:
    20–21.
—. "The Bearslayer—Holt Collier's Recollections of Man and Beast." *The
    Saturday Evening Post*, March 13, 1909: 14–15, 46.
Dobie, J. Frank. *The Ben Lilly Legend.* 9th Printing. Boston, Massachusetts: Little,
    Brown and Company, 1950.
E.G.L. "Gordon, Suh, of Mississippi." *New York Evening Post*, January 1, 1910: 1.
Eder, Bruce. *Emerson Hough.* Rovi. 2013. http://www.allmovie.com/artist/
    emerson-hough-p310551 (accessed April 9, 2013).
Egbert, J. Hobart. "The Horn Snake." *Forest and Stream*, November 4, 1899: 366.
Evening Scimitar. "Bob Bobo Is Dead Today." December 17, 1902: 1.
Fairall, Herbert S. *The World's Industrial and Cotton Centennial Exposition, New
    Orleans, 1884–1885.* Iowa City, Iowa : Republican Publishing Company,
    1885.
Farmer and Mechanic. "The Flood Subsides." June 11, 1912: 1.
Farmers' Register. "History of the Cane." 1842: 288.

Faulkner, William C. "Delta Autumn." In *Go Down, Moses*, 335–365. New York, New York: Random House, Inc., 1942.

"Fincher Gist Bobo." *Find A Grave*. http://www.findagrave.com/cgi-bin/ fg.cgi?page=gr&GRid=21600039 (accessed November 8, 2013).

Florence Montroy, Mrs. Janie Alcorn Cooper, Information from Memoranda of W. A. Alcorn, Sr., Dictated to Judge William A. Alcorn, Jr., August 18, 1911. *Coahoma County History Revised Assignment No. 5, War Assignment No. 18, Project No. 2984.* Historical Research Project of Coahoma County, Clarksdale: Works Progress Administration for Mississippi, 1936.

Fogle, Bruce. *The Encyclopedia of the Dog.* Edited by Cangy Venables. New York, New York: DK Publishing, NYC, 1995.

"Folklore and Customs." *Historical Research Project of Coahoma County.* Clarksdale, Mississippi: Works Progress Administration for Mississippi, August 17, 1937.

Fontaine, Lamar. *My Life and My Lectures.* New York and Washington: The Neale Publishing Company, 1908.

Forest and Stream. "Capt. Bell's Panther Story." September 9, 1880: 110.

Forest and Stream. "Deer in the Southern Floods." April 27, 1882: 248.

Forest and Stream. "Sinnaker Bears." March 25, 1899: 221.

Forest and Stream. "Successful Treatment of Snake Bites." August 19, 1880: 52.

Forest and Stream. "The President Invited to Hunt with Bobo." June 7, 1902: 445.

Forest and Stream. "The Squirrels, The Rifle and Night." January 30, 1897: 88.

Forest and Stream. "Wild Animals in the Flood." March 30, 1882: 169.

Franklin, Scott B. *Bamboo Ecology.* http://www.unco.edu/biology/sfranklin/ bamboo%20ecology.htm (accessed November 14, 2013).

Ganong, Walter S. "Camp Talla-Quit." *Forest and Stream*, February 12, 1898: 122.

"General Information File." *Historical Research Project of Coahoma County.* Clarksdale, Mississippi: Works Progress Administration for Mississippi, 1936.

George F. Maynard. 2013. http://trees.ancestry.com/tree/5690520/ person/5107164213 (accessed September 23, 2013).

George N. Saunders. 2013. http://trees.ancestry.com/tree/11241759/ person/55817941 (accessed September 23, 2013).

Gibson, Wilbur T., interview by Florence F. Montroy. "Coahoma Outlaws." *Historical Research Project of Coahoma County.* Clarksdale, Mississippi: United States Works Progress Administration for Mississippi, (September 23, 1938): Series 447, Box 10677, Outlaws File.

Gibson, Wilbur T., interview by Florence Montroy. "Supplement to Forest & Fauna, Assignment #8, Project No. 2984." *Historical Research Project of Coahoma County*, edited by Florence Montroy. Clarksdale, Mississippi: Works Progress Administration for Mississippi, (1936).

Goodloe, James L. "My First Bear Hunt." *Forest and Stream*, January 1917: 16.

Gordon, James. "How We Went Fishing and Caught a Bear." *Chicago Field*, June 18, 1881: 297.

—. "Bear Dogs." *Forest and Stream*, July 16, 1885: 488.

—. "Bear-Hunting In the South." *Scribner's Monthly*, October 1881: 857–63.

—. "The Bear Hunt." *Turf, Field & Farm*, April 8, 1870: 210.

—. "A Camp Hunt in the Mississippi Bottom." *Turf, Field and Farm*,
    September 8, 1871: 152.
—. "A Panther Hunt In Mississippi." *Turf, Field and Farm*, May 27, 1870: 321.
Graff, John Franklin. "My Bear Hunt with Gen. Wade Hampton." *Turf, Field &*
    Farm, September 27, 1872: 193.
Graham, Joseph A. "The Field Trials of the Fall Circuit." *Outing*, February 1902:
    606–608, 706.
Gray, James G., interview by James T. McCafferty. *Author's interview*
    (February 19, 2014).
Griffith, Edward. *General and Particular Descriptions of Carnivorous Animals.*
—. *General and Particular Descriptions of the Vertebrated Animals.* London:
    Baldwin,Cradock, and Joy, 1821.
Hall, William C. "Mike Hooter's Bar Story." In *Polly Peablossom's Wedding and*
    Other Tales, edited by T. A. Burke, 49–54. Philadelphia, Pennsylvania: T. B.
    Peterson and Brothers, 1851.
—. "Mike Hooter's Bar Story." *New Orleans Delta*, January 26, 1850: 581.
—. "Trout Fishing in Mississippi." *Spirit of the Times*, December 23, 1843: 505.
—. "A Dinner in the Yazoo Swamp." *The Spirit of the Times*, December 30, 1843:
    44.
Hallock, Charles. "Old Bob Gerry, Of Hyde." *Forest and Stream*, January 21,
    1899: 50.
—. "The Sinnaker Bear." *Forest and Stream*, March 4, 1899: 165.
—. *The Sportsman's Gazetteer and General Guide.* 5th ed. New York, New York:
    Forest and Stream Publishing Co., 1880.
Halsell, Willie D. "Protection of Game in Sunflower County One Hundred Years
    Ago." *Journal of Mississippi History*, 1951: 105–107.
Hamilton, Mary. *Trials of the Earth.* Edited by Helen Dick Davis. Jackson,
    Mississippi: University Press of Mississippi, 1992.
Harrell, Susan Haskell. "Letter to Author." June 6, 1987.
Heagney, Adele. "Electronic Mail to Author." St. Louis, Missouri, August 20,
    2013.
Heffernan, Kevin. *A History of Oakland: The Story of Our Village.* 1st ed.
    Charleston, South Carolina: The History Press, 2007.
Hemphilll, Marie M. *Fevers, Floods and Faith, A History of Sunflower County,*
    Mississippi , 1844–1876. Indianola, Mississippi, 1980.
"Hirsch, Baron Maurice De." *JewishEncyclopedia.com.* 1906. http://www.
    jewishencyclopedia.com/articles/7739-hirsch-baron-maurice-de-moritz-
    hirsch-freiherr-auf-gereuth (accessed June 5, 2013).
Holmes, Jack David Laurus. *Gayoso: The Life of a Spanish Governor in the*
    Mississippi Valley 1789–1799. Baton Rouge, Louisiana: Louisiana State
    University Press, 1965.
Hood, Margaret B. "Early County History, Coahoma County." *Historical*
    Research Project of Coahoma County. Clarksdale, Mississippi: Works Progress
    Administration for Mississippi, 1936.
Hope Star. "Red Cross Leader Dispatched to Area Infested By Gnats." April 11,
    1931: 1.
Hough, Emerson. "Bear Dog Wanted." *Field and Stream*, January 1904: 766.
—. "Chicago and the West." *Field and Stream*, March 1904: 965.

—. "A Shootingless Shooting Trip." *Forest and Stream*, March 18, 1899: 209.

—. "All Kinds of a Good Time." *Forest and Stream*, January 27, 1900: 68.

—. "Among Western Sportsmen." *Forest and Stream*, February 24, 1900: 149–150.

—. "Bear Dogs in Old Mexico." *Forest and Stream*, January 3, 1903: 9.

—. "Bobo and Some Bear Stories." *Forest and Stream*, November 17, 1900: 387.

—. "Bobo and Some Bear Stories." *Forest and Stream*, November 10, 1900: 368.

—. "Bobo and the Bear Hunt." *Forest and Stream*, December 20, 1902: 490.

—. "Chicago and the West." *Forest and Stream*, August 22, 1896: 146.

—. "Chicago and the West." *Forest and Stream*, December 25, 1897: 517.

—. "Chicago and the West." *Forest and Stream*, January 21, 1899: 53.

—. "Chicago and the West." *Forest and Stream*, August 27, 1898: 166.

—. "Chicago and the West." *Forest and Stream*, February 24, 1900: 149–150.

—. "Farm Preserves." *Forest and Stream*, October 27, 1900: 328–329.

—. "From the South." *Forest and Stream*, October 16, 1897: 308.

—. "Gates Ajar." *Forest and Stream*, December 19, 1896: 489.

—. "Hunting Knives and Old Timer." *Forest and Stream*, July 15, 1899: 46.

—. "In Old Mississippi." *Forest and Stream*, November 21, 1896: 408–409.

—. "In the West." *Forest and Stream*, November 4, 1899: 366–367.

—. "Learning the Diamond Hitch." *Forest and Stream*, April 20, 1901: 308.

—. "No Mast This Year." *Forest and Stream*, December 19, 1896: 489.

—. "Squirrel Migrations." *Forest and Stream*, February 14, 1903: 125–126.

—. "Still Buying Hound Pups." *Forest and Stream*, September 15, 1900: 207.

—. "Swimming Powers of a Horse." *Forest and Stream*, July 4, 1903: 11.

—. "The Bobo Bear Country Gone." *Forest and Stream*, June 9, 1900: 449.

—. "The Death of Col. Bobo." *Forest and Stream*, December 27, 1902: 513.

—. "The Floods in the South." *Forest and Stream*, April 17, 1897: 307.

—. "The Ivanhoe Club Preserve, of Mississippi." *Forest and Stream*, March 10, 1900: 190.

—. "The President's Bear Hunt." *Forest and Stream*, November 29, 1902: 428.

—. "The President's Mississippi Bear Hunt." *Forest and Stream*, June 14, 1902: 466.

—. "The Sunny South—I." *Forest and Stream*, February 16, 1895: 124.

—. "The Sunny South—II." *Forest and Stream*, February 23, 1895: 144–145.

—. "The Sunny South—III." *Forest and Stream*, March 2, 1895: 162–164.

—. "The Sunny South—IV." *Forest and Stream*, March 9, 1895: 184–185.

—. "The Sunny South—V." *Forest and Stream*, March 16, 1895: 205.

—. "Those Mississippi Squirrels." *Forest and Stream*, January 31, 1903: 85.

—. "Turning Southward." *Forest and Stream*, December 20, 1902: 490.

—. "Visitors." *Forest and Stream*, July 29, 1899: 87.

—. "Winter Hunt in the Rockies." *Forest and Stream*, June 26, 1897: 503–504.

—. "With the Bobo Bear Pack—I." *Forest and Stream*, February 1, 1896: 92–93.

—. "With the Bobo Bear Pack—II." *Forest and Stream*, February 8, 1896: 112–113.

—. "With the Bobo Bear Pack—III." *Forest and Stream*, February 15, 1896: 131–132.

—. "With the Bobo Bear Pack—IV." *Forest and Stream*, February 22, 1896: 151–153.

—. *The Law of the Land.* Indianapolis: The Bobbs-Merrill Company, 1904.

—. *The Story of the Outlaw: A Study of the Western Desperado.* New York, New York: The Outing Publishing Company, 1907.

Hunter, Trader, Trapper. "Questions and Answers." August 1914: 109–112.

Illinois Central Employees' Magazine. "Thomas A. Divine Dead." November 1920: 54–55.

Jackson, Sherry. *Meet Jefferson Davis at the Cross Keys House in Union.* http://www.ourupstatesc.info/meet-jefferson-davis-at-the-cross-keys-h.php?utm_source=Our+Upstate-Newsletter-4.26.2012-noads&utm_campaign=E-Newsletter&utm_medium=archive (accessed September 27, 2013).

James, Ronald Michael, and C. Elizabeth Raymond. *Comstock Women: The Making of a Mining Community.* Reno, Nevada: University of Nevada Press, 1998.

Janie Alcorn Cooper, William A. Alcorn Sr., and William A. Alcorn, Jr. "County History, Supplement to Interviews, #13." *Historical Research Project of Coahoma County.* Clarksdale, Mississippi: Works Progress Administration for Mississippi, 1936.

Johnson, Carole M. "Emerson Hough's American West." *University of Iowa Libraries.* University of Iowa. http://www.lib.uiowa.edu/spec-coll/bai/johnson.htm (accessed December 8, 2013).

Kelley, Arthell. In *The Past Is Not Dead: Essays from the Southern Quarterly*, edited by Douglas B. Chambers. Jackson, Mississippi: The University Press of Mississippi, 2012.

Kephart, Horace. "Lost in the Swamp—II." *Forest and Stream*, August 10, 1895: 112–113.

Kirkby, William. *Annual Report of the Commissioner of Railroads and Telegraphs to the Governor of the State of Ohio for the Year 1892.* Office of the Commissioner of Railroads and Telegraphs, State of Ohio, Norwalk, Ohio: The Lansing Printing Company, 1892, 24.

Koempe, Michael L., and Judy Schneider. *Judy Schneider and Michael L. Koempel, Congressional Desk Book, 6th ed. (Alexandria, Virginia: TheCapitol.Net, Inc., 2012), 200.* Alexandria, Virginia: TheCapitol.Net, Inc., 2012.

Longleaf Alliance. *Longleaf Pine Glossary.* 2002. http://www.auburn.edu/academic/forestry_wildlife/longleafalliance/teachers/teacherkit/glossary.htm (accessed February 15, 2013).

Lowe, E. N. *Mississippi State Geological Survey, Bulletin No. 12.* Bulletin, State Geological Commission, Jackson, Mississippi: Tucker Printing House, 1915, p. 269.

Maloney, Amber. *Napoleon Lewis Leavell (1842–1899).* 2013. http://www.geni.com/people/Napoleon-Leavell/6000000010545275268 (accessed January 11, 2013).

Maynard, Jr., George F., interview by Florence F. Montroy. *Historical Research Project of Coahoma County.* Clarksdale, Mississippi: Works Progress Administration for Mississippi, (March 12, 1937).

Maynard, Sr., George F. "County History, Supplement to Interviews, Assignment #13, Project No. 2984." *Historical Research Project of Coahoma County.* no. Project No. 2984. Clarksdale, Mississippi: Works Progress Administration for Mississippi, October 20, 1936.

McFarland, L. B. "Some Reminiscences of the Memphis Bar." *Proceedings of the of the Fourteenth Annual Meeting of the Bar Association of Tennessee, July 13–14, 1895.* Nashville: Marshall & Bruce Co., 1899. 87–104.

McNab, Chris, ed. *Knives and Swords: A Visual History.* New York, New York: DK Publishing, 2010.

Memphis Daily Avalanche. "Bobo - Prince Marriage." November 26, 1868.

Merriam, C. Hart. "The Yellow Bear of Louisiana, Ursus Luteolus Griffith." *Proceedings of the Biological Society of Washington.* Washington, D. C., 1893. 147–152.

Miller, Gene Ramsey. *A History of North Mississippi Methodism, 1820–1900.* 1st ed. Nashville, Tennessee: The Parthenon Press, 1966.

"Mississippi Marriages, 1776–1935." *Ancestry.com.* 1997–2013. http://search.ancestry.com/cgi-bin/sse.dll?db=MSmarriages_ga&h=671485&indiv=try&o_vc=Record:OtherRecord&rhSource=7602 (accessed June 11, 2013).

Montroy, Florence F. "Historical Facts, Coahoma County." *Historical Research Project of Coahoma County.* Clarksdale, Mississippi: Works Progress Administration for Mississippi.

Morris, Christopher, and Susan Eacker. *Southern Writers and Their Worlds.* Baton Rouge, Louisiana: Louisiana State University Press, 1998.

Nagel, I. E. "The Beaver Dam Club." *Forest and Stream*, January 1884: 446.

National Park Service. *Regimental Details.* March 23, 2013. http://www.nps.gov/civilwar/search-regiments-detail.htm?regiment_id=CMS0018RC (accessed April 2, 2013).

—. *Search for Soldiers.* April 2, 2013. http://www.nps.gov/civilwar/search-soldiers. htm?sdrankin=&sdfname=&sdkeyword=&showall=0&sdunitnumber=&sdlname=&maxrows=20&sort=PER%5FLAST%5FNAME%2CPER%5FFIRST%5FNAME&sdrankout=&sdfunction= &sdoriginstate= &sdsidename=&sdcompany=&sdunitcode=CMS0018RC&submitt (accessed April 2, 2013).

"New Orleans, Louisiana, Marriage Records Index, 1831–1920." *Ancestry.Com.* 1997–2013. http://search.ancestry.com/cgi-bin/sse.dll?rank=1&new=1&MSAV=1&msT=1&gss=angs-g&gsfn=Walter+S.&gsfn_x=XO&gsln=Ganong&gsln_x=XO&msydy=1898&msypn__ftp=New+Orleans%2c+Orleans%2c+Louisiana%2c+USA&msypn=34322&msypn_PInfo=8-%7c0%7c1652393%7c0%7c2%7c3246%7c21%7c (accessed June 5, 2013).

New York Times. "New Senator Once a Fugitive." December 29, 1909.

New York Times. "Wade Hampton Hurt." November 25, 1886.

Omer/Steer/Callahan/Calvert. *Charlotte "Lottie" Amelia Cheesebro.* 1997–2013. http://trees.ancestry.com/tree/8148034/person/44722258 (accessed November 26, 2013).

Ott, Ludwig. *Fundamentals of Catholic Dogma.* Edited by James Canon Bastible. Translated by Patrick Lynch. Rockford, Illinois: Tan Books and Publishers, Inc., 1960.

Otto, John Solomon. *The Final Frontiers, 1880–1930: Settling the Southern Bottomlands.* Westport, Connecticut: Greenwood Publishing Company, 1999.

Parker, H. H. *Alf Daniels.* 1880 Census, U. S. Government, 1880, 16.

Peck, Henry J. "Bears and Bear-Hunting." *Spirit of the Times* 13, no. 48 (January 1844): 572.

Pendleton, William C., ed. "Presidential Bear Hunt." *Tazewell Republican,* June 12, 1902: 4.

Phelan, George R. "A Swamp Hunter." *Forest and Stream,* May 25, 1882: 324.

—. "Camp Fire in the Great Swamp—Part I." *Forest and Stream,* July 13, 1882: 465.

—. "Camp Fire in the Great Swamp—Part II." *Forest and Stream,* July 20, 1882: 486.

—. "Camp Life in the Great Swamp." *Forest and Stream,* October 5, 1882: 192.

—. "The Great Swamp." *Forest and Stream,* July 6, 1882: 444.

—. "The Pack Well Shuffled." *Forest and Stream,* September 7, 1882: 103.

"Pledge of the Am. Temp. Union." *Journal of the American Temperance Union* (American Temperance Union), November 1839: 161.

Polk, Burr H. "The Mississippi Floods." *Forest and Stream,* March 23, 1882: 150.

Polk, William Lancaster. "With the Bears In Coon Bayou." *Forest and Stream,* February 10, 1887: 46–47.

Reid, Frank S. "Special Schedule, Surviving Soldiers, Sailors, and Marines, and Widows, Etc., Supervisor's Disrict 3." *United States Census, 1890, Coahoma County, Mississippi.* United States, June 1890. 1.

Remington Arms Company, LLC. *Company History—Remington Arms Company History of the Firearms Business.* LLC Remington Arms Company. http://www.remington.com/pages/our-company/company-history.aspx (accessed January 13, 2013).

Richard Nelson Harris. 2014. http://trees.ancestry.com/tree/26613694/person/1945204738 (accessed April 10, 2104).

Richter, William L. *Historical Dictionary of the Old South.* Lanham, Mayland: Rowman and Littlefield Publishing Company, 2006.

Riley, Franklin L. *Extinct Towns and Villages of Mississippi.* Vol. 5, in *Publications of the Mississippi Historical Society,* edited by Franklin L. Riley, 311–383. Harrisburg, Pennsylvania: Harrisburg Publishing Company, 1902.

"Robert E. Bobo Obituary." *Clarion Ledger.* April 20, 2013. http://www.legacy.com/obituaries/clarionledger/obituary.aspx?page=lifestory&pid=164329765 (accessed November 9, 2013).

Robert Eager Bobo. http://trees.ancestry.com/tree/44168589/person/6169033534 (accessed April 2, 2013).

Rolinson, Martha. "Archeology along Bayou Bartholomew, Southeast Arkansas." *The Arkansas Archeologist: Bulletin of the Arkansas Archeological Society* 32 (1991): 12, 23.

Roosevelt, Theodore. "In the Louisiana Canebrakes." *Scribner's Magazine,* January 1908: 47–60.

Rowland, Dunbar. *Encyclopedia of Mississippi History: Comprising Sketches of Counties, Towns, Events, Institutions and Persons.* First. Edited by Dunbar Rowland. Vol. 1. Two vols. Madison, Wisconsin: Selwyn A. Brant, 1907.

Rule, D. H. *James & Youngers: The Outlaws.* 2001–2007. http://www.civilwarstlouis.com/history/jamesgangoutlaws.htm (accessed February 11, 2013).

Satchfield, Lamar. "Those Famous Bobo Bear Hunts." *Delta Scene*, February 1974: 4–5.

Schmidt, John L., and Douglas L. Gilbert,. *Big Game of North America: Ecology and Management.* 2nd. Harrisburg, Pennsylvania: Stackpole Books, 1980.

Seale, Lea Leslie. "Indian Place Names in Mississippi." *Master's Thesis.* Baton Rouge, Louisiana: Louisiana State University, 1939. 127.

Shethar-Boznai. "Notes from Mississippi." *Forest and Stream*, January 18, 1877: 370–71.

—. "Trapping in the Southern States." *Forest and Stream*, December 28, 1876: 327.

Shields, Joseph Dunbar, and Seargent Prentiss Knut. *The Life and Times of Seargent Smith Prentiss.* Philadelphia: J. P. Lippincott & Co., 1884.

Silver, James W. "Paul Bunyan Comes to Mississippi." *The Journal of Mississippi History* 19 (1957): 93–119.

Skinner, F. G. "Mississippi in '36—Adventures with an Alligator." *Turf, Field and Farm*, June 16, 1882: 396.

Spirit of the Times. "Game Steaks and Cane Brakes." February 19, 1859: 13–14.

Spirit of the Times. "Panther Fight." December 16, 1843: 498.

Sporting Life. "Remsen Wins the Recreation Cup at the Hackensack Shoot." April 4, 1897: 20.

Sporting Life. "The Trigger." October 26, 1895: 13.

Sporting Life. "The World of Shooters." August 10, 1895: 19.

Sportsman's Magazine and Life In London. "A 'Bad Fix' in a Bear Fight." October 18, 1845: 372.

St. Louis Post-Dispatch. "Why Col. Bob Bobo Was Not in Hunt." November 28, 1902: 16.

Stone County Enterprise. "Illegally Killed Black Bear Results in Citation." September 15, 2010.

Tax. "A Day on the Tennessee." *American Field*, September 7, 1895: 221.

Taylor, Walter Nesbit, and George H. Etheridge. *Mississippi, A History.* Vol. 3. Four vols. Hopkinsville, Kentucky: Historical Records Associatin, 1940.

Thorpe, Benjamin. *Northern Mythology, Comprising the Principal Popular Traditions and Superstitions of Scandinavia, North Germany, and the Netherlands.* Vol. 3. London: Edward Lumley, 1852.

Titus, W. W. "Reminiscences of a Dog Trainer—No. 3." *The American Field*, August 18, 1894.

Tusa, Bob M. *Dabney (Thomas Gregory) Collection.* The University of Southern Mississippi Libraries Special Collections. November 4, 2004. http://www. lib.usm.edu/legacy/archives/m007.htm (accessed June 4, 2013).

U. S. Fish and Wildlife Service. *Louisiana Black Bear (Ursus americanus luteolus).* March 17, 2014. http://ecos.fws.gov/speciesProfile/profile/speciesProfile. action?spcode=A08F (accessed March 17, 2014).

Urbana Union. February 15, 1871: 3.

Urdang, Laurence, ed. *The Timetables of American History.* Millenial. New York, New York: Touchstone, 1984.

Ursussen, Reuben. "The Demon Bear of Tarantula Ridge." *Forest and Stream*, July 5, 1902: 2–4.

Walter S. Ganong. 2014. http://trees.ancestry.com/tree/5656960/ person/70098244 (accessed April 10, 2014).

War Department. *Report of the Chief of Engineers of the U. S. Army Corps of Engineers.* War Department, United States, Washington, D. C.: Government Printing Office, 1899, 1935.

Weathers, Margaret A. "When Coahoma County Had 3 Families and a Hand-Mill." *Clarksdale Press-Register*, March 18, 1928: 8.

Weir, D. B. "After Wild Turkeys in a 'Dugout'." *American Field*, March 25, 1882: 209–210.

—. "An Arkansas Bear Fight—Part 1." *Forest and Stream*, March 23, 1882: 147.

—. "Mississippi Bear Hunting." *The American Field*, November 25, 1882: 357–58.

Whitney, Milton. *Field Operations of the Bureau of Soils, 1902.* United States Department of Agriculture, Bureau of Soils, Washington, D. C.: Government Printing Office, 1903, p. 334.

Wild Fennel. June 7, 2013. http://eattheinvaders.org/blue-plate-special-wild-fennel/ (accessed April 27, 2014).

Willey, Charles H. "The Vermont Black Bear." *Vermont Fish and Wildlife Department.* 2003–2013. http://www.vtfishandwildlife.com/books/Vermont_Black_Bear/_The%20Vt%20Black%20Bear_Section%201.pdf (accessed November 1, 2013).

Williams, Bobby Joe. *The One They Had In 1882 Was "The Big Flood."* June 17, 2012. http://tn-roots.com/tnshelby/history/1882Flood.htm (accessed September 11, 2013).

Wilson, Gregory C. "The Birth of the Teddy Bear." *Bear Tracks*, Fall 1979: 3–5.

—. "How Teddy Bear Got His Name." *The Washington Post Potomac*, November 30, 1969: 33–36.

Wingfield, A. B. "In Jones's Bayou.—I." *Forest and Stream*, October 19, 1895: 332.

—. "In Jones's Bayou.—III." *Forest and Stream*, November 9, 1895: 398.

—. "On Jones's Bayou.—IV." *Forest and Stream*, November 16, 1895: 420.

—. "Outing of the Ozark Club." *Forest and Stream*, January 11, 1902: 26–27.

Woolley, John, and Gerhard Peters. *Grover Cleveland: "Proclamation 379—Thanksgiving Day, 1895," November 4, 1895.* 1999–2013. http://www.presidency.ucsb.edu/ws/index.php?pid=70686 (accessed January 11, 2013).

Yazoo Whig. "Horrible Death." January 21, 1848: 4.

Yerger, Nina Maynard. "Folk Lore & Folk Customs, Assignment No.30, Project No. 6055–4120." *Historical Research Project of Coahoma County.* Clarksdale, Mississippi: Works Progress Administration for Mississippi, August 19, 1937.

Yocum, Jack Harlan. *A History of Theatre in Houston, 1836–1954.* Vol. 2. Madison, Wisconsin, 1954.

Young, Brad. *Conservation and Management of Black Bears in Mississippi.* State of Mississippi, Mississippi Department of Wildlife, Fisheries, and Parks, Mississippi Museum of Natural Sciences, Jackson: Mississippi Department of Wildlife, Fisheries, and Parks, 2006.

Younger, Cole. *The Story of Cole Younger, by Himself.* Chicago, Illinois: The Henneberry Company, 1903.

Zema, Nicole. "Buffalo Gnats a Temporary Annoyance." *Natchez Democrat*, June 1, 2011.

Index

Dickerson, (probably William H.) 34
Dickson, Harris 25, 87
Didymus (pen name of Martin John-
    son Head). *See* Head, Martin
    Johnson
Divine, Thomas A. 1, 3, 36, 39, 43-49,
    65, 113, 117, 127-131,163-
    166, 168, 170, 183, 184, 188,
    266, 277
  description of 44, 266
  negotiation of claim for cattle with
    Robert Eager Bobo 43
  negotiation of death claim against
    railroad 44
Dixie 47, 121, 183
dog(s) 21, 23, 28, 37, 38, 47, 50-59,
    61-63, 66-69, 75, 77, 79-82,
    84-87, 89, 91, 93, 94-96,
    104, 105, 107, 109-111,
    114-116, 118-121, 123, 125,
    128-132, 134, 135, 137-140,
    142-158, 164, 169, 170, 180,
    186, 195, 196
  bear dog(s) 23, 42, 51, 52-58, 66,
    73, 80, 91-93, 96, 129, 133,
    135, 157, 163, 170, 173, 191,
    193, 195, 197, 199
  accidentally killed or injured by
    hunters 86, 92, 95, 96, 140
  bear dog name(s) 135
    Alcorn 140, 164, 165
    Bad-eye 146
    Cleopatra 93
    Clint 53
    Dublin 101
    Guard 53
    Henry 66, 67, 68, 110, 130
    Jolly 153, 159
    Lawyer 57
    Mark Anthony 93, 94, 95, 96
    New York 130
    Old Rapid 92
    Old Rock 155, 159
    Raphael 66, 67, 68, 130
    Rounce 134

dog(s)*continued*
  bear dog(s) *continued*
    bear dog name(s) *continued*
      Scott 139
      Texas 130
    bear fighting styles 53, 54, 57, 58
    breeding bear dogs 55, 56
    fed offal from eviscerated bear 63,
      111
    life expectancy 58
    small dog(s) as 57
    training 66, 91, 147, 148, 195
  Bobo, Robert Eager (1847-1902),
      bear pack 28, 32, 37, 38, 42,
      51, 58, 68, 69, 86, 91, 92,
      110, 112, 114, 115, 118, 119,
      120, 130, 131, 133, 134, 135,
      137, 140, 143, 144, 146, 147,
      148, 150, 151, 152, 153, 154,
      155, 164, 183, 184, 186, 190,
      191, 193
  breed(s)
    beagle(s) 54, 93
    bird dog(s) 53, 54, 92, 130, 195
    bloodhound(s) 54
    bulldog(s) 54, 55
    bull terrier(s) 54
    cur(s) 55, 56, 146
    foxhound(s) 14, 51, 52, 54, 55,
      66, 91, 110, 130, 140, 164
    greyhound(s) 55, 56
    hound(s) 51, 52, 54, 55, 67, 68,
      75, 76, 87, 88, 89, 91, 93, 96,
      109, 110, 115, 116, 117, 118,
      129, 133, 134, 135, 137, 139,
      143, 145, 146, 147, 148, 150,
      151, 152, 153, 154, 155, 159,
      161, 164, 165, 177, 184, 197
    bear hound(s) 54, 91, 189
    mastiff(s) 55
    pointer(s) 54, 130
      pointer names 54
    redbone hound(s) 51
    staghound(s) 55, 56, 130
    terrier(s), rough coated 58

Endnotes

Chapter 1 A Divine Appointment

[1] "The President Invited to Hunt with Bobo," *Forest and Stream*, June 7, 1902, 445; "Current Topics," *Hickman Courier*, June 27, 1902, 6.

[2] Lindsay Denison, "President Roosevelt's Mississippi Bear Hunt," *Outing*, February 1903, 607.

[3] Emerson Hough, "The Sunny South – II," *Forest and Stream*, February 23, 1895, 144.

[4] Bruce Eder, "Emerson Hough," http://www.allmovie.com/artist/emerson-hough-p310551 (accessed April 9, 2013).

[5] Hough, "The Sunny South – II," 144.

[6] *The Evening Scimitar*, "Bob Bobo Is Dead Today," December 17, 1902, 1.

Chapter 2 The Delta

[1] James Gordon, "A Camp Hunt in the Mississippi Bottom," *Turf, Field, and Farm*, September 8, 1871, 152.

[2] George R. Phelan, "The Great Swamp," *Forest and Stream*, July 6, 1882, 444.

[3] Gordon, "Hunting in the Mississippi Bottoms," *Forest and Stream*, October 12, 1907, 574.

[4] James C. Cobb, *The Most Southern Place On Earth: the Mississippi Delta and the Roots of Regional Identity* (Oxford, Mississippi: Oxford University Press, 1994). The region comprised of the Arkansas counties lying close to the Mississippi River is also referred to as "the Delta" in that state. *See*, Charles Bowden, "Return to the Arkansas Delta," *National Geographic*, November 2012, accessed through http://ngm.nationalgeographic.com/2012/11/arkansas-delta/bowden-text (accessed April 5, 2014). That bottomland country of Arkansas is also occasionally referred to herein as "the Delta."

[5] Hennig Cohen, *Humor of the Old Southwest* (Athens, Georgia: University of Georgia Press, 1964), 363–364.

[6] Susan Eacker and Christopher Morris, *Southern Writers and Their Worlds* (Baton Rouge, Louisiana: Louisiana State University Press, 1998), 124, n. 17.

[7] *See, e. g.,* William C. Hall, "Mike Hooter's Bar Story," in *Polly Peablossom's Wedding and Other Tales*, ed. T. A. Burke (Philadelphia: T. B. Peterson and Brothers, 1851), 49–54.

[8] William C. Hall, "A Dinner in the Yazoo Swamp," *The Spirit of the Times*, December 30, 1843, 44; Eacker and Morris, *Southern Writers and Their Worlds*, 124, n. 17.

[9] Hall, "A Dinner in the Yazoo Swamp," 44.

[10] John Franklin Graff, "My Bear Hunt with Gen. Wade Hampton," *Turf, Field & Farm*, September 27, 1872, 193.

[11] James Gordon, "Bear-Hunting In the South," *Scribner's Monthly*, October 1870, 857–63.

[12] The portion of Mississippi that became Coahoma County was ceded by the Choctaw Nation to the United States in 1830 by the terms of the Treaty of Dancing Rabbit Creek. Dunbar Rowland, *Encyclopedia of Mississippi History: Comprising Sketches of Counties, Towns, Events, Institutions and Persons*, vol. 1 (Madison, Wisconsin: Selwyn A. Brant, 1907) 581–82.

[13] L. B. McFarland, "Some Reminiscences of the Memphis Bar," *Proceedings of the Fourteenth Annual Meeting of the Bar Association of Tennessee*, July 13–14, 1895 (Nashville: Marshall & Bruce Co., Printers and Stationers, 1899), 87–104.

[14] George R. Phelan, "The Great Swamp," *Forest and Stream*," July 6, 1882, 444.

[15] Theodore Roosevelt, "In the Louisiana Canebrakes," Scribner's Monthly, January 1908, 47.

[16] "Delta Lands," *Clarion-Ledger*, November 7, 1890.

[17] *Gordon, "Bear Hunting in the South," Scribner's Monthly*, October 1881, 858–859.

[18] *Biographical and Historical Memoirs of Mississippi*, vol. 1 (Chicago: The Goodspeed Publishing Company, 1891), 123.

[19] Milton Whitney, *Field Operations of the Bureau of Soils, 1902*, United States Department of Agriculture, Bureau of Soils (Washington, D. C.: Government Printing Office, 1903), 334.

[20] George R. Phelan, "The Great Swamp—Part II," *Forest and Stream*, July 6, 1882, 486.

[21] "History of the Cane," *Farmers' Register* 10 (1842), 289.

[22] D. B. Weir, "An Arkansas Bear Fight—Part 1," *Forest and Stream*, March 23, 1882, 147, n. 2.

[23] Nina Maynard Yerger, "Folk Lore & Folk Customs," Assignment No. 30, Project No. 6055–4120," *Historical Research Project of Coahoma County*, Clarksdale, Mississippi, 1937, Coahoma County Materials, Mississippi Works Progress Administration Microfilm Collection, Reels A770 and A771, University of Mississippi Library.

[24] Phelan, "The Great Swamp—Part II," 486.

[25] Wilbur T. Gibson, 1936, "Supplement to Forest & Fauna, Assignment #8, Project No. 2984," *Historical Research Project of Coahoma County*, Clarksdale, Mississippi, 1936, Coahoma County Materials, Mississippi Works Progress Administration Microfilm Collection, Reels A770 and A771, University of Mississippi Library.

[26] John James Audubon, "Hunting the Cougar, or American Lion; and Deer Hunting," *The Edinburgh New Philosophical Journal* 11, April-June (1831), 108.

[27] Phelan, "Camp Fire in the Great Swamp—Part II," 486.

[28] William C. Hall, "Trout Fishing In Mississippi," *Spirit of the Times*, December 23, 1843, 505; C. C., "On the Sunflower River," *Forest and Stream*, November 3, 1892, 379.

[29] F. G. Skinner, "Mississippi In '36—Adventures with an Alligator," *Turf, Field and Farm*, June 16, 1882.

[30] Hall, "Trout Fishing In Mississippi," 505.

[31] Raven, "Fishing in this Vicinity," *Turf, Field and Farm*, May 12, 1866, 294.

[32] The current world record alligator gar was caught February 14, 2011, in Mississippi's Lake Chotard, a Mississippi River Oxbow. It was 8 feet, 5 and ⅛ inches long, 47 inches in girth, weighed 327 pounds, and was estimated to be between 50 and 70 years old. http://www.fieldandstream.com/photos/gallery/fishing/2011/02/world-record-gar-alligator-gar-monster-huge-mississippi?photo=6#node-1001383265.

[33] Roosevelt, 48.

[34] George R. Phelan, "Camp Fire in the Great Swamp—Part II," *Forest and Stream*, July 20, 1882, 486.

[35] Yerger, "Folk Lore & Folk Customs," *Historical Research Project of Coahoma County*.

[36] "Wildcat" is the name traditionally used by Mississippi Delta folk for the bobcat, also known as the "bay lynx."

[37] Yerger, "Folk Lore & Folk Customs," *Historical Research Project of Coahoma County*.

[38] Dance, "Supplement to Assignment XXX," *Historical Research Project of Coahoma County*.

[39] Roosevelt, 47.

[40] "Successful Treatment of Snake Bites," *Forest and Stream*, August 19, 1880, 52.

[41] Cooper, Alcorn, and Alcorn, Supplement to Interviews, #13, *Historical Research Project of Coahoma County*.

[42] "Red Cross Leader Dispatched to Area Infested By Gnats," *Hope Star*, April 11, 1931, 1, accessed through http://www.newspapers.com/newspage/4412897/ (accessed March 18, 2014).

[43] Exodus 8:16–19.

[44] "Red Cross Leader Dispatched to Area Infested By Gnats," 1.

[45] "The Flood Subsides," *The Farmer and Mechanic*, June 11, 1912, accessed through http://www.newspapers.com/newspage/57487856/ (accessed March 18, 2014).

[46] A. B. Wingfield, "In Jones's Bayou, pt. III, " *Forest and Stream*, November 9, 1895, 398.

[47] "Red Cross Leader Dispatched to Area Infested By Gnats," 1.

[48] Nicole Zema, "Buffalo Gnats a Temporary Problem," *Natchez Democrat*, June 1, 2011, accessed through http://www.natchezdemocrat.com/2011/06/01/buffalo-gnats-a-temporary-annoyance/# (accessed March 18, 2014).

[49] Marie M. Hemphilll, *Fevers, Floods and Faith, A History of Sunflower County, Mississippi , 1844–1876* (Indianola, Mississippi, 1980), 599.

[50] *New York Times*, "New Senator Once a Fugitive," December 29, 1909.

[51] James Gordon, "How We Went Fishing and Caught a Bear," *Chicago Field*, June 18, 1881, 297.

Chapter 3 Pioneer Ways

[1] Janie Alcorn Cooper, William A. Alcorn Sr., and William A. Alcorn, Jr., Supplement to Interviews, #13, "*Historical Research Project of Coahoma County*," Clarksdale, Mississippi, 1936, Coahoma County Materials, Mississippi Works Progress Administration Microfilm Collection, Reels A770 and A771, University of Mississippi Library.

[2] Arthell Kelley, in *The Past Is Not Dead: Essays from the Southern Quarterly*, ed. Douglas B. Chambers (Jackson, Mississippi: The University Press of Mississippi, 2012), 15.

[3] Cooper, Alcorn, and Alcorn, Supplement to Interviews, #13, *Historical Research Project of Coahoma County.*

[4] Blankenstein's Homepage, 1997–2015, http://www.blankensteingenealogy. net/bobo.htm (accessed 29 January 2015).

[5] Also spelled, "Barham."

[6] "Cross Keys House, Union County (S.C. Hwy. 49, Cross Keys)," http://www.nationalregister.sc.gov/union/S10817744005/ (accessed September 27, 2013).

[7] "Browse Ancestry ArchiveTM By Surname, "Barram Bobo," http://www. mytrees.com/newanc/South-Carolina/Born-1776/Bo/Bobo-family/Barram-Bobo-bo001087-2.html (accessed September 27, 2013).

[8] Fincher was married on April 27, 1837, in Columbus, Mississippi, which would have been on the road between Cross Keys and Panola County. Blankenstein's Homepage, (accessed September 28, 2013).

[9] Sherry Jackson, "Meet Jefferson Davis at Cross Keys in Union," http:// www.ourupstatesc.info/meet-jefferson-davis-at-the-cross-keys-h.php?utm_source=Our+Upstate-Newsletter-4.26.2012-noads&utm_campaign=E-Newsletter&utm_medium=archive (accessed September 27, 2013).

[10] "A large barrel or cask, especially one holding from 100 to 140 gallons." Webster's New World *Dictionary of the American Language*, College Edition, 1966, s.v. "hogshead."

[11] Hough, "The Sunny South—II," 144–145.

[12] Blankenstein's Homepage, http://www.blankensteingenealogy.net/ generation_6_page_1.htm (accessed September 28, 2013).

[13] Weathers, "When Coahoma County Had 3 Families and a Hand-Mill," 8.

[14] University of Virginia Library, Historical Census Browser, http:// mapserver.lib.virginia.edu/php/county.php (19 January 2015). The population increased to 2, 7 80 by 1850. Ibid.

¹⁵ Mrs. James L. McKeown, "General Information and History," 6, *Historical Research Project of Coahoma County*, Clarkdale, Mississippi, 1936, Coahoma County Materials, Mississippi Works Progress Administration, Box 10677, Formation file, Mississippi Department of Archives and History; Franklin Lafayette Riley, "Extinct Towns and Villages," Publications of the Mississippi Historical Society, Volume 5, ed. Franklin Lafayette Riley (Harrisburg, Pennsylvania: 1902), 331.

¹⁶ Kelley, in *The Past Is Not Dead: Essays from the Southern Quarterly*, ed. Douglas B. Chambers, 16.

¹⁷ George F Maynard, Sr., Interview, *Historical Research Project of Coahoma County*, Clarksdale, Mississippi, 1936, Coahoma County Materials, Works Progress Administration for Mississippi, Box 10677, General Information file, Mississippi Department of Archives and History.

¹⁸ Weathers, "When Coahoma County Had 3 Families and a Hand-Mill," 8.

¹⁹ Donna E. Dance, "Supplement to Assignment XXX," *Historical Research Project of Coahoma County*, Clarksdale, Mississippi, 1936, Coahoma County Materials, Works Progress Administration for Mississippi, Microfilm Collection, Reels A770 and A771, University of Mississippi Library.

²⁰ James Gordon, "A Panther Hunt In Mississippi," *Turf, Field and Farm*, May 27, 1870, 321.

²¹ While "switch cane" is understood by many, especially in the botanical science community, to mean a variety of cane considered by some to be a subspecies (*Arundinaria gigantean tecta*) of river cane (*Arundinaria gigantean*) and by others to be a separate cane species (*Arundinaria tecta*), in the old Delta writings the term generally appears to refer simply to the young, tender river cane favored by cattle and horses for grazing. *See, e. g.*, A. B. Wingfield, "In Jones's Bayou.—I," *Forest and Stream*, October 19, 1895, 332 (describing new, shorter cane, in a recently burned portion of a brake as "switch cane").

²² A sedge of the genus *Scirpus*, also known as "bulrushes." Author's telephone interview with U. S. Fish and Wildlife Service botanist Carrie Norquist, April 16, 2014.

²³ Wingfield, "In Jones's Bayou.—I," 332.

²⁴ Weathers, "When Coahoma County Had 3 Families and a Hand-Mill," 8.

²⁵ Very young shoots or sprouts of cane, called "mutton" cane, continued to appear for some while after the brake was cut and burned to make way for crops and had to be hoed out like weeds. "History of the Cane," *Farmers' Register*, 288–90. The old canebrakes made for the most fertile agricultural fields. Ibid. *See also*, Cooper, Alcorn, and Alcorn, Supplement to Interviews, #13, *Historical Research Project of Coahoma County.*

²⁶ Weathers, "When Coahoma County Had 3 Families and a Hand-Mill," 8.

²⁷ Dance, "Supplement to Assignment XXX," *Coahoma County WPA Microfilm Collection, Reels A770 and A771.*

²⁸ George R. Phelan, "The Great Swamp—Part II," *Forest and Stream*, July 6, 1882, 486.

[29] Phelan, "The Great Swamp—Part II," 486.

[30] D. B. Weir, "After Wild Turkeys in a 'Dugout,'" *American Field*. March 25, 1882, 209–210.

[31] George R. Phelan, "Camp Life in the Great Swamp," *Forest and Stream*, October 5, 1882, 192.

[32] Yellow poplar.

[33] D. B. Weir, "After Wild Turkeys in a 'Dugout,'" 209–210.

[34] Tax, "A Day on the Tennessee," *American Field*, September 7, 1895, 221.

[35] Meaning "pirogue." The author does not recall having seen the term "pirogue" used in reference to Mississippi Delta dugouts anywhere else.

[36] A. B. Wingfield, "In Jones's Bayou.—I," *Forest and Stream*, October 19, 1895, 332.

[37] By the age of 32, McPeak had been elected to the board of police, the former name of the county governing body now known in Mississippi as the board of supervisors. Barbara Russell Chesser, *Remembering Mattie* (Waco: Sunstone Press, 2008), 269; "1880 United States Census About I. Shelby McPeak," accessed through Ancestry.com, (accessed, September 14, 2013).

[38] Phelan, "The Great Swamp," *Forest and Stream*, July 6, 1882, 444.

[39] Gibson, "Supplement to Forest & Fauna," *Historical Research Project of Coahoma County.*"

[40] Phelan, "Camp Life in the Great Swamp," 192.

[41] Dr. Emile S. Gardiner and Dr. James S. Meadows, both research foresters at the U. S. Department of Agriculture's "Center for Bottomland Hardwoods Research" at Stoneville, Mississippi, say that "bottle ash" is another name for the "pumpkin ash," a species native to the Mississippi Delta. The tree receives both its names from the buttressing along its lower trunk, common among some bottomland tree species, that swells into what apparently has been perceived by some as a pumpkin-like shape. This lower trunk enlargement also gives the tree a bottle-like profile. Emile S. Gardiner, electronic mail to author, March 27, 2014. The wood from the "bottled" portion of the tree, according to Dr. Gardiner, tends to be lighter due to its cell structure. Author's telephonic interview with Emile Gardiner, March 26, 2014. That light weight, combined with the strength of ash, made it an ideal stock for canoe paddles.

[42] "Flag" is a common name for several species of the genus *Iris*, e. g., *Iris virginica*, commonly called "blue flag," that grow in shallow waters in swamps and marshes in the eastern United States. "Blue Flag," Center for Aquatic and Invasive Plants, accessed at http://plants.ifas.ufl.edu/node/206 (accessed April 20, 2014).

[43] Phelan, "Camp Life in the Great Swamp," 192.

[44] Burr H. Polk, "The Mississippi Floods," *Forest and Stream*, March 23, 1882, 150.

[45] *Forest and Stream*, "Deer in the Southern Floods," April 27, 1882, 248.

[46] "Capt. Bell's Panther Story," *Forest and Stream*, September 9, 1880, 110.

[47] *Forest and Stream*, "Wild Animals in the Flood," March 30, 1882, 169.

[48] Hough, "The Sunny South—II," 145.

⁴⁹ Florence F. Montroy, "Historical Facts, Coahoma County," Clarksdale, Mississippi, 1936, Coahoma County Materials, Works Progress Administration for Mississippi, Box 10676, Formation file, Mississippi Department of Archives and History.

⁵⁰ "Walter S. Ganong," http://trees.ancestry.com/tree/5656960/person/70098244 (accessed April 10, 2014).

⁵¹ Montroy, "Historical Facts, Coahoma County WPA *Materials, Box 10676.*

Chapter 4 Bears Before Breakfast

¹ Maynard, Interview, *Historical Research Project of Coahoma County.*

² "George F. Maynard," http://trees.ancestry.com/tree/5690520/person/5107164213 (accessed September 23, 2013).

³ Dance, "Supplement to Assignment XXX," *Coahoma County WPA Microfilm Collection, Reels A770 and A771.*

⁴ Maynard, Interview, *Historical Research Project of Coahoma County.*

⁵ Cooper, Alcorn, and Alcorn, Supplement to Interviews, #13, *Historical Research Project of Coahoma County.*

⁶ Maynard, Interview, *Historical Research Project of Coahoma County.*

⁷ "Col George N. Saunders," http://www.findagrave. com/cgi-bin/fg.cgi?page=gr&GSln=SAU&GSpartial=1&GSbyrel=all&GSst=27&GScntry=4&GSsr=1361&GRid=15924942&(accessed September 27, 2013).

⁸ One might wonder if Mr. Maynard was confusing Fincher Bobo with his son, Robert Eager Bobo. Probably he was not. Fincher Bobo was born in 1815 and died in 1856. "Fincher Gist Bobo," http://records.ancestry.com/Fincher_Gist_Bobo_records.ashx?pid=14659015 (accessed November 8, 2013). George N. Saunders was born in 1792 and died in 1875. Saunders, Ancestry.com. Robert E. Bobo, Fincher's son, was born in 1847. "Spreading Branches," Robert E. Bobo, /cgi-bin/igm.cgi?op=GET&db=wilson%2Dtempleton&id=I11785 (accessed November 8, 2013). Col. Saunders's grandson, George F. Maynard, Sr., was born in 1853. "George F. Maynard, Sr.," http://trees.ancestry.com/tree/5690520/person/5107164213 (accessed November 8, 2013). Given Col. Saunders's age, it makes more sense that the Colonel would have hunted with Fincher Bobo rather than his son, Robert. Moreover, Mr. Maynard, being a contemporary of Robert E. Bobo, no doubt knew the difference between the two men and intended to describe incidents involving Fincher, not Robet Eager, Bobo.

⁹ Dance, "Supplement to Assignment XXX," *Coahoma County WPA Microfilm Collection, Reels A770 and A771.*

¹⁰ Maynard, Interview, *Historical Research Project of Coahoma County.*

¹¹ Charles Hallock, "The Sinnaker Bear," *Forest and Stream*, March 4, 1899, 165.

¹² George Douglas Alexander, "Hunting Sketches—No. 2. Booby's Encounter with a Ten-Year Old He Bear," *American Field*, November 11, 1882, 329.

¹³ "How Much Do a Bear's Guts Weigh?," http://biggamehoundsmen.com/forum/how-much-do-a-bear-s-guts-weigh-t25268.html (November 1, 2013). Ten

ff8ffggffgg

percent is a very conservative factor. According to the Vermont Fish and Wildlife Department, a Montana study found that the viscera of a black bear typically make up anywhere from 11.6 to 20.7 percent of the bear's live weight. The Vermont Black Bear, http://www.vtfishandwildlife.com/books/Vermont_Black_Bear/_The%20Vt%20Black%20Bear_Section%201.pdf (November 1, 2013).

[14] Charles Hallock, "The Sinnaker Bear," 165.

[15] Baron Cuvier, Edward Griffith, Edward Pidgeon, and Charles Hamilton Smith, *The Animal Kingdom*, vol. 2 (London: George B.Whittaker, 1827), 228–29; Charles Hallock, *A Sportsman's Gazetter and General Guide* (New York: Forest and Stream Publishing Company, 1880), 23. C. Hart Merriam, "The Yellow Bear of Louisiana, Ursus Luteolus Griffith," *Proceedings of the Biological Society of Washington* 8: 148–49 (1893).

[16] Merriam, 148.

[17] "Black Bear Color Phases," http://www.bear.org/website/bear-pages/black-bear/basic-bear-facts/16-black-bear-color-phases.html (accessed November 11, 2013).

[18] Lea Leslie Seale, "Indian Place Names in Mississippi" (master's thesis, Louisiana State University, 1939), 127, citing Choctaw Indian Simpson Tubby.

[19] Harris Dickson, "The Bearslayer—Holt Collier's Recollections of Man and Beast," *Saturday Evening Post*, March 13, 1909, 14.

[20] Remington Kellogg and Gerrit Smith Miller, List of North America's Recent Mammals (Washington:Smithsonian Institution, 1955), 693 (called *Euarctos americanus luteolus*, by Kellogg and Miller).

[21] "Louisiana Black Bear (Ursus americanus luteolus)," http://ecos.fws.gov/speciesProfile/profile/speciesProfile.action?spcode=A08F (accessed March 17, 2014).

Chapter 5 Young Bob Bobo

[1] Fincher Gist Bobo, http://www.findagrave.com/cgi-bin/fg.cgi?page=gr&GRid=27502692 (accessed September 27, 2013).

[2] Thomas G. Dabney, writing under the nom de plume, Coahoma, incorrectly reported that Bob Bobo's mother died when he was young and that Curt Clark was the son of Bob's stepmother. Thomas G. Dabney, "Bruin in the Canebrake," *Forest and Stream*, March 28, 1887, 179.

[3] William L. Richter, *Historical Dictionary of the Old South* (Lanham, Maryland: Rowman and Littlefield, 2006), xxvii.

[4] Dabney, "Bruin in the Canebrake," 179.

[5] 1890 United States Census (Veterans Schedule), s.v. "Robert E. Bobo," Coahoma County, Mississippi, accessed through *Ancestry.com* (accessed February 13, 2014).

[6] National Park Service "Search for Soldiers," s. v., "Robert E. Bobo," accessed through http://www.nps.gov/civilwar/search-soldiers.htm (accessed April 2, 2013).

[7] National Park Service, "Regimental Details," http://www.nps.gov/civilwar/search-regiments-detail.htm?regiment_id=CMS0018RC (accessed April 2, 2013).

[8] Hough, "The Sunny South—II," 145.

[9] Hough, "The Sunny South—II," 144; George D. Alexander, "The Big Mound Near the Hushpuckany," *The American Field*, August 25, 1883, 17.

[10] Hough, "The Sunny South—II," 145.

[11] Also called "Annis" Brake. See, MS HomeTownLocator, "Annis Brake Coahoma County," http://mississippi.hometownlocator.com/maps/feature-map,ftc,1,fid,666278,n,annis%20brake.cfm (accessed September 10, 2013).

[12] *The Evening Scimitar*, "Bob Bobo Is Dead Today," 1.

[13] "Richard Nelson Harris," http://trees.ancestry.com/tree/26613694/person/1945204738 (accessed April 10, 2014).

[14] "Mississippi Marriages," 1776–1935, s.v. "R. N. Harris," Coahoma County, Mississippi, accessed through *Ancestry.com* (accessed November 2013).

[15] "Bobo-Prince Marriage," *The Memphis Avalanche*, November 26, 1868, accessed through Archiver.rootsweb.ancestry.com (accessed Feburary 13, 2014).

[16] Dabney, "Bruin in the Canebrake," 179.

[17] D. B. Weir, "Mississippi Bear Hunting," *The American Field*, November 25, 1882, 357–58.

[18] The age given for Fincher in the 1880 census indicates his birth year to be 1871. "1880 Census about Fincher Gist Bobo," accessed through Ancestry.com (accessed November 8, 2013). The 1900 census lists his birth as occurring in March 1870. "1900 Census about Fincher Gist Bobo," accessed through Ancestry.com (accessed November 8, 2013). The 1910 census indicates his birth year as 1868. 1910 Census about Fincher Gist Bobo, accessed through Ancestry.com (accessed November 8, 2013).

The Blankenstein genealogy page says he was born March 7, 1872. Blankenstein's Homepage, Generation 8, Page 4, http://www.blankensteingenealogy.net/generation_8_page_4.htm (accessed September 28, 2013). The year 1872 is also given as his birth year on his grave stone. "Fincher Gist Bobo," http://www.findagrave.com/cgi-bin/fg.cgi?page=gr&GRid=21600039 (accessed November 8, 2013). It is doubtful, then, that we can know the exact year of Fincher's birth. Neither can it be determined with 100 percent accuracy that Fincher was the couple's first born. Family tradition holds that a daughter named Sara Clara who had but a short life was also born to Bob and Anna Bobo, but there is no tradition as to her place in the family birth order. The author has been unable verify from any records the birth of any daughter to the Bobos. Mrs. Fincher Gist Bobo, Interview for "Historical Research Project of Coahoma County," Interview by Florence F. Montroy, November 20, 1936; Fincher G. (Jack) Bobo, electronic mail to author, September 18, 2013.

Chapter 6 The Bandits' Bear Hunt

[1] There are those who doubt that Dalton was a part of the James Gang. Dalton claimed also to have ridden with the Missouri-based Quantrill's Raiders, the notorious Confederate guerrilla band. According to Ancestry.com and records cited there, however, Daniel Webster "Kit" Dalton was born in Kentucky in

January 1852, which would have made him no more than 13 at the end of the Civil War—very young to have written with hard-bitten guerrillas like Quantrill's men. On the other hand, even at 13, he would not have been the youngest man to have fought in the Civil War. Still, there are those who believe his memoir, *Under the Black Flag*, was fiction pretending to be autobiography. That said, Dalton's account, whether based on his own experiences or those of others, appears to tell fact when it comes to the gunfight at the Louisiana racetrack, which is the reason Dalton gives for the James Gang's hiding out in Coahoma County. Certainly the racetrack incident was reported as true by the Chicago *Tribune*. Given that, even if Dalton had never ridden with the James-Younger outfit but was only telling stories he had heard about the gang, it is still quite likely that the story of the bear hunt is true except perhaps for Dalton's claim to have been there.

[2] *See*, Cole Younger, *The Story of Cole Younger, by Himself* (Chicago: The Henneberry Company, 1903), 76, 78–79.

[3] Daniel Webster "Kit" Dalton, *Under the Black Flag* (Memphis: Lockard Publishing Company, 1914), 181–182.

[4] D. H. Rule, "James & Youngers: The Outlaws," http://www.civilwarstlouis.com/history/jamesgangoutlaws.htm (accessed February 11, 2013).

[5] *The Chicago Tribune*, "The Younger Boys," March 27, 1875, 7.

[6] Dalton, *Under the Black Flag*, 181–183.

[7] *The Chicago Tribune*, "The Younger Boys," March 27, 1875, 7.

[8] Younger, *The Story of Cole Younger, by Himself*, 78, 81–85.

[9] Dalton, *Under the Black Flag*, 183–184.

[10] Gibson, "Supplement to Forest & Fauna," *Historical Research Project of Coahoma County*."

[11] "Jefferson B. Snyder," *New Orleans Times-Picayune*, April 15, 1938, accessed through http://files.usgwarchives.net/la/madison/bios/snyderjb.txt (accessed February 27, 2013).

[12] This Dickerson was probably William H. Dickerson. *See*, Vladimir Alexandrov, *The Black Russian* (New York: Atlantic Monthly Press, 2013), 13.

[13] Jesse James was murdered in 1882. Joseph A. Dacus, *Illustrated Lives and Adventures of Frank and Jesse James and the Younger Brothers, the Noted Western Outlaws* (New York and St. Louis: N. D. Thompson and Company, 1882), 435–36.

[14] Bobby Joe Williams, "The One They Had In 1882 Was 'The Big Flood,'" *Shelby County, Tennessee, History and Genealogy*, Tennessee Roots , http://tn-roots.com/tnshelby/history/1882Flood.htm (accessed September 11, 2013).

[15] Dacus, 435–436.

[16] Old Citizen, Interview, Mrs. J. L. McKeown, August 4, 1936, County History, Supplement to Interviews, Assignment #14, Project No. 2984, Clarksdale, Mississippi, *Historical Research Project of Coahoma County*, Works Progress Administration for Mississippi, Box 10677, Outlaws File, Series 447, Mississippi Department of Archives and History. Coahoma County had a rich outlaw history that at one time apparently involved some prominent names in the community. When the

WPA oral histories were taken in the late 1930s, the memories of the outlaw days
were still fresh enough to make the older men and women interviewed reluctant to
name names and, in the case of the Old Citizen, to reveal his own.

   [17] Ibid., 183.

Chapter 7 Bobo's Reputation Expands

   [1] How Bobo attracted the attention of an Urbana, Ohio, paper, is unknown.
He already may have had friends in that area. Certainly, by the time of his death,
he had friends in the Midwest, including some in Champaign, Illinois, who
would visit and hunt with him in Coahoma County. "Bob Bobo is Dead Today,"
The Evening Scimitar, 1.

   [2] Mrs. Fincher Gist Bobo, Interview for "Historical *Research Project of
Coahoma County*," Interview by Florence F. Montroy, November 20, 1936;
Fincher G. (Jack) Bobo, electronic mail to author, September 18, 2013; Betty
Bobo Pearson, electronic mail to author, September 6, 2015.

   [3] James G. Chism, "Editors Appeal," *The Memphis Daily Appeal*, November 15, 1876, 4.

   [4] Weir, "Mississippi Bear Hunting," *The American Field*," November 25, 1882,
357.

   [5] "Throughout the Southern States, from east to west, every man is a colonel."
Commonwealth of Australia, Parliamentary Debates, House of Representatives,
vol. 19, June 8, 1904, accessed through Googlebooks.com (February 13, 2014).

   [6] John Solomon Otto, *The Final Frontiers, 1880-1930: Settling the Southern
Bottomlands* (Westport, Connecticut: Greenwood Publishing Company, 1999), 22.

   [7] Emerson Hough, "In Old Mississippi," *Forest and Stream*, November 21,
1896, 408-409.

   [8] *Biographical and Historical Memoirs of Mississippi*, vol. 1 (Chicago: The
Goodspeed Publishing Company, 1891), 123.

   [9] Robert Lowry, *Biennial Report of the Commissioner of Immigration and
Agriculture to the Legislature of Mississippi, for the Years 1884-'85* (Jackson,
Mississippi: J. L. Power, State Printer, 1886).

   [10] *Biographical and Historical Memoirs of Mississippi*, vol. 1 (Chicago: The
Goodspeed Publishing Company, 1891), 123.

   [11] *Forest Products of the United States* (Washington, D. C.: Government
Printing Office, 1909), 120, 123.

   [12] Cavalier, "Arkansas Game Grounds," *Forest and Stream*, May 27, 1886, 349.

   [13] Dabney, "Bruin in the Canebrake," 179.

   [14] Weir, "Mississippi Bear Hunting," 357. Dabney, "Bruin in the Canebrake,"
179.

   [15] Dabney, "Bruin in the Canebrake," 179.

   [16] J.D.H., "A Mississippi Fish Fry." *Forest and Stream*, 1879, 97.

   [17] Betty Bobo Pearson, electronic mail to author, September 6, 2015.

   [18] Fincher G. (Jack) Bobo, electronic mail to author, September 19, 2013.

[19] The 1880 census shows Mrs. Bobo still in the Bobo home, and the 1887 Dabney article in *Forest and Stream* refers to "Mrs. Bobo." Dabney, who lived and worked in Coahoma County, would not have mistaken a housekeeper for "Mrs. Bobo." Clearly, she had not left Coahoma County at that time.

[20] C. C., "On the Sunflower River," *Forest and Stream*, November 3, 1892, 379.

Chapter 8 Mashed up Cattle

[1] Hough, "In Old Mississippi," 408–409.

[2] The Illinois Central railroad acquired the Louisville, New Orleans and Texas's Mississippi line in 1892. Otto, *The Final Frontiers, 1880–1930: Settling the Southern Bottomlands,* 27.

[3] I. E. Nagel, "The Beaver Dam Club," *Forest and Stream*, January 1884, 446.

[4] "The World of Shooters," *The Sporting Life*, August 10, 1895, 19.

[5] In 1894, the year of Hough's hunt, a car load of midwestern men, including Civil War veteran Col. D. B. Henderson, of Dubuque, Iowa, left Memphis for a two day Delta hunt. "At Panther Burn (a village in Sharkey County, Mississippi)," wrote Hough, "someone fired a shot or two at the car, which caused Col. Henderson, who lost an arm in the war, to say it reminded him of old times." Emerson Hough, "The Sunny South—V," *Forest and Stream*, March 16, 1895, 206.

[6] Emerson Hough, *The Story of the Outlaw: A Study of the Western Desparado*, (New York: The Outing Publishing Company, 1907), 16.

[7] Emerson Hough, "The Death of Col. Bobo," *Forest and Stream*, December 27, 1902, 513.

[8] Hough, "The Sunny South—II," 144.

[9] Hough, *The Law of the Land*, 33. Divine was probably smaller and thinner than the fictional character in Hough's novel said to have been based on him. *Illinois Central Employees' Magazine*," Thomas A. Divine Dead," November 1920, 54–55. A pair of "knee breeches" belonging to Noel Money and borrowed by Divine for a deer hunt fit Divine "to a T" as full length pants. Hough, "In Old Mississippi," 408–409. Also, Hough's telegram to friends in Memphis on the occasion of Divine's death described Divine as "of frail physique." *Illinois Central Employees' Magazine*," Thomas A. Divine Dead," November 1920, 54–55.

[10] Hough, *The Law of the Land*, 33.

[11] Hough, "The Sunny South—II," 144–145.

Chapter 9 The Writer Down South

[1] Emerson Hough, "The Sunny South—I," *Forest and Stream*, February 16, 1895, 124. Peabody was Secretary of the Baltimore and Ohio Southwestern Railroad. William Kirkby, *Annual Report of the Commissioner of Railroads and Telegraphs to the Governor of the State of Ohio for the Year 1892*, Office of the Commissioner of Railroads and Telegraphs, State of Ohio (Norwalk, Ohio: The Lansing Printing Company, 1892), 24.

[2] Hough, "The Sunny South—I," 124.

[3] "Farm Preserves." *Forest and Stream*, October 27, 1900, 329.

[4] Hough, "The Sunny South—II," 144.

[5] Hough, "The Sunny South—I," 124.

[6] Ibid. The debate was far from over on the pages of *Forest and Stream*, however. Among others holding forth on the subject in future issues of the magazine would be T. G. "Coahoma" Dabney. Thomas G. Dabney, "The Horn Snake," *Forest and Stream*, November 4, 1899, 365.

[7] Hough, "The Sunny South—II," 144.

Chapter 10 A Few Dogs

[1] Hough, "The Sunny South—II," 144.

[2] This figure most likely applies to the acres under cultivation and not to the total acreage owned. Bobo's obituary, written some eight years later, places his land holdings at 2000 acres. "Bob Bobo Is Dead Today," *The Evening Scimitar*, 1.

[3] Hough, "The Sunny South—II," 144.

[4] Satchfield, "Those Famous Bobo Bear Hunts," 5.

[5] Hough, "The Sunny South—II," 144.

[6] Robert (Bob) Bobo (1924–2013) of Clarksdale, Mississippi, died April 19, 2013. *Clarion Ledger*, "Robert E. Bobo," http://www.legacy.com/obituaries/clarionledger/obituary.aspx?page=lifestory&pid=164329765 (accessed November 9, 2013).

[7] Lamar Satchfield, "Those Famous Bobo Bear Hunts," *Delta Scene Magazine*, Spring, 1974, 4–5.

[8] "Extinction of Large Game," *Commercial Appeal*, November 17, 1895, 11.

[9] Hough, "The Sunny South—II," 144.

[10] James Gordon, "Bear Dogs," *Forest and Stream*, July 16, 1885, 488.

[11] Henry J. Peck, "Bears and Bear-Hunting," *Spirit of the Times*, January 27, 1844, 572.

[12] George D. Alexander, "The Black Bear," in *The Big Game of North America*, ed. George O. Shields (Chicago: Rand, McNally & Company, 1890), 258.

[13] Gordon, "Bear Dogs," 488.

[14] George D. Alexander, "Hunting Sketches—No. 4. The Death of the Big He Bear.—Fishing in the Hushpuckany," *The American Field*, November 25, 1882, 359.

[15] W. T. Block, "The Big Thicket Bear Hunters Club of Kountze," ed. William T. Block III, http://www.wtblock.com/wtblockjr/BearHunters.htm (accessed May 23, 2013).

[16] W. W. Titus, "Reminiscences of a Dog Trainer—No. 3," *The American Field*, August 18, 1894, 154.

[17] Peck, "Bears and Bear-Hunting," 572.

[18] A. B. Wingfield, "In Jones's Bayou.—IV," *Forest and Stream*, November 16, 1895, 420.

[19] Peck, "Bears and Bear-Hunting," 572.

[20] George R. Phelan, "A Swamp Hunter," *Forest and Stream*, May 25, 1882, 324.

[21] Alexander, "The Black Bear," 247–278.

[22] Peck, "Bears and Bear-Hunting," 572.

[23] Gordon, "Bear Dogs," 488.

[24] Hough, "The Sunny South—II," 144.

[25] Alexander, "The Black Bear," 247–278.

[26] Gordon, "Bear Dogs," 488.

[27] Emerson Hough, "With the Bobo Bear Pack—I," *Forest and Stream*, February 1, 1896, 92.

[28] "Kind hearts are more than coronets, and simple faith than Norman blood." Alfred Lord Tennyson, "Lady Clara Vere de Vere," *The Works of Tennyson*, ed. Hallam Lord Tennyson (New York: The MacMillan Company, 1913), 48.

[29] Gordon, "Bear Dogs," 488.

[30] Here Gordon seems to be using the term "cur," not in its specialized sense, i. e., as the name for a specific type or breed of dog, but in its historic sense of "a dog of mixed breed, mongrel"; Webster's New World *Dictionary of the American Language*, College Edition, 1966, s.v. "cur"; "[a] mongrel," The American Kennel Club, *The Complete Dog Book* (New York: Wiley Publishing, Inc., 1998), 738.

[31] Gordon, "Bear Dogs," 488. In Greek mythology, Hyperion was one of the Titans, superiors and predecessors to the gods. He was "the father of the sun, the moon, and the dawn… ," while a satyr was an ugly, goat-man, minor god of the wastelands and deserted places. Edith Hamilton, *Mythology* (New York: New American Library, 1969), 25, 42.

[32] Gordon, "Bear Dogs," 488.

[33] Weir, "Mississippi Bear Hunting," 357–58.

Chapter 11 The Right Place for a Hunt

[1] Hough, "The Sunny South—II," 144.

[2] Satchfield, "Those Famous Bobo Bear Hunts," 5; Hough, "The Sunny South—II," 144.

[3] The Bobo family has a photo, almost certainly taken by Hough, of Bob Bobo feeding a young bear, presumably this same Alice, standing on its hind legs.

[4] Hough, "The Sunny South—II," 144.

[5] Hough called the younger Bobo, "Horace." Emerson Hough, "The Sunny South—III," *Forest and Stream*, March 2, 1895, 164. There is no record of Bobo having any son by that name. The Bobo son on this hunt almost certainly was Robert E. Bobo, Jr., since, at the time, Fincher, the older son, was occupied in running his father's logging camp on the Sunflower River. Ibid. Perhaps Bob, Jr., was nicknamed Horace, to distinguish him from his father. Hough may have heard Bobo call his nephew or brother-in-law by their surnames—Harris—and mistook Bobo, with his Delta accent, for saying Horace. Or, perhaps Huff was simply mistaken as to the name he heard. What is almost certain is that R. E. Bobo had no son named Horace.

[6] Hough, "The Sunny South—II," 144.

[7] Dabney, "Bruin in the Canebrake," 179

[8] Alexander, "The Black Bear," 248.

[9] Dabney, "Bruin in the Canebrake," 179

[10] Hough, "The Sunny South—II," 144.

[11] Deer were not always plentiful. Some years—particularly after severe floods, which were hard on deer—deer were in short supply. Weir, "Mississippi Bear Hunting," 357–58.

[12] Hough, "The Sunny South—II," 145.

[13] "Bears," *Fur Trade Review*, June 1, 1894, 260.

[14] Hough, "The Sunny South—II," 145. A Kentucky weekly reported in 1902 that R.E. Bobo "killed 43 bears last year and has a total to his credit of over 2000." "Current Topics," *Hickman Courier*, June 27, 1902, 6.

[15] "Meat" is the word used in the original publication, but it almost certainly was supposed to have been "mast." Such errors were not unusual in nineteenth century periodicals like *Forest and Stream*. Manuscripts were typeset from handwritten copy, in all probability. A type setter not familiar with the term "mast" might well have read it as "meat" and set the type accordingly, especially if Hough's handwriting was difficult to read, as that of a journalist on a deadline might well have been.

[16] Emerson Hough, "The Sunny South—II," 145.

[17] Harris was married to Bob Bobo's sister, who provided many of the early historical details concerning the Bobo family during the course of a local history project reported in the *Clarksdale Press-Register* in 1928. Mrs. Harris was still living at that time. Weathers, "When Coahoma County Had 3 Families and a Hand-Mill," 8. *See also,* Graye Harris Carter, "Untitled Reminisences."

[18] "Bears," *Fur Trade Review*, 260. The Indiana hunter, C. C., said Bobo killed the 304 bears in 1879, but that could have been C. C.'s mistake or an editor or a typesetter confusing a 4 for a 9. C. C., "On the Sunflower River," *Forest and Stream*, November 3, 1892, 379.

[19] Weir, "Mississippi Bear Hunting," 358.

[20] Lindsay Denison, "President Roosevelt's Mississippi Bear Hunt," *Outing*, February 1903, 603.

[21] Hough, "The Sunny South—II," 144.

[22] Alexander, "Hunting Sketches—No. 4. The Death of the Big He Bear.—Fishing in the Hushpuckany," 358.

[23] Hough, "With the Bobo Bear Pack—I," 92.

[24] These "100 souls" included Bobo's family but consisted mostly of sharecroppers or hired hands. Hough, "The Sunny South—II," 144.

[25] Hough, "With the Bobo Bear Pack—I," 92.

[26] Hough, "The Sunny South—II," 144.

[27] *See, e. g.,* Hough, "The Sunny South—III," 164.

[28] "Bears," *Fur Trade Review*, June 1, 1894, 260.

[29] Hough, "The Sunny South—II," 145.

Chapter 12 The First Strike

[1] Hough, "The Sunny South—III," 162.

[2] Hough, "The Sunny South—IV." *Forest and Stream*, March 9, 1895, 184.

[3] Again, in his "Sunny South" articles, Hough apparently incorrectly calls the younger Bobo "Horace."

[4] Hough, "The Sunny South—III," 162–63.

[5] Longleaf Alliance, *Longleaf Pine Glossary* (2002), s.v. "Dummy Line," http://www.auburn.edu/academic/forestry_wildlife/longleafalliance/teachers/teacherkit/glossary.htm (accessed February 15, 2013).

[6] Hough, "The Sunny South—III," 163.

[7] Emerson Hough, "The Sunny South—IV," *Forest and Stream*, March 9, 1895, 184.

[8] Hough, "The Sunny South—III," 162.

[9] Fincher G. (Jack) Bobo, electronic mail to author, November 22, 2013.

[10] George D. Alexander, "My First Bear Hunt," *The American Field*, 1882, 291.

[11] *Knives and Swords: A Visual History*, ed. Chris McNab (New York: DK Publishing, 2012), 238–39, 256.

[12] Peck, "Bears and Bear-Hunting," 572.

[13] *Knives and Sword: A Visual History*, 238–39, 256.

[14] Peck, "Bears and Bear-Hunting," 572.

[15] Emerson Hough, "The Sunny South—V," 205.

[16] Hough, "The Sunny South—II,"144.

[17] Horace Kephart, "Lost in the Swamps.—II," *Forest and Stream*, August 10, 1895, 112.

[18] Hough, "The Sunny South—IV," 184.

[19] George R. Phelan, "The Pack Well Shuffled," *Forest and Stream*, September 7, 1882, 103.

[20] Hough, "The Sunny South—IV," 184.

[21] Hough, "The Sunny South—III," 163.

Chapter 13 Into the Sunflower Wilderness

[1] Hough, "The Sunny South—III," 163. Often, there is no hard freeze in Mississippi before early November, and much green foliage can still be seen at that time.

[2] "Whippers-in" are the members of the hunting party charged with keeping the pack together and orderly by whipping straying hounds back into the group or punishing misbehaving dogs, *e. g.*, those that open on something other than the intended game. Delabere Pritchett Blaine, *An Encyclopaedia of Rural Sports*, 3rd (London: Longmans, Green, Reader, and Dyer, 1870), 486. The shortened version of this term, "whip," is used to describe the member of a political party who serves an analogous function in a legislative body. Judy Schneider and Michael L. Koempel, *Congressional Desk Book*, 6th ed. (Alexandria, Virginia: TheCapitol.Net, Inc., 2012), 200.

[3] Bobo called the Tallahatchie the "Hatchee." Hough, "The Sunny South—III,"163.

⁴ Hough, "Bobo and Some Bear Stories," *Forest and Stream*, November 10, 1900, 368.

⁵ Backwoodsman, "The Ferocity of the Black Bear," *The American Field*, December 18, 1886, 383.

⁶ Emerson Hough, "Gates Ajar," *Forest and Stream*, December 19, 1896, 489.

⁷ Hough, "The Sunny South—III," 163–164. Fincher was erroneously called "Fitcher" by Hough.

⁸ In 1911 Coahoma County pioneer W. A. Alcorn, Sr., described "raftsmen" as "thieves and thugs" in a reminiscence dictated to his son, Judge William A. Alcorn, Jr. *See*, Cooper, Alcorn, and Alcorn, Supplement to Interviews, #13, *Historical Research Project of Coahoma County.*

⁹ Dobie, *The Ben Lilly Legend*, 186. One wonders if this hide was still a bit fresh and elastic when measured, or if it was dry.

¹⁰ Hough, "The Sunny South—III," 164.

¹¹ Dabney, "Bruin in the Canebrake," 179.

¹² Hough, "The Sunny South—III,"164.

¹³ Emerson Hough, "With the Bobo Bear Pack—II," *Forest and Stream*, February 8, 1896, 113.

¹⁴ Backwoodsman, "The Ferocity of the Black Bear," 383.

¹⁵ Gordon, "Bear-Hunting In the South," 861.

¹⁶ Hough, "Bobo and Some Bear Stories," November 10, 1900, 368.

¹⁷ Paul J. Rainey, "The Royal Sport of Hounding Lions," *The Outing Magazine*, November 1911, 145.

¹⁸ Hough, "Bobo and Some Bear Stories," November 10, 1900, 368.

¹⁹ Phelan remembered William as Shelby McPeak's brother-in-law in his recollection of the story. The biographer of Shelby McPeak's granddaughter, however, correctly identified William as Shelby's nephew, which is verified by the 1880 U. S. Census, which records that, at that time, a 40 year old William McPeak lived in the household of a 60 year old I. Shelby McPeak. Barbara Russell Chesser, *Remembering Mattie* (Waco: Sunstone Press, 2008), 328–329; "1880 United States about I. Shelby McPeak," accessed through Ancestry. com, (accessed, September 14, 2013); Phelan, "A Swamp Hunter," 324. Phelan contributed to the outdoor press of his day under the pseudonym, "A Mule." "George R. Phelan," *Forest and Stream*, Oct. 12, 1882, 202.

²⁰ Peck, "Bears and Bear-Hunting," 572.

²¹ *Yazoo Whig*, "Horrible Death," January 21, 1848, 4. Theodore Roosevelt recounted the death of Dr. Hamberlin in a 1908 article for *Scribner's Magazine*, though he, assuming a contemporaneous newspaper account was correct, misstated a number of details, including giving the bear's weight as 640 pounds, which seems to be quite an overstatement for a lean bear that field dressed at 310. He also called Dr. Hamberlin, whose Christian name was Isaac, by the name of his nephew, Monroe Hamberlin. Theodore Roosevelt, "In the Louisiana Canebrakes," *Scribner's Magazine*, January 1908, 52–53.

Chapter 14 The Right Weapon

[1] Willie D. Halsell, "Protection of Game in Sunflower County One Hundred Years Ago," *Journal of Mississippi History* 13 (1951), 105.

[2] Kephart, "Lost in the Swamps.—II," 113.

[3] See, e. g., "Pledge of the Am. Temp. Union," *Journal of the American Temperance Union* (November 1839), 161: "We, the undersigned, do agree that we will not use intoxicating liquours as a beverage and will not traffic in them; that we will not provide them as an article of entertainment, or for persons in our employment; and that, in all suitable ways, we will discountenance their use throughout the community."

[4] Don Johnson, *Thirteen Months at Manassas/Bull Run* (Jefferson, North Carolina: McFarland & Company, Inc., Publishers, 2013), 53.

[5] Dobie, *The Ben Lilly Legend*, 62.

[6] Jack David Laurus Holmes, *Gayoso: The Life of a Spanish Governor in the Mississippi Valley 1789–1799* (Baton Rouge: Louisiana State University Press, 1965), 59.

[7] *Knives and Swords: A Visual History*, 220, 256. Rezin Bowie is buried in the cemetery of St. Joseph Catholic Church, Port Gibson, Mississippi.

[8] Halsell, 105.

[9] James Gordon, "The Bear Hunt," *The Turf, Field, and Farm* (August 8, 1870), 210.

[10] Col. James L. Goodloe was the first cousin of the great-grandfather of the Honorable William F. Winter, former governor of the state of Mississippi, making Col. Goodloe a first cousin thrice removed to Gov. Winter. William F. Winter, letter to author, February 14, 2014.

[11] James L. Goodloe, "My First Bear Hunt," *Forest and Stream*, January 1917, 16.

[12] Hough, "The Sunny South—III," 163.

[13] Wingfield, "In Jones's Bayou.—IV," 420.

[14] Alexander, "The Black Bear," 259.

[15] Fincher G. Bobo, electronic mail to author, November 22, 2013.

[16] Susan Haskell Harrell, letter to author, June 6, 1987.

[17] Dabney, "Bruin in the Canebrake," 179.

[18] Dickson, "The Bearslayer—Holt Collier's Recollections of Man and Beast," 14.

[19] Hough, "The Sunny South—III," 164. Bobo's descendants have to this day a Winchester model 1892 .44-40 that belonged to Bob Bobo, almost certainly the very one carried by Bob Bobo on this hunt. Fincher G. Bobo, letter to author, January 12, 2013.

[20] Gordon, "Bear-Hunting in the South," 862.

[21] Phelan, "A Swamp Hunter," 324; *Remembering Mattie*, 328–329.

[22] Cavalier, "Arkansas Game Grounds," 349. Daniels was born "about 1846," making him the approximate age of Bobo. *U. S. Census, Cache Township, Monroe County, by H. H. Parker,* (page 16, Supervisor's District 1, Enumeration District 207) 1880.

[23] Hough, "The Sunny South—III," 164.

[24] Dabney, "Bruin in the Canebrake," 179.

[25] *The Sportsman's Magazine and Life in London*, "A 'Bad Fix' in a Bear Fight," October 18, 1845, 372.

Chapter 15 The Life of the Bear Dog

[1] *See, e. g.,* "Questions and Answers," *Hunter, Trader, Trapper*, August 1914, 110: "Dog bread (home-made) is to be made of meat scraps boiled, shorts and corn meal stirred into broth, after meat portion has been well stirred to shreds, till stiff dough is formed, then filled into pans and baked in a slow oven. This makes a very good, nutritious, relished food for dogs of all ages... ." Betty Bobo Pearson, the great-granddaughter of the Bear Hunter, says that the food for Bob Bobo's bear dogs was prepared by cooking "table scraps, corn meal, meat, etc., in a large cast iron pot... ." Bobo kept one such vessel at the plantation house "in the back and one at the hunting camp." Mrs. Pearson "ended up" with those two kettles. One has been converted into a fountain in the backyard of one of the Bear Hunter's descendants. Betty Bobo Pearson, electronic mail to author, September 6, 2015.

[2] Hough, "With the Bobo Bear Pack—I," 93.

[3] The author has known bird dog owners who did not permit the petting of their dogs.

[4] Hough, "With the Bobo Bear Pack—I," 93.

[5] William Lancaster Polk, "With the Bears In Coon Bayou," *Forest and Stream*, February 10, 1887, 46–47.

[6] Gordon, "Bear Dogs," 488.

[7] Hough, "In Old Mississippi," 408–409.

[8] A. B. Wingfield, "In Jones's Bayou.—III," *Forest and Stream*, November 9, 1895, 398.

[9] A. B. Wingfield, "In Jones's Bayou.—I," *Forest and Stream*, October 19, 1895, 332.

[10] A. B. Wingfield, "On Jones's Bayou.—IV.," *Forest and Stream*, November 16, 1896, 420.

[11] Hough, "The Sunny South—III," 164.

Chapter 16 Wolves, Panthers, and Squirrel Hunting at Night

[1] Hough, "The Sunny South—III," 164.

[2] C. C., "On the Sunflower River," 379.

[3] James G. Chism, "Editors Appeal," *The Memphis Daily Appeal*, November 15, 1876, 4.

[4] The animal called "panther" in the southern and eastern U. S., of course, is the same species (*puma concolor*) called "cougar," or "mountain lion," in the west. Victor H. Cahalane, "The American Cats," In *Wild Animals of North America*, ed. Merle Severy (Chicago: National Geographic Society, 1960), 212–213.

[5] J. Frank Dobie, *The Ben Lilly Legend*, 9th (Boston: Little, Brown and Company, 1950), 186.

[6] "Panther Fight," *Spirit of the Times*, December 16, 1843, 498.

[7] Dobie, *The Ben Lilly Legend*, 237.

[8] Cahalane, "The American Cats," In *Wild Animals of North America*, 212–213.

[9] Chism, "Editors Appeal," 4.

[10] Hough, "The Sunny South—III," 164. Morgan Furore, a friend of the author's daughter, can verify this aspect of the panther's character. While jogging near her college campus along a trail in the Los Padres Mountains north of Santa Paula, California, Morgan came upon a mother cougar and her half grown cub. The young lady immediately stopped, turned, and began walking back toward campus. The two cats followed the college student until she reached a paved road.

[11] Gordon, "A Panther Hunt In Mississippi," 324. Gordon may have sacrificed some accuracy on the altar of drama in so describing the call of the panther.

[12] Dobie, *The Ben Lilly Legend*, 116. Thanks to modern technology, we can hear the cry of a panther and decide for ourselves whether it sounds like a woman's scream. *See*, Max Allen, ed. Yiwei Wang, "Female Mountain Lion Screaming for Mates in Front of Trail Camera," http://www.youtube.com/watch?v=hM2Sw8dsMDQ (accessed November 22, 2013).

[13] Hough, "The Sunny South—III," 164.

[14] Lamar Fontaine, *My Life and My Lectures* (New York and Washington: The Neale Publishing Company, 1908), 275.

[15] Lamar Fontaine, "Golden Spot of the Delta," *Cincinnati Enquirer*, August 29, 1896, 12.

[16] The author is uncertain which night of the hunt this incident occurred. The account of it that appears in *Forest and Stream* states only that "Mr. Hough forgot to incorporate [the story] in his charming sketches of the 'Sunny South.'" Since "The Sunny South" was the name of Hough's series of articles on his 1894 hunt, the author has assumed that the incident here related occurred during that hunt and has placed the story on this particular night out of convenience and cannot confirm the chronological accuracy of such placement.

[17] *Forest and Stream*, "The Squirrels, The Rifle and Night," 88.

[18] Hough, "The Sunny South—III, 164.

Chapter 17 Riding Cane

[1] Hough, "The Sunny South—IV," 184. Richard Sanders, of New Albany, Mississippi once told the author that in the years immediately following World War II he made a number of deer hunting trips to the lower Mississippi Delta. At that time, Mr. Sanders said, goat horns were preferred by many Delta hound men for their hunting horns.

[2] A whitetailed deer's hooves are cloven and consist of four parts, the two larger main hooves, and smaller rear hooves, called dewclaws.

[3] Author's telephonic interview with James G. Gray (great-grandson of James G. Norwood), February 19, 2014.

[4] W. L. Polk, "With the Bears In Coon Bayou," 46–47.

[5] Hough, "The Sunny South—IV," 184.

[6] The author's search of old and modern maps and inquiries in Coahoma and surrounding counties disclose no known location called "Surveyor's Lake." There was and is, however, between the site of the old Bobo Plantation and the Sunflower River a body of water—today, little more than a bayou—named "Sevier Lake" and called "Sevier's Lake" on at least one old map. In all probability Hough's Midwestern ear heard the word "surveyor" when his Southern hosts, with their strong, Mississippi Delta accents, said "Sevier." Either that, or the typesetter at *Forest and Stream* misread "Sevier" in Hough's manuscript and typeset "surveyor" in its place, as a typesetter apparently set "meat" for "mast" in one of Hough's articles. It is doubtful that Hough and the party hunted around Sevier Lake on the day in question, for the Bobo party had already crossed to the east side of Sunflower. They would have had to have crossed back to the west side of the river in order to hunt along Sevier Lake, and Hough almost certainly would have mentioned such a crossing, but he describes none that day. More probably, Hough, in his recollections, confused Sevier Lake with Roundaway Lake or Plummer Lake, both of which are in southern Coahoma County near Black Bayou on the east side of the Sunflower, where the Bobo party was hunting. Or, he could have confused his days. The party plainly hunted on the west side of the Sunflower the first day. They very well could have hunted along Sevier Lake that day and probably did.

[7] Hough, "The Sunny South—III," 163.

[8] A. B. Wingfield, "In Jones's Bayou.—IV," *Forest and Stream*, November 16, 1895, 420.

[9] Hough, "The Sunny South—III," 163.

[10] Hough, "The Sunny South—IV," 184.

[11] Hough, "The Sunny South—V," 205.

[12] *New York Times*, "Wade Hampton Hurt," November 25, 1886.

[13] Hough gives Leavell's name as "N. L. Leavell." Hough, "With the Bobo Bear Pack—I," 92. This Leavell is almost certainly Napoleon Lewis Leavell, no doubt called "Boney" as short for "Bonaparte," probably a nickname given him due to his Christian name of Napoleon. *See* Amber Maloney, "Napoleon Lewis Leavell (1842–1899)," http://www.geni.com/people/Napoleon-Leavell/6000000010545275268 (accessed January 11, 2013). The Leavell family had settled in the same area of Coahoma County as the Bobo family and at about the same time. Weathers, "When Coahoma County Had 3 Families and a Hand-Mill," 8. The friend who accidentally shot Bobo was most likely Leavell. Certainly, Hough suggests no other member of the party. Hough, who knew Leavell, would have been unlikely to name him as the negligent shooter in the national press. Hough, "Bobo and Some Bear Stories," November 10, 1900, 368.

[14] Hough, "Bobo and Some Bear Stories," November 10, 1900, 368.

[15] Hough, "The Sunny South—IV," 184. Again, Hough calls this son "Horace," but, as explained elsewhere, the youngster almost certainly was Robert Eager Bobo, Jr.

[16] Hough, "The Sunny South—IV," 184.
[17] See Psalm 22:12.
[18] Hough, "The Sunny South—II,"144.
[19] Hough, "The Sunny South—IV," 184–185.
[20] "History of the Cane," *Farmers' Register*, 288.
[21] Montesano, *Spirit of the Times*, "Game Steaks and Cane Brakes," February 19, 1859, 14.
[22] Hough, "The Sunny South—I," 124.
[23] Hough, "The Sunny South—IV," 184.

Chapter 18 Fresh Tracks

[1] Hough, "The Sunny South—IV," 184.

Chapter 19 Bear Hunt Looking Up

[1] Hough, "The Sunny South—V," 205. "Old River" is a term generally applied to old runs and cutoffs of the Mississippi River. Here it names an old channel of the Sunflower River rather than the specific oxbow of the Mississippi known today in Coahoma County as "Old River" and less commonly as "Horse Shoe Bend Cutoff." *See,* Franklin Lafayette Riley, "Extinct Towns and Villages of Mississippi," *Publications of the Mississippi Historical Society*, vol. 5, ed. Franklin Lafayette Riley (Harrisburg: Harrisburg Publishing Company, 1902), 331, describing "Old River," and Margaret B. Hood, "Early County History, Coahoma County," 1936, Clarksdale, Mississippi, Box 10676, Formation File, Series 447, Mississippi Department of Archives and History, describing the same ox bow lake as "Horse Shoe Bend cut off." As a boy the author often fished the "Old River" cutoff of the Mississippi with his father.
[2] Emerson Hough, "The Sunny South—V," 205; *The Evening Scimitar*, "Bob Bobo Is Dead Today," 1.
[3] Emerson Hough, "The Sunny South—V," 205.
[4] Hough "From the South," 308.

Chapter 20 The Great Delta Bear Rush

[1] Hough, "The Sunny South—II," *Forest and Stream*, February 23, 1895, 144–145; "The Sunny South—III," *Forest and Stream*, March 2, 1895, 162–164; "The Sunny South—IV," *Forest and Stream,* March 9, 1895, 184–185; "The Sunny South—V," *Forest and Stream*, March 16, 1895, 205.
[2] Emerson Hough, "The Sunny South—V," 205.
[3] Hough, "With the Bobo Bear Pack—I," 92–93.
[4] Laurence Urdang, ed., *The Timetables of American History* (New York: Touchstone, 1984), 260.
[5] Emerson Hough, "The Sunny South—V," 205.
[6] E. G. L., "Gordon, Suh, of Mississippi," *New York Evening Post* (January 8, 1910), p. 1.

[7] Hough, "The Sunny South—V," 205. Only since the last ten or 15 years of the 20th century have guided hunts been readily available in the Mississippi Delta. Guides still are not as common in the Mississippi Delta as in other popular hunting locales.

[8] Hough, "The Sunny South—V," 205–206.

[9] Hough, "With the Bobo Bear Pack—I," 92–93.

[10] Emerson Hough, "The Bobo Bear Country Gone," *Forest and Stream*, June 9, 1900, 449.

[11] Hough, "With the Bobo Bear Pack—I," 92–93.

Chapter 21 Hough's Return

[1] Hough, "With the Bobo Bear Pack—I," *Forest and Stream*, 92.

[2] "Cabinet Card Photos," http://historic-memphis.com/memphis/cabinet-cards/cabinet-cards.html (accessed April 13, 2014).

[3] "Extinction of Large Game," *Commercial Appeal*, November 17, 1895, 11.

[4] The dates given by Hough are somewhat confusing, and it is not entirely clear whether he left Chicago on Wednesday, November 20, or Thursday, November 21, or whether he left the following Wednesday, November 27, or the following Thursday, November 28, 1895, which was Thanksgiving Day. "Grover Cleveland," *The American Presidency Project*, http://www.presidency.ucsb.edu/ws/index.php?pid=70686 (accessed January 11, 2013). As best the author can determine, Hough left on Thursday, November 21.

[5] Hough, "With the Bobo Bear Pack—I," *Forest and Stream*, 92.

[6] The camps on the first and second Hough hunt, of course, could have been at different locations. The similarity between the two could be because Bobo owned both logging camps and set them up the same way.

[7] Hough, "With the Bobo Bear Pack—I," 93.

[8] According to Hough, the members of the party were

> Capt. R. E. Bobo, Fincher Bobo, and Mr. Felix Payne, of Bobo Station, Mr. T. A. Divine and Mr. L. J. Lockwood, of Memphis, Tennessee; Mr. R. W. Foster, of New Orleans, Louisiana; Col. Dick Payne, of the Yazoo Valley, Mississippi; Capt. N. L. Leavell, of Clarksdale, Mississippi; Col. Bob Edwards, M. James Dunn, and Mr. James Dailey, of Coahoma County, Mississippi; Mr. Noel Money, of the E. C. Powder Co., of Oakland, New Jersey, and a dozen or so others who joined the party after they left the railroad or after they had gone to camp.

Irby Bennett, a well known Memphis sportsman and close friend of Tom Divine, was also present. "Extinction of Large Game," *Commercial-Appeal,* November 17, 1895, 11. Bennett was a representative of The Winchester Repeating Arms Company. "Old Guard Southern Hardware Salesmen," *The Iron Age,* January 28, 1909, 350. There were also a number of hired hands in camp in the employ of Bobo and of his guests. Hough, "With the Bobo Bear Pack—I," 93.

[9] Hough, "With the Bobo Bear Pack—I," 92.

[10] "Noel Ernest Newberry Money," http://trees.ancestry.com/tree/60003740/person/30054689179 (accessed April 13, 2014).

[11] Kevin Heffernan, *A History of Oakland: The Story of Our Village,* (Charleston: The History Press, 2007), 71.

[12] *Sporting Life*, "The Trigger," October 26, 1895, 13.

[13] Nash Buckingham, *De Shootinest Gent'man and Other Tales* (1934; reprint, New York, New York: Rowman & Littlefield, 2000), 1–15.

[14] Hough, "With the Bobo Bear Pack—I," 92.

[15] Hough, "With the Bobo Bear Pack—II," 113.

[16] Hough, "With the Bobo Bear Pack—I," 92–93.

[17] *The Evening Scimitar*, "Bob Bobo Is Dead Today," 1.

[18] Hough, "The Sunny South—II," 144.

[19] *The Evening Scimitar*, "Bob Bobo Is Dead Today," 1.

[20] Hough, "With the Bobo Bear Pack—I," 92.

Chapter 22 Bobo Sings

[1] Kephart, "Lost in the Swamps.-II," 113.

[2] Hough, "With the Bobo Bear Pack—I," 93.

[3] "Extinction of Large Game," *Commercial Appeal*, November 17, 1895, 11.

[4] Hough, "With the Bobo Bear Pack—I," 92.

[5] Hough, "With the Bobo Bear Pack—II," 112–113.

[6] Mary Hamilton, *Trials of the Earth* (Jackson, Mississippi: University Press of Mississippi, 1992), 83.

[7] Hough, "With the Bobo Bear Pack—II," 112.

[8] Hamilton, 82.

[9] Hough, "With the Bobo Bear Pack—II," 112.

[10] Mary Hamilton, *Trials of the Earth* (Jackson, Mississippi: University Press of Mississippi, 1992), 83; "Memphis and the South," *Packages,* November 1904, 64.

[11] Hamilton, 83.

[12] 1900 Census about Leo Minkus. accessed through Ancestry.com (accessed January 22, 2014).

[13] Hamilton, 101–103.

[14] "Memphis and the South," *Packages*, November 1904, 64.

[15] "Memphis," *The Barrel and Box*, December 1904, 40.

[16] Hough, "With the Bobo Bear Pack—II," 112.

[17] That is, to position themselves in front of the bear's path in order to force it to run in a different direction. Hough, "With the Bobo Bear Pack—II," 112.

[18] Benjamin Thorpe, *Northern Mythology, Comprising the Principal Popular Traditions and Superstitions of Scandinavia, North Germany, and the Netherlands*, vol. 3 (London: Edward Lumley, 1852), 158, 219.

[19] Hough, "With the Bobo Bear Pack—II," 112–113.

[20] Emerson Hough, *The Law of the Land* (Indianapolis: The Bobbs-Merrill Company, 1904), 40.

Chapter 23 Rainbound

[1] Hough, "With the Bobo Bear Pack—II," 113.

[2] Gordon, "The Bear Hunt," 210.

[3] Hough, "With the Bobo Bear Pack—II," 113.

[4] Hough, "In Old Mississippi," 408–409.

[5] Hough, "With the Bobo Bear Pack—II," 112–113.

[6] Dabney, "Bruin in the Canebrake," 179.

[7] Emerson Hough, "Chicago and the West," *Field and Stream*, March 1904, 965.

[8] Dabney, "Bruin in the Canebrake," 179.

[9] Hough, "With the Bobo Bear Pack—II," 113.

[10] Harris Dickson, "Bear Stories," *Saturday Evening Post*, April 10, 1909, 20–21.

[11] Hough, "With the Bobo Bear Pack—II," 112.

[12] Emerson Hough, "With the Bobo Bear Pack—III," *Forest and Stream*, February 15, 1896, 131.

[13] Hough, "With the Bobo Bear Pack—II," 113.

[14] Hough, "With the Bobo Bear Pack—III," 131.

Chapter 24 The Bull of the Woods

[1] Hough, "With the Bobo Bear Pack—III," 131.

[2] Emerson Hough, "With the Bobo Bear Pack—IV," *Forest and Stream*, February 22, 1896, 151–152.

Chapter 25 Moonlight Bear

[1] Emerson Hough, "With the Bobo Bear Pack—IV," 151–2.

Chapter 26 Insubordination

[1] Alexander, "The Black Bear," 262.

[2] Peck, "Bears and Bear-Hunting," 572.

[3] *Yazoo Whig*, "Horrible Death," January 21, 1848, 4.

[4] Emerson Hough, "Bobo and Some Bear Stories," *Forest and Stream*, November 17, 1900, 387.

[5] A. B. Wingfield, "In Jones's Bayou.—IV," *Forest and Stream*, November 16, 1895, 420.

[6] A Latin phrase meaning "from the chair." According to Catholic teaching, papal pronouncements are infallible when made ex cathedra, i. e., meeting certain conditions required for an infallible definition on a matter of faith and morals. Ludwig Ott, *Fundamentals of Catholic Dogma*, trans. Patrick Lynch, ed. James Canon Bastible (Rockford, Illinois: Tan Books and Publishers, Inc.,1960), 286–87.

[7] Emerson Hough, "Bobo and Some Bear Stories," *Forest and Stream*, November 17, 1900, 387.

[8] Hough, "With the Bobo Bear Pack—IV," 152.

[9] Union Metallic Cartridge Company, the ammunition manufacturing sister company to Remington Arms, later was merged into Remington. Remington Arms Company, LLC, "Company History—Remington Arms Company History

of the Firearms Business," http://www.remington.com/pages/our-company/
company-history.aspx (accessed January 13, 2013).

¹⁰ Hough, "With the Bobo Bear Pack—IV," 152.

¹¹ Emerson Hough, "Learning the Diamond Hitch," *Forest and Stream,*
April 20, 1901, 308.

¹² James Gordon, "A Bird Hunt with Guyon," Vol. *Forest and Stream*
(February 24, 1876), pp. 33–34.

¹³ Hough, "With the Bobo Bear Pack—IV," 152.

Chapter 27 A Year Goes By

¹ Hough, "With the Bobo Bear Pack—I," February 1, 1896, *Forest and
Stream,* 92–93; "With the Bobo Bear Pack—II," *Forest and Stream,* February
8, 1896, 112–113; "With the Bobo Bear Pack—III," *Forest and Stream,*
February 15, 1896, 131–132; "With the Bobo Bear Pack—IV," *Forest and
Stream,* February 22, 1896, 151–153.

² Hough, "Chicago and the West," *Field and Stream,* March 1904, 965.

³ Emerson Hough, "Chicago and the West," *Forest and Stream,* August 22,
1896, 146.

⁴ Hough, "In Old Mississippi," 408–409.

⁵ Hough, "The Sunny South—I," 124.

⁶ Hough, "In Old Mississippi," 408–409.

⁷ Satchfield, "Those Famous Bobo Bear Hunts," 5.

⁸ Hough, "In Old Mississippi," 408–409.

⁹ Hough, "Bobo and Some Bear Stories," November 10, 1900, 368.

¹⁰ Shethar-Boznai, "Trapping in the Southern States," *Forest and Stream,*
December 28, 1876, 327. Shethar-Boznai, "Notes from Mississippi," *Forest and
Stream,* January 18, 1877, 370–71.

¹¹ Augustine Lee Dabney, "In Bear-Trap Peril," *Forest and Stream,* February 1,
1896, 94.

¹² Hough, "With the Bobo Bear Pack—III," 131.

¹³ Emerson Hough, "In Old Mississippi," 408–409.

¹⁴ Emerson Hough, "No Mast This Year," *Forest and Stream,* December 19,
1896, 489

¹⁵ Emerson Hough, "The Floods in the South," *Forest and Stream,* April 17,
1897, 307.

¹⁶ Hough, "Winter Hunt in the Rockies," 504.

¹⁷ Hough, "From the South," 308. The convention was almost certainly
the Convention on the Improvement of the Western Waterways, Davenport,
Iowa, held October 5–6 of that year. War Department, *Report of the Chief of
Engineers of the U. S. Army Corps of Engineers, United States* (Washington, D. C.:
Government Printing Office, 1899), 1935.

¹⁸ Hough, "From the South," 308.

¹⁹ Hough, "Bobo and Some Bear Stories," November 10, 1900, 368.

20 Emerson Hough, "Chicago and the West," *Forest and Stream*, December 25, 1897, 517. It is assumed by the author that Hough referred to the Baron Maurice de Hirsch, the German philanthropist and business man who financed the original oriental railway linking western Europe with Istanbul (then, Constantinople). "Hirsch, Baron Maurice De," JewishEncyclopedia.com, 1906. Capt. Money must have been bear hunting with that gentleman considerably before Hough wrote those words, since the Baron died on April 21, 1896. *JewishEncyclopedia.com*, s.v. "Hirsch, Baron Von Maurice de (Moritz Hirsch, Freiherr auf Gereuth)," http://www.jewishencyclopedia.com/articles/7739-hirsch-baron-maurice-de-moritz-hirsch-freiherr-auf-gereuth (accessed June 5, 2013).

21 "Charlotte "Lottie" Amelia Cheesebro," http://trees.ancestry.com/tree/8148034/person/44722258 (accessed November 26, 2013).

Chapter 28 Bobo's House in the Hills

1 Walter S. Ganong, "Camp Talla-Quit," *Forest and Stream*, February 12, 1898, 122.

2 Montroy, "Historical Facts," Coahoma County WPA *Materials, Box 10676.*

3 Emerson Hough, "Chicago and the West," *Forest and Stream*, January 21, 1899, 53.

4 Hough, "Bobo and Some Bear Stories," November 10, 1900, 368.

5 Emerson Hough, "A Shootingless Shooting Trip," *Forest and Stream*, March 18, 1899, 209. It is not clear from Hough's writing whether the meeting with Bobo was planned for the trip to New Orleans or the return trip. From the order of Hough's article, the author is assuming it was the latter.

6 Hough, "A Shootingless Shooting Trip," 209.

7 Emerson Hough, "All Kinds of a Good Time," *Forest and Stream*, January 27, 1900, 68.

8 Hough, "A Shootingless Shooting Trip," 209.

9 Emerson Hough, "Hunting Knives and Old Timer," *Forest and Stream*, July 15, 1899, 46.

10 Emerson Hough, "Visitors," *Forest and Stream*, July 29, 1899, 87.

11 Hough said the "right eye" was the one with problems in this reference, but he almost certainly meant "left eye," for it was Bobo's left eye that was affected by a tumor and eventually required surgery. There is no other indication anywhere that Bobo ever had problems with his right eye.

12 Emerson Hough, "In the West," *Forest and Stream*, November 4, 1899, 367.

13 W. A. Powel's residence, according to the 1900 census, was Desoto County, Mississippi, (1900 United States Federal Census About W. A. Powell 1997–2013), and his first name was William. Ancestry.com, "Mississippi Marriages, 1776–1935, http://search.ancestry.com/cgi-bin/sse.dll?db=MSmarriages_ga&h=671485&indiv=try&o_vc=Record:OtherRecord&rhSource=7602 (accessed June 11, 2013).

14 Emerson Hough, "The Ivanhoe Club Preserve, of Mississippi," *Forest and Stream*, March 10, 1900, 190.

[15] Emerson Hough, "Farm Preserves," *Forest and Stream*, October 27, 1900, 328–329.

[16] Hough, "All Kinds of a Good Time," 68.

[17] Emerson Hough, "The Ivanhoe Club Preserve, of Mississippi," *Forest and Stream*, March 10, 1900, 190.

[18] Gordon, "Bear Dogs," 488.

[19] Hough, "All Kinds of a Good Time," 68.

[20] Hough, "The Ivanhoe Club Preserve, of Mississippi," 190.

[21] Hough, "All Kinds of a Good Time," 68.

[22] Emerson Hough, "Farm Preserves," *Forest and Stream*, October 27, 1900,, 329.

[23] Question One of the *Westminster Shorter Catechism* asks, "What is the chief end of man." The answer is, "Man's chief end is to glorify God, and enjoy him forever." James Robert Boyd, *The Shorter Westminster Catechism* (Philadelphia: The Presbyterian Board of Publication, 1859), 19.

Chapter 29 Bobo's Trials

[1] Emerson Hough, "Among Western Sportsmen," *Forest and Stream*, February 24, 1900, 150.

[2] "Fincher G. Bobo, electronic mail to author, September 18, 2013. The wedding was Fincher's second marriage. According to Fincher's granddaughter, Betty Bobo Pearson, Fincher's first wife was "a woman from Arkansas named Hallie Garrett." Hallie and Fincher had one child, a girl named "Hallie." After her mother's death, "she was sent to live with her grandparents in Arkansas." The younger Hallie eventually grew up, married one Charlie Keeler, and had two children, Elizabeth and Bobo Keeler, who were very close to the Bobo Family. Betty Bobo Pearson, electronic mail to author, September 6, 2015.

[3] Emerson Hough, "Chicago and the West," *Forest and Stream*, February 24, 1900, 150.

[4] Emerson Hough, "All Kinds of a Good Time," 68.

[5] William C. Faulkner, "Delta Autumn," in *Go Down, Moses*, 7th ed (New York: Random House, Inc., 1942), 364.

[6] Hough, "The Bobo Bear Country Gone," 449.

[7] Emerson Hough, "Still Buying Hound Pups," *Forest and Stream*, September 15, 1900, 207.

[8] Hough, "Bobo and Some Bear Stories," November 10, 1900, 368.

[9] Hough, "In the West," 367.

[10] Emerson Hough, "Bobo and Some Bear Stories," *Forest and Stream*, November 17, 1900, 387.

[11] Emerson Hough, "Visitors," *Forest and Stream*, July 29, 1899, 87.

[12] Emerson Hough, "Bobo and Some Bear Stories," November 17, 1900, 387

[13] Hough, "The Sunny South—II," 144.

[14] Hough, "Learning the Diamond Hitch," 308.

[15] "Current Topics," *Hickman Courier*, June 27, 1902, 6.

[16] According to the piece that appeared in *Forest and Stream*,

> The names of members who booked for this year's hunt were as follows:
> From Nashville—Governor Benton McMillin, Dr. Duncan Eve,
> Dr. J. Y. Crawford and Dr. W. W. Core.
> From Memphis—A. B. Wingfield, A. H. Murray, Page M. Patterson, Albert
> Swind, and Philip Fransioli.
> From Union City, Tenn.—John H. McDowell, Fulton Haward,
> J. S. Glover, D. A. Edwards and Harry Edwards.
> From Rives, Tenn.—Bob Wade, Frank Caldwell, Joel Shores, Oscar
> Clemmons, R. J. Barnett and John Mores.
> From Newberne, Tenn.—W. J. Flatt and Ed. Brady.
> From Rosedale, Miss.—O. Y. McGuire. Last, but by no means least,
> Judge M. D._ Smallman, of McMinnville, Tenn., the Socrates and Diogenes of
> the party.

A. B. Wingfield, "Outing of the Ozark Club," *Forest and Stream*, January 11,
1902, 26–27. R. E. Bobo, Jr., and his brother F. G. Bobo, joined the others at
Sunflower Landing.

[17] Wingfield, "Outing of the Ozark Club," 26–27.

[18] *Clarksdale Challenge*, "Died," January 24, 1902, 3.

Chapter 30 Bobo and the President

[1] Denison, 605.

[2] Joseph Dunbar Shields and Seargent Prentiss Knutt, *The Life and Times of Seargent Smith Prentiss* (Philadephia: J. B. Lippincott & Co., 1884), 314. Politics was not the stated purpose of Prentiss's bear hunt nor the topic of his speech, but the mere presence of Prentiss, who was a well-known Whig partisan and former member of Congress from Mississippi, rendered it a political occasion.

[3] Gregory C. Wilson, "How Teddy Bear Got His Name," *Potomac*, November 30, 1969, 33–34.

[4] "The President Invited to Hunt with Bobo," *Forest and Stream*, June 7, 190, 445.

[5] "Letter from Theodore Roosevelt to Stuyvesant Fish, 1902-10-21, Library of Congress Manuscript Division, http://www.theodorerooseveltcenter.org/ Research/Digital-library/Record/Image Viewer.aspx?libID=o183336&imageNo=1 (accessed September 12, 2015).

[6] *The Evening Scimitar*, "Bob Bobo Is Dead Today," 1.

[7] *St. Louis Post-Dispatch*, "Why Col. Bob Bobo Was Not in Hunt," November 28, 1902, 16. In Bobo's absence Washington County, Mississippi, bear hunter Holt Collier served as chief huntsman to the presidential party. An incident during the hunt in which Roosevelt declined to kill a bear captured by Collier resulted in the naming of the teddy bear. That story is told in the author's children's book, *Holt and the Teddy Bear* (Gretna, Louisiana: Pelican Publishing Company, 1991).

[8] *The Evening Scimitar*, "Bob Bobo Is Dead Today," 1.

[9] Emerson Hough, "Turning Southward," *Forest and Stream*, December 20, 1902, 490.

¹⁰ See, *e. g.*, Ronald Michael James and C. Elizabeth Raymond, eds., *Comstock Women*, (University of Nevada Press, 1998) p. 172; Jack HarlanYocum, "A History of the Theatre in Houston,1836–1954" (PhD Diss, University of Wisconsin, 1954), 33.

¹¹ Hough, "Turning Southward," 490.

Chapter 31 The Curtain Falls

¹ Hough, "The President's Mississippi Bear Hunt," *Forest and Stream*, June 14, 1902, 466.

² Graye Harris Carter, "Untitled Reminisences."

³ *The Evening Scimitar*, "Bob Bobo Is Dead Today," 1.

⁴ Hough, "The President's Mississippi Bear Hunt," 466.

⁵ Hough, "The Death of Col. Bobo," 513.

⁶ *The Evening Scimitar*, "Bob Bobo Is Dead Today," 1.

⁷ An announcement of Bobo's death appeared in the *Post-Dispatch* on December 18, 1902. Adele Heagney (Reference Librarian, St. Louis Public Library) electronic mail to author, August 20, 2013.

⁸ Hough, "The Death of Col. Bobo," 513.

⁹ Otto, *The Final Frontiers, 1880–1930: Settling the Southern Bottomlands*, 31–32.

¹⁰ Hough, "The Death of Col. Bobo," 513.

EPILOGUE

¹ Emerson Hough, "Chicago and the West," *Field and Stream*, March, 1904, 965.

² Emerson Hough, "Bear Dogs in Old Mexico," *Forest and Stream*, January 3, 1903, 9.

³ Cristadoro, "An Embarrassment of Literary Riches," 24.

⁴ Hough, "Turning Southward," 490.

⁵ Kephart, "Lost in the Swamps.-II," 113.

⁶ Hough, "Turning Southward," 490.

⁷ John 20:24–25.

⁸ Emerson Hough, "Those Mississippi Squirrels," *Forest and Stream*, January 31, 1903, 85

⁹ Emerson Hough, "Squirrel Migrations," *Forest and Stream*, February 14, 1903, 125–126.

¹⁰ B. E. Birge, "Squirrel Migrations," *Forest and Stream*, March 28, 1903, 245.

¹¹ "Gray Squirrel Migration," *Forest and Stream*, March 14, 1903, 205.

¹² Hough, "Squirrel Migrations," 125–126.

¹³ "Gray Squirrel Migration," *Forest and Stream*, 205.

¹⁴ Hough, "Squirrel Migrations," 125–126.

¹⁵ Emerson Hough, "Swimming Powers of a Horse," *Forest and Stream*, July 4, 1903, 11.

¹⁶ Hough, "Swimming Powers of a Horse," 11.

[17] Emerson Hough, "Bear Dog Wanted," *Field and Stream*, January 1904, 766.

[18] *Historical Research Project of Coahoma County*, Clarksdale, Mississippi, 1936, Coahoma County Materials, Mississippi Works Progress Administration, Box 10677, General Information file, Mississippi Department of Archives and History.

[19] Hough, "The Death of Col. Bobo," 513.

[20] David Evans, "Afro-American Folk Music from Tate and Panola Counties, Mississippi," http://www.loc.gov/folklife/LP/AfroAmFolkMusicMissL67_opt.pdf (November 9, 2013).

[21] Betty Bobo Pearson, electronic mail to author, September 6, 2015. Mrs. Pearson still has her great-grandmother's trunk.

[22] Joseph A. Graham, "The Field Trials of the Fall Circuit," *Outing*, February 1904, 607.

[23] James W. Silver, "When Paul Bunyan Came to Mississippi," *Journal of Mississippi History* 19, (1957): 115–16.

[24] "Mrs. Duryea Kills a Bear," *Charlotte News*, October 28, 1905, 3.

[25] Silver, "When Paul Bunyan Came to Mississippi," 115–16.

[26] David Evans, "Afro-American Folk Music from Tate and Panola Counties, Mississippi," http://www.loc.gov/folklife/LP/AfroAmFolkMusicMissL67_opt.pdf (November 9, 2013).

[27] Silver, "When Paul Bunyan Came to Mississippi," 118, quoting from *The Hardwood Recorder*.

[28] John B. Cullen, *Old Times in Faulkner* Country (Baton Rouge: Louisiana State University Press, 1976), 26,27.

[29] Mrs. Fincher Gist Bobo, Interview, *Historical Research Project of Coahoma County*, Interview by Florence F. Montroy, Clarksdale, Mississippi, 1936, Coahoma County Materials, Mississippi Works Progress Administration Microfilm Collection, Reels A770 and A771, University of Mississippi Library.

[30] Silver, "When Paul Bunyan Came to Mississippi," 118, quoting from *The Hardwood Recorder*.

[31] Silver, "When Paul Bunyan Came to Mississippi," 118–19.

[32] "One Potato Weighed 30 Pounds and Another Weighs 32 Pounds," *Commercial-Appeal*, November 17, 1917, 12.

[33] Thus passes the glory of the world.

[34] Carole M. Johnson, "Emerson Hough's American West," http://www.lib. uiowa.edu/spec-coll/bai/johnson.htm (accessed December 8, 2013).

[35] Hough, "With the Bobo Bear Pack – I," 93.

[36] Betty Bobo Pearson, electronic mail to author, September 6, 2015; Fincher G. (Jack) Bobo, electronic mail to author, September 18, 2013; Fincher G. (Jack) Bobo, electronic mail to author, September 19, 2013.

[37] Mrs. Fincher Gist Bobo, Interview for "Historical *Research Project of Coahoma County*," Interview by Florence F. Montroy, November 20, 1936.

[38] "Historic Delta Research Changed Cotton Farming," http://msucares.com/news/print/agnews/an08/ 080103.html, March 21, 2012 (accessed April 14, 2014).

[39] Betty Bobo Pearson, electronic mail to author, September 6, 2015.

Appendix III

[1]Emerson Hough, "Bobo and Some Bear Stories," *Forest and Stream*, November 10, 1900, 368.

[2]*Weekly Panola Star*, October 21, 1871, 3, reprinted from the *Friars Point Delta*.

[3]Peter Bobo in the 1870 Census, Ancestry.com, https://www.ancestry.com/discoveryuicontent/view/36260016:7163 (accessed October 20, 2022).

[4]*Memphis Daily Appeal*, September 13, 1883, 2.

[5]Emerson Hough, "The Sunny South – III," *Forest and Stream* (March 2, 1895), 164

[6]"The Boss Panther," *Magnolia Gazette*, November 5, 1880, 2.

[7]J. Frank Dobie, *Ben Lilly Legend*, 9th (Boston: Little, Brown and Company, 1950), 186.

[8]James G. Chism, "Editors Appeal," *Memphis Daily Appeal*, November 15, 1876, 4.

[9]"Through Train," *Memphis Daily Appeal*, September 18, 1884, 4.

[10]"In the Yazoo Valley," *Evening Star*, April 25, 1905, 13.

[11]"Joseph Purcell Prince," Ancestry.com, https://www.ancestry.com/family-tree/person/tree/161224397/person/112105922681/facts (accessed October 20, 2022).

[12]A Friend, "Married," *Memphis Appeal*, November 25, 1868, 2.

[13]"Clarksdale, Jonestown, and County," *Friars Point Gazette*, March 20, 1885.

[14]"In the Yazoo Valley," *Evening Star*, April 25, 1905, 13.

[15]"Clarksdale, Jonestown, and County," *Friars Point Gazette*, March 20, 1885.

[16]Daniel Byrne Weir, "Mississippi Bear Hunting," *American Field*, November 25, 1882, 357.

[17]Tuckahoe, "Dave's Medical Experience," *Forest and Stream*, May 24, 1883, 322.

[18]"Arkansas Military Institute," *Encyclopedia of Arkansas*, https://encyclopedia of arkansas.net/entries/arkansas-military-institute-4582/ (April 20, 2023); "Arkansas Military Institute," *Gazette and Democrat*, January 31, 1851, 4; George D. Alexander, "Genealogical Table and History of the Great Grandparents of Col. George Douglas Alexander," 1 (Unpublished two page manuscript, 1889).

[19]"Civil War Veteran," *Shreveport Times*, July 3, 1907, 10.

[20]*Journal of George Douglass Alexander*, January 22, 1848, 110.

[21]*Indianapolis News*, October 13, 1890, 6.

[22]"Delta Farmers Association," *Greenville Times*, May 21, 1887, 1.

[23]"Fourth Judicial District Convention," *Democrat-Times*, June 18, 1887, 1.

[24]*Weekly Clarion-Ledger*, July 13, 893, 4.

[25]"Delta Experiment Station," *Democrat-Times*, November 3, 1894, 5.

[26]"Historical,"*Daily Commercial Herald*, November 8, 1896, 5.

[27]"Proceedings of the District Executive Committees," *Greenwood Commonwealth*, July 28, 1898, 4.

[28]Emerson Hough, "South South – VI," *Forest and Stream*, March 23, 1895, 225; Emerson Hough, "Big Bear Foot from Bobo," *Forest and Stream*, May 4, 1895, 347; Emerson Hough, "Story of the Big Bear Foot," *Forest and Stream*, May 18, 1895, 391.

[29]Robert Eager Bobo, "Big Bear on the Sunflower," *Forest and Stream*, May 18, 1895, 391.

[30]"First Annual Sportsmen's Exposition," *Forest and Stream*, May 25, 1895, 416-430.

[31] *Clarion-Ledger*, November 23, 1895, 4.

[32]"Cleveland as a *Nimrod*," *Chicago Tribune*, November 10, 1895, 39.

www.ingramcontent.com/pod-product-compliance
Lightning Source LLC
Chambersburg PA
CBHW021353090426
42742CB00009B/838